PASQUINADES IN E

Slaughtering Some Sacred Cows

Gilles Paquet

Invenire Books

INVENIRE is an Ottawa-based "idea factory" specializing in collaborative governance and stewardship. Invenire and its authors offer creative and practical responses to the challenges and opportunities faced by today's complex organizations.

INVENIRE welcomes a range of contributions – from conceptual and theoretical reflections, ethnographic and case studies, and proceedings of conferences and symposia, to works of a very practical nature – that deal with problems or issues on the governance and stewardship front. INVENIRE publishes works in French and English.

This is the thirty-sixth volume published by INVENIRE.

INVENIRE is associated with La Maison Gouvernance and publishes a quarterly electronic journal, found at *www.optimumonline.ca*, which reaches more than 10,000 readers.

Editorial Committee
Ruth Hubbard
Daniel Lane
Gilles Paquet (chair)

The titles published by INVENIRE are listed at the end of this book.

PASQUINADES IN E

Slaughtering Some Sacred Cows

Gilles Paquet

INVENIRE

Ottawa, Canada

2017

University of Ottawa **Press**
Les **Presses** de l'Université d'Ottawa

The University of Ottawa Press (UOP) is proud to be the oldest of the francophone university presses in Canada and the oldest bilingual university publisher in North America. Since 1936, UOP has been enriching intellectual and cultural discourse by producing peer-reviewed and award-winning books in the humanities and social sciences, in French and in English.

www.Press.uOttawa.ca

Library and Archives Canada Cataloguing in Publication

Title: Pasquinades in E : slaughtering some sacred cows / Gilles Paquet.
Names: Paquet, Gilles, author.
Description: Reprint. Originally published: Ottawa, Canada : Invenire, 2017. | Includes bibliographical references.
Identifiers: Canadiana (print) 20220394946 | Canadiana (ebook) 20220395012 | ISBN 9780776638492 (softcover) | ISBN 9780776638508 (PDF) | ISBN 9780776638515 (EPUB)
Subjects: LCSH: Democracy. | LCSH: Power (Social sciences) | LCSH: Consensus (Social sciences)—Political aspects. | LCSH: Political culture—Canada. | LCSH: Canada—Politics and government.
Classification: LCC JC423 .P2517 2022 | DDC 321.8—dc23

Legal Deposit: Library and Archives Canada, Third Quarter 2022
© University of Ottawa Press 2022, all rights reserved.

This book was initially published by Invenire Books in 2017. The initial cover design, layout and design were produced by Sandy Lynch. Cover photo: Lalupa. The University of Ottawa Press reissued this book thanks to the support of Ontario Creates.

Invenire

Invenire Books, an Ottawa-based idea factory that operated from 2010 to 2019, specialized in collaborative governance and stewardship. Invenire and its authors provide creative practical and stimulating responses to the challenges and opportunities faced by today's organizations. The list is now carried by the University of Ottawa Press.

Profession: Public Servant
The Entrepreneurial Effect: Practical Ideas from Your Own Virtual Board of Advisors
La flotte blanche : histoire de la compagnie de navigation du Richelieu et d'Ontario
Tableau d'avancement II : essais exploratoires sur la gouvernance d'un certain Canada français
The Entrepreneurial Effect: Waterloo
The Unimagined Canadian Capital: Challenges for the Federal Capital Region
The State in Transition: Challenges for Canadian Federalism
Cities as Crucibles: Reflections on Canada's Urban Future
Gouvernance communautaire : innovations dans le Canada français hors Québec
Through the Detox Prism: Exploring Organizational Failures and Design Responses
Cities and Languages: Governance and Policy – An International Symposium
Villes et langues : gouvernance et politiques – symposium international
Moderato Cantabile: Toward Principled Governance for Canada's Immigration Policy
Stewardship: Collaborative Decentred Metagovernance and Inquiring Systems
Challenges in Public Health Governance: The Canadian Experience
Innovation in Canada: Why We Need More and What We Must Do to Get It
Challenges of Minority Governments in Canada
Gouvernance corporative : une entrée en matières

Tackling Wicked Policy Problems: Equality, Diversity and Sustainability
50 ans de bilinguisme officiel : défis, analyses et témoignages
Unusual Suspects: Essays on Social Learning
Probing the Bureaucratic Mind: About Canadian Federal Executives
Tableau d'avancement III : pour une diaspora canadienne-française antifragile
Autour de Chantal Mouffe : le politique en conflit
Town and Crown: An Illustrated History of Canada's Capital
The Tainted-Blood Tragedy in Canada: A Cascade of Governance Failures
Intelligent Governance: A Prototype for Social Coordination
Driving the Fake Out of Public Administration: Detoxing HR in the Canadian Federal Public Sector
Tableau d'avancement IV : un Canada français à ré-inventer
A Future for Economics: More Encompassing, More Institutional, More Practical
Pasquinade en F : essais à rebrousse-poil
Building Bridges: Case Studies in Collaborative Governance in Canada
Scheming Virtuously: The Road to Collaborative Governance
A Lantern on the Bow: A History of the Science Council of Canada and its Contributions to the Science and Innovation Policy Debate
Fifty Years of Official Bilingualism: Challenges, Analyses and Testimonies
Irregular Governance: A Plea for Bold Organizational Experimentation
Pasquinade in E: Slaughtering Some Sacred Cows

The University of Ottawa Press gratefully acknowledges the support extended to its publishing list by the Government of Canada, the Canada Council for the Arts, the Ontario Arts Council, the Social Sciences and Humanities Research Council and the Canadian Federation for the Humanities and Social Sciences through the Awards to Scholarly Publications Program, and by the University of Ottawa.

ONTARIO ARTS COUNCIL
CONSEIL DES ARTS DE L'ONTARIO
an Ontario government agency
un organisme du gouvernement de l'Ontario

Canada Council   Conseil des arts
for the Arts   du Canada

Canadä

uOttawa

Table of Contents

To John Meisel, mentor and friend,

from whom I received *savoirs, savoir-faire* and *savoir-être*,
but who should never be held responsible for my
truancy and waywardness,
even though I owe much of my gumption to
his encouragement …

avec mon amitié et mon affection.

Pasquinade:
a satire traditionally posted in
a public place in ancient Rome;
in particular, on the statue of Pasquino

"Common sense is the most fairly distributed thing
in the world, for each one thinks he is so well-endowed
with it that even those who are hardest to satisfy
in all other matters are not in the habit of desiring
more of it than they already have."

– René Descartes

Driving Out Uncritical Thinking

" [...] most organizations would rather risk obsolescence than make room for the non-conformist in their midst."

– Warren Bennis

These essays are exercises in critical thinking. They aim at exorcising a number of 'mental prisons' about aspects of governing, and at denouncing pathologies in our ways of thinking and governing ourselves, by exposing their toxic nature. This sort of work is inspired by Frédéric Bastiat, the master debunker of sophistry in the 19th century. Unfortunately, the gods have blessed me with neither his wit nor his corrosiveness. Yet silence on such matters connotes tacit agreement with toxic nonsense, and therefore guilt by association for the ensuing malgovernance.

Provocations and purposes

Dealing with the issues discussed later in this book is a matter of legitimate defense. The bunk producers have been on the attack first, and always very sanctimoniously! When pressed politely to explain a bit more clearly the rationale for their exhortations or concatenations, those aggressors have used one of three conventional tactics: (1) to repeat the argument louder and even more sanctimoniously so as to make it sound more self-evident (intimidation); (2) to turn to a neighbourly coalition of complicit colleagues for moral comfort with a view to democratically mauling the witless questioner (mobbing); or (3) to adopt a sanctimonius and contemptuous pose, and ostracize the fool who has dared to challenge the purported canonical view (exclusion).

This has been sufficient for many critical observers, perplexed by nonsensical utterances or absurd governance choices, to choose routinely not to attack such nonsense or contraptions, even when they were aware that, by such failure to confront, the silent observers were becoming complicit with the bunk producers.

The requisite antidote most likely to be effective in the face of provocative bunk is a mix of critical thinking and irony. That is what this book proposes.

I have a three-level target audience for this book:

- my intellectually honest acquaintances and friends (with whom I have had conversations about these issues in the past) that I would like to persuade to react forcefully in the face of such nonsense or aberration by showing how easily it might be done;

- a broader group of reasonable readers whom I would like to make aware of the toxic consequences of their intellectual numbness in the face of so many vacuous arguments and proposals for dysfunctional and pathological governance arrangements, so as to trigger in their souls the emergence of a powerful rejection syndrome – powerful enough to override their tendency to silently concur when nonsense is uttered, or absurd arrangements are defended;[1] and

- the group of intellectual imposters in academe and the media that has been taking advantage of the intellectual indolence and the lack of gumption of the silent majority to disinform and deceive the unsuspecting, and using all their sophistry to defend the most toxic governance arrangements; these operatives, boldly calling themselves progressives in recent decades, and coming mainly from political science and law, have dissolved the notion of governance into an all-purpose weaselword, and have used all the venomous dirty tricks in the book (misrepresentation, calumny, denunciation of governance as a form of neo-liberalism, etc.) to vilify their 'unenlightened' colleagues working within the

---

[1] In the vernacular of the diplomatic circles, this is referring to the use of the "French protocol": a well-known strategy of French diplomats (I am told by colleagues from those circles) to ensure, by effective techniques, that they make those defending views contrary to their own feel more and more uncomfortable.

governance problematique with toxic intimidation and censure; this toxic group deserves to be exposed.[2]

Whether it takes the form of nudging, persuading, or exposing, on these three fronts, the message will be the same: one must practice critical thinking and the relentless asking 'why' and 'how' – the sort of questions that have a corrosive effect on sophistry and any defense of the indefensible.

One additional benefit of this sort of coaxing and challenge function is that it might generate a modicum of annoyance, especially on the part of the members of the third group: this may make them careless, and prone to reveal, in the heat of conversation, the poverty of their arguments.

Critical thinking plus

This book deals with the consequences of problems generated by failures to think critically and to confront. Yet critical thinking is not a simple notion (Paquet 2014: chapter 1). When an international group of experts was asked to develop a consensus about the meaning of critical thinking, the outcome was akin to the proverbial horse drawn by a committee.[3]

[2] These fundamentalist individuals remind one of the central character in a Wiliam Saroyan's fable (Saroyan 1941: fable xxiv). This fable features a man who plays a cello with one string over which he draws the bow for hours at a time holding his finger in one place. When his wife observes that other players play the instrument with four strings and move their fingers about continuously, the man shakes his head and says "They are looking for the place. I've found it." The difference between the fundamentalist apostles of conservatorship (Terry 2003) and Saroyan's cellist is that the cellist neither declared war on four-string cellists nor chose to malign them viciously.

[3] "We understand critical thinking to be purposeful, self-regulatory judgment which results in interpretation, analysis, evaluation, and inference, as well as explanation of the evidential, conceptual, methodological, criteriological, or contextual considerations upon which that judgment is based. CT is essential as a tool of inquiry. As such, CT is a liberating force in education and a powerful resource in one's personal and civic life. While not synonymous with good thinking, CT is a pervasive and self-rectifying human phenomenon. The ideal critical thinker is habitually inquisitive, well-informed, trustful of reason, open-minded, flexible, fair-minded in evaluation, honest in facing personal biases, prudent in making judgments, willing to reconsider, clear about issues, orderly in complex matters, diligent in seeking relevant information, reasonable in the selection of criteria, focused in inquiry, and persistent in seeking results which are as precise as the subject and the circumstances of inquiry permit. Thus, educating good critical thinkers means working toward this ideal. It combines developing CT skills with nurturing those dispositions which consistently yield useful insights and which are the basis of a rational and democratic society" (quoted in Facione 2009).

Less verbose, but not less daunting, is the definition of what critical thinkers do: raise vital questions, formulating them clearly, gather relevant information, and interpret it effectively, come to well-reasoned conclusions and decisions, testing them on relevant criteria, thinking open-mindedly about alternative perspectives, assessing as need be their assumptions and consequences, and communicating effectively with others in figuring out correctives.

More succinctly, one may choose Schafersman's definition of critical thinking as "reasonable, reflective, responsible, and skillful thinking that is focused on deciding what to believe or do" (Schafersman 1991: 3); or the analytical definition proposed by Gabennesch that focuses on the three dimensions of critical thinking: thinking skills (analyzing, synthesizing, interpreting, explaining, evaluating, generalizing, abstracting, illustrating, comparing, recognizing logical fallacies); a skeptic's worldview (things are not always entirely what they seem as the first wisdom of critical thinking); and intellectual due process (more integrity, humility, tolerance of uncertainty, and raw courage than most of us find easy to summon) (Gabennesch 2006).

Whatever the definition used, critical thinking is not something that everyone practices, or anything that everyone is good at all the time. Most agents do not have the combination of skills, worldview and vigilance required to meet this sort of standard of reasonableness, self-awareness, honesty, reflexivity and open-mindedness. Yet this is what one needs.

But making citizens aware of the iron cage of the mental prisons that they often unwittingly carry with them, and of the pathological governance arrangements they unduly tolerate, cannot suffice. Besides opening the gates of mental prisons, and exposing pathologies of governance, one must suggest ways to get these wrongs righted in the name of harm reduction.[4]

---

[4] While, on the surface, promoting good things and working at reducing bad things may look the same, they are not. At the operational level, it makes a considerable difference, and entails substantially different ways of thinking: "scrutinizing the harms themselves, and discovering their dynamics and dependencies, leads to the possibility of sabotage. Cleverly conceived acts of sabotage, exploiting identified vulnerabilities of the object under attack, can be not only effective, but extremely resource-efficient too" (Sparrow 2008: 27).

This book is all about sabotaging the dynamics of harms generated by the failure to confront nonsense and governance aberrations. Promoting better understanding and better governance arrangements is the object, but it will often be done in an oblique way by suggesting the elimination of the sources of blockages and dysfunctions that effectively prevent the search for better understanding and better governance arrangements. Without such decontamination and clearing of the ground, it is often impossible to proceed successfully with the construction of preferable governance arrangements.

Some words of caution

Before the sabotage work can begin, two points need to be clarified. First, what philosophy of governance will guide us in this work? And second, how does one avoid confusing truly pathological arrangements with creative arrangements that are unusual, paradoxical, and/or baroque?

(1) In our complex, uncertain, and surprise-generating world, nobody is really fully in charge. Governing requires a process of effective coordination of the activities of the persons and groups who have a portion of the power, resources and information. This means effectively mobilizing every one of the potentially significant partners as a co-producer of governance.

Governing requires more than fiduciary sentinels to prevent things from going financially awry. It also calls for much more than the search for elusive consensual strategies (*consensus mous*) as a way to cope with external shocks. What governance commands most importantly is a capacity for individuals and organizations to learn, i.e., to tap effectively into the knowledge located in the experience of all partners, to learn by reflections on our own experience and to make sense of it, and to retool, restructure and even reframe the basic questions facing the organization in order to generate more effective ways to discern and grapple with the generative challenge of continuous organizational learning (Cleveland 2002; Chait *et al.* 2005).

The requirements for that sort of task are well-known to practitioners of collaborative and reflexive governance: learning by doing; reflexive self-criticism; capacity for long run probing of systemic effects; adaptiveness of strategies and institutions;

iterative experimental and participatory definition of broad directions; and interactive strategy development (Voß *et al.* 2006).

At the foundation of these requirements is a bold capacity for critical thinking, and this, in turn, requires a willingness to overcome the fear of conflict, and its corollary, the failure to confront.

We propose to dispatch this daunting task with a certain degree of levity. Not because the problems dealt with are not serious. They are. But because the easiest way to get the readers to see the importance of reframing crucial perspectives and modifying certain governing arrangements is to provide an opportunity to confront two frames of reference, as humour does, and to appreciate the insights such confrontation generates.

Humour and humourists have operated at this frontier for a long time, and they have much to teach us. They often provide the only sort of viable narrative that can bridge the chasm between radically different frames of reference, and open minds to critical thinking.[5]

Jon Stewart's *The Daily Show* has been an interesting illustration of this use of humour; it made the show a rallying point for much critical thinking. Academic snobs may not regard this approach as the ideal venue for critical thinking, but, in an age of fundamentalism, distrust and anti-intellectualism, it is a promising one.

(2) It must be made clear that it cannot be presumed that anything unusual or peculiar or paradoxical is necessarily pathological, even though it will be declared so by intellectually-challenged fundamentalists. As the reader will soon discover, the very complexity of the world of governance (where power, resources and information are widely distributed, and where no one is in charge) constantly generates surprise situations that challenge belief systems in good currency and governance

---

[5] Arthur Koestler considers that the essence of creativity and humour is the perceiving of an idea or situation in two self-consistent but habitually incompatible frames of reference. He illustrates his view with a story reported by Chamfort of a "Marquis at the court of Louis XIV who, on entering his wife's boudoir and finding her in the arms of a Bishop, walked calmly to the window, and went through the motions of blessing the people in the street. "What are you doing ?" cried the anguished wife. 'Monseigneur is performing my functions' replied the Marquis, 'so I am performing his' (Koestler 1964: 96).

arrangements in place. Indeed, such situations call for belief systems to evolve, and for existing governance arrangements to be modified often in peculiar, unusual and paradoxical ways. Such new belief systems may be perplexing, and the new governance arrangements required may be baroque. This does not in any way make them pathological, *per se*.

In a complex and turbulent world, the effective capacity to transform is a survival trait. Innovation and experimentation are powerful forces in the adjustment process that brings views of the world, organizations and institutions in line with the evolving environment. Consequently, such experiments must be encouraged. But encouraging innovation and experimentation automatically generates the exploration of heretofore unknown territories, and therefore straying away from comfortable canonical forms. Some of these new ways of thinking or new organizational arrangements are bound to turn out to be both unusual and even counterintuitive, and therefore to generate instant rejection by fundamentalists.

An interesting example of such a surprising organizational change is the way in which the Mexican cement giant Cemex reorganized itself to deal with the chaotic reality of delivering cement to different construction sites in Mexico City – a context where weather, traffic, delays in construction, etc. made it almost impossible to get the cement at the required place at the required time. The new governance design that resolved the problem was simply to match chaos with chaos. Borrowing the taxicab model, Cemex decided to send a number of trucks, approximately in keeping with the expected demand for the day, roaming through town. Through walkie-talkies, roaming trucks were then dispatched to the closest construction site requiring cement as effective demand materialized. While the usual planned delivery system generated disastrous results, this chaotic approach, *à la* taxicab, succeeded in delivering cement just in time (Katel 1997).

In the best of all worlds, a new environment triggers new beliefs, new contraptions and new arrangements that may be unorthodox and paradoxical, but arrangements that work. The paradox is 'resolved' by some additional information, through which it becomes clear that what seemed to be absurd *a priori* is not so absurd after all.

Fundamentalists presume that anything unorthodox or baroque (because of its being in violation of orthodoxy: i.e., of what they define in the light of the canon as the only right way) is pathological. This is what fundamentalism is about. Our view is radically at odds with this sort of traditionalism. There is not necessarily one right way to act in most circumstances: different ways may be more or less effective for the job at hand, depending on context and circumstances. Good governance is therefore fundamentally 'contingent': it depends on circumstances, and calls for experimentation, for trial-and-error in the search of a good fit between structure and circumstances.[6]

Some sort of order

Voluntary servitude need not be only servile submission to a person or group supposedly doing the thinking for the rest of the collectivity. It may be submissiveness to an idea, a canonical text, or a bad habit. Such servitude imposes a *manière de voir* that selectively focuses on some aspects of the context only. As such it becomes a form of automatic self-censorship that constrains the realm of relevant knowledge. This sort of crippling epistemology (a mode of acquisition of knowledge that is reductive and/or distorted) underpins false consciousness and ideologies, and condemns the governing to be wrong-headed as a result of the truncated view of the world (Paquet 2009).

In many cases, the seemingly commonsensical nature of the proposed particular canonical view of the world may be such that members of the indoctrinated cult are led to uncritically and unwittingly make assumptions they are not even aware they are making, and come to consider *'les autres'* – those who do not share

[6] One must recognize the difference between the problems caused by crippling epistemologies (ascribable to ideologies and mental prisons) and problems caused by pathogenic structures and processes. Crippling epistemologies command major 'reframing' – i.e., repairs to the somewhat reductive and distorted view of reality – a modification in the belief systems, in the worldview. Maladjusted structures and processes may often be repaired by mere 'restructuring and retooling'. But, as will become obvious in the rest of the book, this distinction is anything but determinate. Most of the issues discussed here will clearly reveal that theory, structure and technology are so intermingled that there is often no way to escape from crippling epistemologies and governance failures without engaging in reframing, restructuring and retooling.

their views – as simply uttering nonsense, being feeble-minded, or revealing moral failure. The capacity for reflexive examination of one's own assumptions and of one's actions is therefore often stunted. Critical thinking subversively exposes the propensity of the members of any cult of being only capable of rationalizing their own mythologies, and of denouncing the actions of others as erroneous by definition.

It is the main thesis of this introduction that reflexive governance (i.e., governance based on vigilant ongoing experimentation, learning by doing and self-critical assessment of assumptions and results all the way) is the foundation of a workable social order, and that critical thinking is part and parcel of what makes reflexive governance work. Consequently, anything attenuating the extent of critical thinking weakens reflexive governance, and generates pathologies of governance. This may be extremely costly. Therefore, attacking the forces at work in eroding critical thinking is of fundamental importance in ensuring that possibilities of pathologies of governance are eliminated or attenuated.

In the next sections, four ensembles of pathologies are considered.

First, *institutional pathologies*: the toxic effect of the Charter of Rights, of certain special commissions of inquiry, of the creeping power of super-technocracy, and of the rampant invasion of legal corruption.

Second, *impostures and sophistry* that have derailed the democratic conversation: weasel words, academism, fundamentalisms, demonization and psychosis.

Third, *toxic trends* that are crippling the democratic process: the rhetoric of promiscuity, oikophobia, hyper-toleration and the politics of guilt.

Fourth, a sample of *design challenges* difficult to meet because of social blindness and powerful interest groups standing in the way: the National Capital Region, higher education in Ontario, the Armed Forces, the RCMP, the Office of the Auditor General, and the culture of the federal public service.

In each case, the vacuity of some popular views that have come to be in good currency are exposed, along with the sacred labels attached to these ill-founded principles, the bizarrerie of the arrangements built on these false premises, the peculiar assumptions on which these oddities have been built, and the pathological behaviour and awful consequences that have ensued from such unchallenged pathologies.

In the conclusion, a moment is taken to draw attention to the new cosmology *en émergence* that promises to better deal with these challenges.

In earlier books, I have always been very careful to thank colleagues for their continuous support and intellectual stimulation. In this case, keeping most of these colleagues anonymous will ensure that none may be found guilty by association for my attempts at slaughtering so many sacred cows. There are four exceptions to this rule: Gary Caldwell, my *co-équipier* for chapter 11, Robin Higham, my co-author for chapters 4 and 17, Lorna Marsden, my partner in chapter 18, and Andrea E. Courtney, my heteronym, as Fernando Pessoa would have called her, who has haunted Part II of this book.

Yet there is no way to deny the contribution of all the colleagues and friends who, at some time or another, have shared their thoughts with me at **La Maison Gouvernance** – a privileged if evolving locus of critical thinking in governance studies from the late 1980s to the present. Their *compagnonnage*, as they will undoubtedly recognize here and there, has had much tonic impact on my evolving thinking.

As for those readers who are coming to this material anew, I will be delighted if you are startled and amused by this book, and saddened if you are not.

References

Chait, R.P. *et al.* 2005. *Governance as Leadership*. New York, NY: Wiley.

Cleveland, H. 2002. *Nobody in Charge*. San Francisco, CA: Jossey-Bass.

Facione, P.A. 2009. "Critical Thinking: what it is and why it counts," www.insightassessment.com.

Frankfurt, H.G. 1988. *The importance of what we care about*. Cambridge, UK: Cambridge University Press.

Gabennesch, H. 2006. "Critical Thinking...What is it good for? (In fact, what is it?)," *Skeptical Inquirer*, 30(2): 36-41.

Katel, Peter. 1997. "Bordering on Chaos: The Cemex Story," *WIRED*, issue 5.07, July.

Koestsler, A. 1964. *The Art of Creation*. London, UK: Hutchinson.

Koestler, A. 1978. *Janus: A Summing Up*. London, UK: Picador.

Paquet, Gilles. 2009. *Crippling Epistemologies and Governance Failures: A Plea for Experimentalism*. Ottawa, ON: The University of Ottawa Press.

Paquet, Gilles. 2014. *Unusual Suspects – Essays on Social Learning Disabilities*. Ottawa, ON: Invenire.

Saroyan, William. 1941. *Saroyan's Fables*. New York, NY: Harcourt, Brace & Company.

Schafersman, S.D. 1991. "An Introduction to Critical Thinking," www.creeinquiry.com/critical-thinking.html.

Sparrow, M.K. 2008. *The Character of Harms*. Cambridge, UK: Cambridge University Press.

Terry, Larry D. 2003. *Leadership of Public Bureaucracies – Administrator as Conservator*. Armonk, NY: M.E. Sharpe.

Voß, J.P. *et al.* (eds.). 2006. *Reflexive Governance for Sustainable Development*. Cheltenham, UK: Edward Elgar.

PART I
Institutional Pathologies

CHAPTER 1

The Charter as Governance Story

"As the morality of rights displaces the morality of consent,
the politics of coercion replaces the politics of persuasion."

– F.L. Morton and Rainer Knopff

The context

The last 25 years have witnessed major changes both in the nature and valence of the state, and in the configuration of government. Pressures generated by globalization, accelerated technological change, greater socio-ethnic diversity, heightened citizens' expectations, crises in public finances, and so forth, have generated considerable turbulence, a requirement for the institutional order to adjust faster to ever more complex and always evolving circumstances, and have eaten away at many basic assumptions upon which the traditional forms of governing were built.

To simplify, one might say that the Welfare State is in the process of being replaced around the world by the Strategic State: governing has been drifting from a pattern dominated by Big G (government) towards a pattern dominated by small g (governance). This latter pattern of governance is less state-centric, more decentralized, polycentric and network-based than the previous regime.

The dominant features of the Big G world are a presumption that the state is more effective than other mechanisms in the pursuit of the public good, and that redistribution should proceed as a matter of right toward an objective of egalitarianism

– that can be achieved only through a centralized governing that brings the loot to the centre to begin with.

As for the small g world, its dominant features are a belief that the state cannot be presumed to be more effective than market or solidarity mechanisms in all circumstances, that the primary objective should be to reduce waste, and that redistribution should proceed on the basis of needs, and be guided by a philosophy of subsidiarity that operates bottom-up, and in a decentralized fashion – allowing intervention at the higher and more distant level only if the work cannot be done at a lower and more proximate level.

The Charter revolution

My hypothesis is that the 1982 Charter has considerably slowed down the drift from Big G to small g. It has done so by dramatically changing both the Canadian mindset, and the rules of the democratic game in Canada. These impacts have not been well understood.

First, the positive opinion of Canadians about the Charter is not an informed opinion. It is an impressionistic and emotional attachment to a contraption that has been effectively marketed by politicians as an empowerment of the citizens. As soon as the citizens are informed that two thirds of the Charter decisions by the Supreme Court involve the rights of those accused of crimes or of special interest groups, Canadian citizens are often astonished, and much less enthralled. This ignorance explains why more than half of polled Canadians in 2007 thought that the Charter had had a positive effect on Canada in the past, and was moving Canadian society in the right direction for the future.

In fact, the fuzziness of the public mind on Charter matters has allowed interest groups to take advantage of the new instrument to advance their causes by *defining their wants or their preferences as rights*. Rights are claimed without any concern as to whether such claims relate to basic needs or rather to luxury privileges, without any concern for the consequences, and without asking if the population agrees to it and is ready to take on the burdens associated to such rights.

Second, such claims have been routinely supported by the courts, often for specious reasons, and have acquired thereby a sacred character, and thereby a degree of permanency that they would never have acquired through Parliament. So as court decisions accumulated, the courts have gained the upper hand in their dialogue with the legislatures and Parliament.

While it has been argued that the legislatures can always use the 'notwithstanding clause' to neutralize the actions of the courts, the extraordinary degree of political correctness of the population, and their undue deference to the courts, have led to a chill when the possibility of using the notwithstanding clause has been raised – even in the face of the most Kafkaesque decisions of the courts. Such deference *vis-à-vis* the judiciary has generated a new despotism. Consequently, democratic governance has been eroded by the new fundamentalism of rights talk, and by the fact that, through the Charter, judicial adjudication has come to trump the democratic conversation.

The new fundamentalism of rights talk

Fundamentally, rights are social entities: they are a man-made system of rules, granting some privileges to persons with a particular status. When they become formalized – either because they are widely morally endorsed and/or embedded in law – they define expectations. Despite its lofty formulation, the Charter has generated considerable pressure to establish and formalize rights: it has contributed to judicializing certain rules, and to making the related rights distilled by the courts on the basis of the lofty text both inalienable and inextinguishable.

Like all charters of rights, the Canadian Charter was purported to ensure *negative freedom*, i.e., to protect citizens from their governments. But, through various devices – of which judicial activism is only one – the Canadian Charter has morphed into a machine that has produced an inflation of entitlements The courts used it to force government to accept new responsibilities in the name of *positive freedom* – i.e., the obligation to provide citizens with the security and support necessary to help them "develop" to their fullest extent (whatever it may mean) – all in the name of imaginary shared values and the ideology of egalitarianism.

The shift from a focus on negative freedom to one on positive freedom is a change of kind.

While the pursuit of negative freedom entails a reduction of oppressive rules, the focus on positive freedom leads to an increase in the *number of rules* (1) as there seems to be no limit on the 'capacities' that may be presumed necessary for the optimal development of the individual; and (2) therefore no limit to the entitlements that one may 'legitimately' claimed to ensure that one's 'capacities' are fully developed. It has also been argued that the degree of formality, and the permanency of the arrangements necessary for positive freedom to be assured, is such that only formal legal arrangements will do.

This inflation of new rights to symbolic and real resources has re-enforced the centrality of the state, and in so doing, slowed down the drift from Big G to small g in Canada.

Although the new fundamentalism that emerged from the rights talk of the Charter has been denounced from the very moment when the project of a charter was discussed, to the present – from Smiley (1969) to Ignatieff (2001) – and even though it was clear that the vague Rorschackian language of charters would be 'interpreted' by activist judges as legitimizing limitless entitlements, it has proved impossible to counter the ideological support for this philosophy of entitlement.

The notion of needs might have helped in establishing limits on those entitlements. David Braybrooke has shown that, to the extent that one is able to tame the notion of needs (through lists of matters of need, minimal standards, the principle of precedence of needs over preferences, and a revisionary process to modify either lists or standards as circumstances evolve), this may serve to anchor discussions about entitlements, and help to keep them within bounds (Braybrooke 1987). For, contrary to the notion of rights – which is a conversation stopper – the notion of needs is an invitation to conversation and deliberation.

Charter as adjudication trumping politics

In the post-Charter years, the drifts from the rule of law to the idolatry of rights (and toward a deference to the infallibility of the judges and commissars charged with their interpretation) have not been innocent. It would appear that the quest for certainty and clarity knows no bounds, so the political process has been found too unreliable to be counted on in such matters of governance. Better a clear bad rule than a good fuzzy one, we are told.

An elite of super-bureaucrats has been called upon to interpret the laws, to define what is acceptable or not, to make decisions for the citizens, because the citizens have been declared incapable (as were their elected representatives) of doing that. This drift toward legal formalism and administrative adjudication has grown exponentially. It is such that one can hardly go through a week in the life of the country without one commissar or another making an adjudication report that is meant to force a representative government to do something it would prefer not to do.

Such developments, with the complicity of parliamentarians whose lack of courage has, at times, led them (1) to delegate to judges and commissars some of the wicked problems they were faced with, and (2) never to challenge their diktats even when they were absurdly destructive – has tended to slow down the drift to small g governance.

This state of affairs reached a bizarre climax in 2004 when the then federal Minister of Justice developed a new doctrine in the *Ottawa Citizen*, in the midst of the electoral campaign (Cotler 2004). This new gospel stated openly that democracy does not work; and the courts and commissars must be the bulwarks to protect Canadian governance.

The matter under discussion at the time was the decision of appellate courts in British Columbia, Ontario and Quebec to strike down the legislation limiting marriage to a man and a woman. Irwin Cotler regarded appellate court judges as infallible, even though the majority in the House of Commons would appear not to agree, and had said so very clearly. It is difficult to understand why the Minister of Justice did not even feel the need to obtain the Supreme Court's view about whether the traditional definition of marriage was indeed in violation of the Charter – an opinion that whimsically, one may add, the Supreme Court has refused to give.

Whatever the Supreme Court's final decision might have been, what is most surprising is to see a federal Minister of Justice so obsessed with limiting the damages that democracy might inflict on minorities, that he is willing (1) to fall into an idolatry of court-interpreted rights (as if they were sacred), (2) to pronounce the ultimate authority of the courts over Parliament in a representative democracy, and (3) to suggest that Parliament should not dare to use the notwithstanding clause – thereby arguing for the judiciary to be allowed complete license.

As Michael Ignatieff has rightly underlined, "we need to stop thinking of human rights as trumps and begin thinking of them as a language that creates a basis for deliberation" (Ignatieff 2001: 95). Rights are not a set of trump cards to bring political disputes to closure. Parliament is the place of last resort for deliberation about all governance issues in a democracy.

The idea that Parliament is not to be trusted, and that judges, as super-bureaucrats, are like shamen whose views cannot be contested is anti-democratic.

The Charter is a creature of Parliament.

Rights have been defined by Parliament, as Michael Ignatieff reminds us. They are a "tool kit against oppression" and one should not automatically "define anything desirable as a right," because that would erode the legitimacy of core rights (*Ibid.*: 57).

The courts are not infallible in interpreting the Charter either. And there is nothing sinister, in a free and democratic society, in Parliament's using the notwithstanding clause to suspend for a short period the application of a decision by the courts that does not pertain to oppression, and with which the majority of freely elected parliamentarians does not agree.

To allow minority groups to obtain everything they would prefer to have as a matter of rights, and to make rights into a secular religion, and the courts into its only authorized clergy, is taking Canada back into dangerous territory. And when it is a minister of the Canadian government who trivializes Parliament as the ultimate authority in a representative democracy, one has cause for concern.

One might be tempted to take Cotler's views as extreme and marginal, and to discount them accordingly. That would be a mistake. The activism of the courts and the willingness of judges and commissars to indulge in intellectual acrobatics in interpreting Article 15 of the Charter – the equality clause – (for instance), and in philosophizing about what may touch or leave untouched "dignity, feelings and self-respect" of a person can only leave one somewhat uncomfortable.

The thrusting of the language of rights into democratic conversations, and the further displacement of Parliament by judges and commissars, have imposed onto discussions about more or less (that characterize most of the democratic discourse) a sort of either-or yoke. Practical issues (that ought to be discussed taking into account context and circumstances) are adjudicated in the absolute and in the abstract, within an adversarial venue. This is not what all Canadians accept as what democracy is.

Hopes and fears

At first, many were enthusiastically favourable to the idea of the Charter, on the grounds that the Supreme Court would exercise the same restraint in interpreting the Charter that it had exercised in interpreting the Bill of Rights of 1960. This has proven not to be the case. The dual forces of the fundamentalism of rights and judicial activism have unleashed a major attack on representative democracy.

The saga of this successful attack has been eloquently told by Rory Leishman.

This is a cautionary tale.

Our institutional order has been transformed while the citizens slept. It has now been established that the courts have a right (when they wish) to review and strike down policies supported by the citizens' elected representatives, and to define their own rules for doing so (Oakes' test) – in complete ignorance or blatant contradiction of earlier jurisprudence when they wish to do so, as Leishman shows (Leishman 2006).

Whether this is an irreversible trend is the key question.

Let us just say that, for an observer from the mezzanine, it is difficult to see how this *dérapage* will be stopped (1) until judges go back to their duty of *jus dicere* instead of indulging in *jus dare;* and this will not happen until there is a change of the guard; and (2) until parliamentary democracy has been strengthened; and this will not happen until there is a change in the activism of the citizenry.

References

Braybrooke, David. 1987. *Meeting Needs*. Princeton, NJ: Princeton University Press.

Cotler, Irwin. 2004. "The Charter is here to stay," *Ottawa Citizen*, June 16.

Ignatieff, Michael. 2001. *Human Rights as Politics and Idolatry*. Princeton, NJ: Princeton University Press.

Leishman, Roy. 2006. *Against Judicial Activism*. Montreal, QC: McGill-Queen's University Press.

Morton, F.L. and R. Knopff. 2000. *The Charter Revolution and the Court Party*. Toronto, ON: Broadview Press.

Smiley, Donald. 1969. "The Case Against the Canadian Charter of Human Rights," *Canadian Journal of Political Science*, 2: 277-291.

CHAPTER 2

Bouchard-Taylor
as Hyper-tolerance

The Bouchard-Taylor report, like 15th century maps, is elegant but not very helpful to navigation in rough times. To throw light on debates and to help arriving at better decisions, it is not sufficient to generate an indigestible tome, and to put forward dozens of recommendations. Often, in such ventures, the commissioners have a propensity to arrive at certain conclusions in their haste to bring the conversation to a halt, and to impose what experts call 'final solutions'. This is an anti-democratic resolution.

What has emerged from the report is nothing more than the inconsiderate promotion of hyper-tolerance.

This hyper-tolerant attitude is anchored in:
- a phenomenal amnesia (about the common public culture in Quebec and all that has contributed to it);
- certain assumptions that claim not only that all cultures are equivalent (which is immensely contestable), but also that the maintenance of original cultures is absolutely necessary for the full personal development of any individual wherever he or she may move in the world (which is equally contestable); and
- the view that the host society must shoulder most, if not all, of the adjustment required to accommodate the newcomer on this front (which is eminently contestable).

Most of the readers of the Bouchard-Taylor report have interpreted it as a call for an excessive accommodation that might lead the host society to lose its soul. Polls show that some

55 percent of the host country population believes that the newcomers should shoulder the adjustment completely.

The Canadian population's common sense has come to see that there should be a moral contract defining the mutual expectations (something that goes much beyond the edicts of common law) of the host country population and the newcomers. Canadians feel that it is legitimate for the host country to define its expectations, and to negotiate entrance requirements that constitute the *quo* corresponding to the *quid* that is made up of the generous benefits the newcomers are entitled to in the *quid pro quo* of the moral contract.

Not to negotiate a moral contract would be irresponsible for two reasons: first, because uncertainty in these matters generates apprehension in the short run, and unhelpful and toxic frictions in the long haul; second, because the lack of a moral contract can only generate unfortunate reactions by the host society to acts of provocation by radical newcomers who insist on bringing into our social context some of the former practices of the old country that are incompatible with local mores, and threaten to erode the common public culture. These tensions may turn ugly because the courts of law, crippled by the elusive language of the charters of rights, are often incapable of taking into account the common public culture of the host society in the resolution of such conflicts and, therefore, are likely to err predictably in directions that do violence to the host society.

The fact of being able to interact with members of our community *à visage découvert* is an example of the usefulness of the moral contract. The idea of living in a society where one wears a mask is not tolerable for Canadians. It is therefore legitimate that this imperative be part of the moral contract to which newcomers are invited to subscribe. Otherwise, as has been the case with polygamy and young girls' excision (something that the criminal code prohibits but that the police forces have ceased to track down with determination for fear that the courts might indeed make them legal), there is a likelihood that our society might be surreptitiously infiltrated by practices that would not only modify our culture, but pervert it.

The content of the moral contract between the host society and newcomers should be continuously debated, and the moral contract must evolve through time. But the systematic refusal to honour such a moral contract should be considered a lack of *affectio societatis* – a lack of commitment to engage fully and creatively in the construction of a better host society. In the private sector, lack of *affectio societatis* entails the dissolution of the flawed partnership. In the public sphere, lack of *affectio societatis* could translate into an invitation to those who do not feel capable of *affectio societatis* for the host society to exert one of the most fundamental rights in a democratic society – the right to leave.

In these sorts of files, the Bouchard-Taylor report is inconsequential, and it may even have contributed to generating some additional mental prisons.

At the end of the day, Bouchard-Taylor as a process of deliberation has been useful in order to ensure that certain sensitive topics would cease to be regarded as taboo topics. But Bouchard-Taylor as a report has only attempted in a futile way (and badly at that) to impose some 'final solutions' in matters where only continuous conversation can be regarded as a workable *modus vivendi* in a democracy. The Bouchard-Taylor report attempt – like Joshua's attempt to stop the sun – has failed.

References

Bouchard, Gérard and Charles Taylor. 2008. *Fonder l'avenir – Le temps de la conciliation*. Rapport de la Commision de consultation sur les pratiques d'accommodement réliées aux différences culturelles. Québec, QC: Gouvernement du Québec.

Paquet, Gilles. 1990. "De l'État-protecteur au contrat moral," *Le Devoir*, December 15.

CHAPTER 3

The Betrayal of Super-bureaucrats

One of the most paradoxical Biblical parables, found in the Gospel of Luke, is that of the dishonest servant who, being asked to render account of his misadministration to his master, realizes that he will be dismissed. Therefore, he assembles his master's debtors, and commits forgeries which dramatically reduce their debts. It is said that, following his dismissal, he was held in high esteem, and supported by the debtors with whom he had conspired to rob his master, but was also cynically admired by his master for having shown such good sense as an *"enfant du siècle"*.

This sacred text, which I must admit I find somewhat puzzling, will serve as a starting point in my analysis of the relationship between elected officials and super-bureaucrats (deputy ministers, agents of Parliament, and the like). For *"enfants du siècle"* are also present among them.

Modest general proposition

According to the conventional model, super-bureaucrats serve government and Parliament. In the case of deputy ministers, they must inform government to the best of their knowledge, give advice, and then must proceed to carry out government's wishes with loyalty, imagination and creativity, as long as those wishes do not run counter to the laws of the country. In the case of agents of Parliament, the burden of office is more complex. Since they are the 'guardians of the guardians', they must not only make their views known, but, if they detect anything untoward, they must also identify the culprits and suggest remedy. A large majority of super-bureaucrats, we are told, fulfill this function loyally and creatively.

However, at the same time, in a subtle way, this model is being put into question. Some deputy ministers and other super-bureaucrats like the Auditor General (AG) or the Parliamentary Budget Officer (PBO) have allowed it to be believed in their communications (or at the very least in what they have allowed to be said about them without contradicting it) that their mandate goes much beyond simply informing and assisting government and Parliament, in their social learning (and in the case of agents of Parliament to nudge the institution to which they report to take action). They have, to different degrees, allowed themselves to be presented to the general citizenry as the privileged and most reliable interpreters of the public interest, and as having the responsibility of standing on guard for the country when facing elected representatives whose legitimacy – according to these super-bureaucrats – would appear to have become questionable.

This has happened more or less by design, depending on the particular super-bureaucracies: some explicitly saying that their own legitimacy is greater than the legitimacy of elected officials; others allowing such things to be said in the media without feeling the need to correct such statements.

One would expect that such weird theorizing would be denounced by academics and the media. Far from it, a large number of members of these brotherhoods have expressed their support for such a view, and have been arguing in favour of reducing the margin of maneuverability of elected officials, and of much more power being granted to super-bureaucrats. The reasons evoked in making these arguments have been the corruption of a political system that allows for all and sundry to act as broker and to seek to influence the government – active citizens … what a horror! This is the reason why they have demanded that the superior moral authority of super-bureaucrats be recognized as uncontestable by granting them additional powers.

This seed of counter-democracy (one of the best guarded secrets in Ottawa) has begun to germinate and flourish. Empowered by the moral support of right-thinking journalists and academics, these newly minted crusaders – deputy ministers, 'independent' adjudicators of all types, and agents of Parliament

– have come to consider themselves to be justified in their active or passive disloyalty to the elected masters in the name of the higher interests of the country.

Such theorization is undermining parliamentary democracy as we know it.

Fortunately, the vast majority of super-bureaucrats and deputy ministers may not subscribe to these views. They are aware of the impropriety of such a claim on the part of bureaucrats who should not attempt to usurp the role of those who are the preeminent and even exclusive interpreters of the highest interests of the country. *A contrario*, such a position is vigourously defended by a clutch of activist super-bureaucrats – direct descendants of the dishonest servant. The worm has entered the apple, and this has consequences since it is often difficult to know who in the tribe of super-bureaucrats subscribes to this philosophy.

What happens when one does not know who is an honest guardian?

There are hundreds of adjudicators and commissars, dozens of deputy ministers, and many agents of Parliament. Even if only a small fraction of these officials consider themselves authorized to be disloyal to the institutions they report to because, in their own view, they are better equipped than elected officials to interpret the higher interests of the country – especially if we do not know who they are – this may completely transform the relationship between super-bureaucrats and elected officials. If one out of 20 is potentially passively or actively disloyal (and no one knows who belongs in that category), a general paranoia of the elected officials becomes understandable: one no longer knows whom to trust! Some striking examples of this paranoia have occurred recently.

The pressures from adjudicators (such as Judge Gomery and some of his academic epigons) seeking to institutionalize such a high moral and legal authority for super-bureaucrats is indicative of this trend. Even though the late Arthur Kroeger and some senior bureaucrats denounced such proposals, they did not succeed in stemming the tide.

A far-reaching process of counter-democracy has ensued. The number of crusading super-bureaucrats who proclaim that in our present age of distrust, they are the only line of defense capable of protecting citizens, has grown. Knights Templar are in the process of knocking our democratic machinery off-balance.

Elected representatives have attempted to take measures to protect themselves from such disloyalty by clarifying the role of super-bureaucrats and constraining their power. However, such measures have been timid and not well received. Those who have installed such measures have exposed themselves to the disapproval of the media and academics, as well as to the displeasure of their subordinates (including those who are loyal).

Two-fold negative impact

The situation is even more critical in a circumstance where some super-bureaucrats like the agents of Parliament have pushed the envelope yet further, and have chosen both to abuse their position by extending unduly their interpretation of their mandate, and to do so in a less than responsible way.

For instance, the Parliamentary Budget Officer (PBO) has performed a useful function in questioning the inaccuracy of certain financial calculations put forward by the government, but when it took unto itself to second guess the government on the putative impact of its forthcoming spending cuts on front line services, it went much beyond its mandate and its capabilities. Its speculation to counter the government speculations, and the unreasonable request of detailed information about the exact impact, at the departmental level, of a broad process of reduction in spending, as it was mechanically unfolding, transformed the PBO into a tool of the Opposition in the House of Commons. It was no longer providing a non-partisan service to Parliament.

Moreover, the PBO, in allowing all his criticisms about the budgetary glitches to be directed to the elected government (when much if not most of it could reasonably be ascribed to public servants) not only tended to re-enforce the view that the office had unduly politicized its function, but also that it had become a paravent to immunize the senior federal executives from criticism. While this has been celebrated by bureaucracy-friendly academics, this was a most unwise strategy on the part of the PBO.

Super-bureaucrats have super powers, but they must exercise them with super prudence. When they do not, they contribute to endangering the very survival of the institution.

By failing to exercise wise restraint, and to accept to live by the imperatives of the four cardinal virtues:

i) *temperantia* – an awareness and sense of limits;

ii) *fortitudo* – a capacity to take into account context and long term;

iii) *justitia* – a sense of what is good and an inclination to search for it;

iv) *prudentia* – a sense of what is practical and reasonable,

the PBO has contributed to the constriction and containment that befell it. But by failing to point the finger at the source of the difficulties, and allowing the media to ascribe all things untoward to the government, the PBO was a disloyal servant: it displayed a higher loyalty to the bureaucratic tribe than to Parliament – a Parliament that would have needed to be informed more fully about the sources and causes of the financial inaccuracies detected.[7]

In an era when the official Opposition in the House of Commons has been in disarray, the temptation for agents of Parliament to become something like the official Opposition is understandable, but reprehensible. In this context, allowing the citizenry to be misinformed by the media about the real source of the glitches is equally reprehensible. It is in such a compost heap that this new dogma of the super-bureaucrat, supposedly more trustworthy and independent than an elected representative, has been allowed to germinate, and the protective belt supplied by the PBO for the senior bureaucracy is also reprehensible.

The real tragedy created by the lack of punishment for deception and irresponsibility at the top of the bureaucracy resides in the climate of distrust which has been implanted. One

---

[7] By some drama-queenesque histrionics at the time of the sponsorship affair, a recent Auditor General has had the same deleterious effect on the office. One may also point to cognate dysfunctions in other single-purpose entities at the federal level in Canada like Canadian Nuclear Safety Commission and the Office of the Commissioner of Official Languages (Hubbard and Paquet 2013).

would expect that agents of Parliament could serve Parliament without having to allow such sabotage of the work of Parliament to prevail.

In the meantime, back at the farm ...

Meanwhile, if the wishes of the government and Parliament are to be carried out each day and if the elected representatives are to succeed in enacting the promises made to the electorate, it is through the efforts of senior public servants and of the public service as a whole. A conflictive equilibrium is thus in place: elected representatives and bureaucrats need each other; they are complementary; they have to work together.

It is therefore essential to take a moment to clarify the burden of office of one and all, and to rid the system not only of the *saboteurs* (who are destroying the capital of trust and professionalism required to ensure that the public service contributes to good governance), but also of the theory promoting 'sabotage as a way to better serve the people'.

But before such an exercise of clarification can be undertaken, the alarm must be sounded and citizens must be persuaded that there is some urgency. For the moment, cognitive dissonance is omnipresent and allows one to continue denying that any disloyalty exists in the federal bureaucracy. And when, with supporting evidence, its existence becomes undeniable, legions continue to insist on calling it an abominable exception, on arguing that errors of judgment should be allowed, etc.

As if we were not all well aware of the impact of one rotten apple in a basket of apples!

The same may be said about *"un enfant du siècle"*. And if there is anything clear about the role of agents of Parliament as 'guardians of guardians', it is that they have to smoke out *"les enfants du siècle"* and not fall under the spell of the *'idol of the tribe'*.

References

Hubbard, Ruth and Gilles Paquet. 2013. "Single-Purpose Entities in the Governance of a Multiplex World" in Christopher Stoney and G. Bruce Doern (eds.). *How Ottawa Spends 2013-2014 – The Harper Government: Mid-Term Blues and Long-Term Plans.* Montreal/Kingston, QC/ON: McGill-Queen's University Press, p. 196-298.

Hubbard, Ruth and Gilles Paquet. 2017. "The penumbra of super-bureaucracies in Canada," *www.optimumonline.ca* , 47(3): 11-36.

Paquet, Gilles. 2010. "Disloyalty," *www.optimumonline.ca,* 40(1): 23-47.

Paquet, Gilles. 2014. "Super-bureaucrats as *enfants du siècle, " www. optimumonline.ca*, 44(2): 4-14.

CHAPTER 4

Unmasking Legal Corruption and Legal Extortion[8]

Pneumopathological ... the state of "those who are morally insane, 'living', as it were, in a fantasy-world of self-righteousness"

– Robert Sibley

The Canadian public culture appears to stand on two wobbly stilts – 'moral numbness' and 'entitlements'. This may sound innocuous until one realizes that it has driven us to pneumopathology. Together, they have triggered our failure to challenge the most egregious decisions entailing important costs to the community, while underpinning our self-serving rationalizations to justify the most indefensible entitlements to private personal benefits from the public purse.

On the moral numbness front, there has been a significant change over the last decades. Some 20 years ago, Neil Nevitte wrote on the decline in deference in Canada. He detected a fault line in the evolution of Canadian public culture: from a tradition of deference to authority, to one of refusal to defer, i.e., to yield to the opinions and decisions of others supposedly better informed or in authority. If one were to conduct the same sort of study today, one would find evidence that this decline of deference has now morphed not only into a total indifference to the opinions and decisions of others, but also into a willingness to silently tolerate and seemingly condone the most abject decisions, having a far-

---

[8] This chapter has been co-authored with Robin Higham.

reaching negative impact on the community. Canadians appear now to take pride in their own disengagement – seeing nothing, hearing nothing and saying nothing in the face of the most reprehensible situations – unless their narrow and immediate personal interests are at stake.

This is when our national entitlement mentality kicks in. How often have we seen a large plurality of Canadians claiming entitlement to equality of outcome whatever their own contribution? They also react negatively to attempts to ascertain each case on its own merit: they regard it as unacceptable discrimination – for it might lead to punishing the shirkers and rewarding the contributors. Consequently, treating blindly all citizens identically and overly generously – whatever their contribution – is the new ethic in our no-fault/ no-merit society. This ethos underpins our most unreasonable sense of entitlements.

Some illustrations

On the moral numbness front, recall the legally corrupt arrangement (Kaufmann and Vicente 2005) that led to a 30-year contract through which Quebecor will manage the new arena in Quebec City. Quebecor will pay an overall annual rent for control of the facility that is a fraction of the price paid by comparable renters in other cities in the country. A few *Parti Québécois* MLAs (to their credit) resigned over this arrangement, but there was none of the open public dissent that one would have expected from such a scandalous deal that will line the pockets of a private sector firm with hundreds of millions of dollars at public expense (Frigon 2011).

On the entitlement front, consider the 17 public service unions in Ottawa that are currently suing the government of Canada for undue "disguised discipline" as a result of a request by the employer that public servants be evaluated on the basis of four seemingly commonsensical criteria: "showing integrity and respect; thinking things through; working effectively with others; and taking initiative and being action-oriented" (May 2014). When it comes to lining their pockets, the self-righteous federal public service unions would seem to have no hesitation to claim that they are entitled to receive their considerable benefits without any meaningful basic evaluation of performance. This is not unlike the reaction of the Alberta teachers' refusing to accept that their members be recertified every five years so that bad teachers can be weeded out. This proposal has been denounced by the union as an "assault" on its members (Mason 2014). Both cases are evidence of a culture of entitlement, legitimizing the extortion of private benefits from the public purse.

The two faces of Janus: same philosophy, many masks

The tolerance of legal corruption on the one hand, and the practice of the legal extortion of benefits on the basis of imaginary entitlements on the other, can be said to be the two faces of Janus, revealing some deep commitment to the same fundamental philosophy of private interests at public expense.

Since these faces are not always charming, a variety of masks hide the willful blindness of the citizens in one case, and the greed of individual groups in the other.

The first mask is legal corruption masquerading as the rule of law – the 'it is legal' mantra is brandished, however wasteful a blind application of the letter of the law might be, given the circumstances. It is applied with gusto to cover, with a legalistic blanket, the most mischievous acts. This calls for a robust public denunciation of the legal corruption phenomenon.

The second mask is legal extortion masquerading as a legitimate defense of self-defined unalienable entitlements – a fantasy through which some privileges, granted in much different circumstances in the past, are presented as unalienable rights having to be honoured in perpetuity whatever the circumstances. This is the mask routinely worn by labour leaders when extorting concessions from senior technocrats – often rather disloyal servants of shareholders or elected governments who are too often tempted to pay less attention to their responsibility to ensure the high performance of their underlings than to their own quiet lives as less than fully responsible bosses. This phenomenon of legal extortion also calls for public denunciation.

Wake-up time

Citizens have been unduly blind to these phenomena of legal corruption and legal extortion that have characterized the work of bureaucrats even more than the work of politicians, but can be better ascribed to entrenched systems than to individuals. Effective action against these phenomena requires some reframing of perspectives.

First, there must be a redirection of the hunt from its quasi-exclusive focus on elected politicians and their transgressions toward a greater attention to the bureaucracy and the systems they operate, where so much of the corruption and extortion occurs. The political tip is only a small portion of the iceberg – the most visible part of the iceberg, but not the most important part in extent or materiality.

Second, there must be also a redirection of the inquiry away from the legal profession's fixation exclusively on individual acts to be exposed by judicial pit bulls, toward a focus on 'systemic governance failures', calling for organizational and institutional redesign. Certainly, such systemic investigations create more difficult challenges than the parading in court of a personalized corruptor or extortionist. Even though courtroom drama seems to satisfy the media-driven appetite for scapegoats, it can never constitute a meaningful strategy to address embedded administrative pathologies.

In the case of corruption (like in the cases of education or health care), the central objective should not be to hang a rogue but to expose the hidden part of the iceberg, where systemic corruption and extortion are niched, in order to be able to suggest ways to repair the system. Lawyers with their sole fixation on establishing personal guilt appear to be ill-equipped to work at exposing the roots of system failures, nor to undertake the redesign of systems that have proved prone to fail. This is the real job of the students of governance.

References

Frigon, Gaétan. 2011. "Un cadeau qui vaut des centaines de millions de dollars," http://gaetanfrigon.com.

Kaufmann, Daniel and Pedro C. Vicente. 2005. "Legal Corruption," *Economics and Politics,* 23(2): 195-219.

Mason, Gary. 2014. "Imagine the uproar if we weeded out bad teachers," *The Globe and Mail,* May 9.

May, Kathryn. 2014. "Unions grieve new PS performance rules," *Ottawa Citizen,* April 7, A1-2.

PART II
Impostures and Sophistry

CHAPTER 5

The Don Quixote Syndrome: Weasel Words as Guideposts

... croire plus vraie son idée que ce que le réel montre ...

– Michel Onfray

Introduction

In a recent book, French philosopher Michel Onfray exposes what he calls the 'Don Quixote principle' – the way Don Quixote sees the world, substituting his idea or perception for whatever exists out there – all this leading Don Quixote to consider his idea of reality as truer and more real than reality itself (Onfray 2014). According to Onfray, this is a bias that has afflicted many Western luminaries.

This is a bias that is also plaguing many observers of the contemporary scene: individuals becoming so mesmerized by their view of the world as to cease seeing reality altogether, and retaining only the bizarre idea of reality concocted by their own troubled minds.

As a result of this false or distorted perception of reality, these luminaries become prisoners of their idea of reality, and become puppets of these ideas – these deceptive ideas becoming their puppeteer. This furious passion for ideas to the detriment of reality transforms their behaviour in ways that ordinary beings can only find disturbing, as when Quixote falls in love with his sublime Dulcinea – in fact a rather ugly and smelly wench – or as he insists on presenting a barber's copper basin as the golden helmet of a knight.

When intellectuals or opinion-moulders or persons in authority become afflicted by this Quixotic syndrome, their discourse acquires a pneumopathological quality, and becomes an echo of the state of mind of "those who are morally insane, 'living' as it were, in a fantasy-world of self-righteousness" (Sibley 2013). Their utterances become at best perplexing, and at worst confusing and toxic.

When such utterances come from those at the very top of organizations and falsely claim to have a canonical quality, they become *mentir-vrai* (Eyries 2013) that serves their partisan goals and underpins their exercise of power. Their impact on the public discourse and policy making are not unlike what would ensue if the Bank of Canada were to decide to issue counterfeit money.

What is most catastrophic about this *mentir-vrai* is the extent to which such utterances fail to generate any strident denunciation on the part of those who know better. It is as if, in our world, stating that the king is naked, that the argument is groundless, that the issue brought forth is an imposture, etc. were no longer part of the menu of legitimate responses to asinine statements from persons in authority suffering from the Don Quixote syndrome. Yet, in such circumstances, silence can only mean consent and, therefore, complicity with deception. This criminal failure to confront Don Quixotisms is responsible for much corruption of the public discourse.

The plight of unchallenged *mentir-vrai* emanating from supposed authoritative sources would appear to have grown exponentially of late. The purpose of this paper is to provide a sample of these utterances, to underline their toxic nature, and to suggest that such bunk needs to be debunked. The sample is drawn from recent 2015 pronouncements, and has been chosen because of the particularly toxic implications of these sophistries.

A sample of sophistries

Most of the intellectual impostures of the sort mentioned above are stylized in the following way:

- the presentation of an imaginary problem purported to be at the source of the level of discomfort and *malaise* experienced in an organization or a socio-economy;
- some evasive storytelling about the toxicity of impact of the problem purported to have been identified, crafted in a way likely to generate some populist appeal while deflecting attention from the real problems crying for repairs;
- the focalization on some policy directions or gimmicks claiming to be a full response to the imaginary problem when, in fact, it leaves the real problems occluded, untouched or worsened.

In this sort of discourse, the more fuzziness the better, obviously!

Justin Trudeau and the imaginary plight of the Canadian middle class

The middle class is a darling of democratic politics. Most people perceive themselves as members of the middle class, and most of them have been led by the media to feel mistreated in a world where supposedly income inequality is growing, and is standing as a challenge to our belief in egalitarianism. Therefore it is not difficult to understand that one leading federal political party (the Liberal Party of Canada) discovered in May 2015 the plight of the middle class as the most important problem of the day. Supposedly, the middle class is struggling, falling behind, doing most of the heavy lifting in this socio-economy of ours, and it is now time that an enlightened government stop the few in the upper class from continuing to take from the many in this struggling middle class.

As Andrew Coyne has shown, this idea of the struggling middle class is a myth: "every line of the Liberal story is a fraud. The middle class isn't struggling: the $53,000 the median family earned after tax in 2012 is an all-time high – 24% more than in 1997, after inflation." As for the rich (top 1 percent), its share of income has been declining since 2006 (Coyne 2015: C5).

Given the groundlessness of the premises on which the problem is manufactured, it is hardly surprising that the solution put forward by Justin Trudeau in May 2015 – some sort of Robin Hood sounding redistribution purported to be benefiting the middle class – turns out to be a *canard* that can be shown to benefit only the top one-third of the tax filers, and not those at the bottom of the income distribution.

This sort of fuzzy thinking is based on the confusion between the notions of inequality and fairness. Reasonable people do not find inequality revulsive: they are offended by unfairness. By deliberately making the weasel word "inequality" a policy target while babbling about unfairness, the Trudeau scheme is a fraud: it does nothing about unfairness and/or poverty, but, by a sleight of hand, it only produces benefits for the top third of the tax filers.

In a country where the battle over inequality would appear to be a phoney war (Coyne 2014), such sophistry is doubly counterproductive: (1) it fuels envy among segments of the middle class to draw attention away from the real repairs needed to the socio-economic apparatus to make it more productive; and (2) it feeds the basest populist passion for equality of outcomes, and the discourse of a zero-sum game, that undermines the fundamental need for cooperation if we are to become more productive.

Janice Charette and the imaginary plague of mental illness in the federal public sector

While some politicians are fantasizing about the imaginary plight of the middle class, it would appear that the Clerk of the Privy Council (also charged with the responsibility for the federal public service) has a myth of her own to fantasize about: the myth of an epidemic of mental illness in the federal bureaucracy being the central problem for the federal public sector.

In the 22nd Annual Report to the Prime Minister on the Public Service of Canada, and in many statements sprinkled at the time of the release of the report, Janice Charette has defined three priorities for the coming year:

- to re-invigorate the recruitment of new entrants,
- to meet mental health challenges, and
- to reinforce the policy community as a profession.

In a very significant number of interviews, the mental health challenges have been singled out as the main source of concern.

No hard evidence has been provided in support of the existence of this mental health epidemic, nor to explain why the federal public service is suffering from it to a greater degree than any other large organization – to the point that it has to be made a key priority. Nor has any analysis been provided to identify the causes behind that supposed epidemic. Yet, it is quite revealing that, in talking about the issue, Charette has been insistent on harassment and discrimination being present, and on the need for "compassion as well as focus on preventing harm" being mentioned as the sort of action required.

If mental illness exists to a high degree (a fact that has not been clearly established), could it be because claiming stress and mental fatigue are such an easy ploy to get access to time off in a world where the employer is more interested in presenting itself as 'model employer' than in extracting high performance from the employees? Or might it be a symptom of a very poor organization of work in the federal public sector as has been suggested by some recent studies (Hubbard and Paquet 2014), but also by earlier reports to the Prime Minister? If it were the case, the answer might not be a romantic call for compassion but a call for a serious redesign of the workplace and a tightening of the rules.

A more realistic and less naïve assessment of the lack of productivity and innovation of the federal public employees might be ascribable to bad matching between competencies required and capabilities of public servants, bad management of human resources (HR) in general, etc. – all things that require an overhauling of the HR system much more than opening the faucet of compassion.

Legitimizing the mental illness myth, on the sole basis of self-serving answers to fluffy questionnaires is reprehensible, and proposing to treat this imaginary problem with compassion can only be regarded as a way to divert attention from the reframing, restructuring and retooling necessary to refurbish the federal public service to make it perform better (Hubbard and Paquet 2015: Part III). The Charette diagnosis would appear to hide more than it reveals, and the moral comfort she promises to those claiming to be mentally challenged and their union leaders may simply encourage yet more X-inefficiency in the Canadian federal public sector (Leibenstein 1978).

Is the federal government workplace akin to a salt mine ... really?

The new unanimity from the Clerk down in the federal ethos – that cushy jobs in the federal public service need to be made cushier with yet better working conditions as compensation for the morbidity of the workplace – appears to many observers as pure fantasy and pathetic indulgence.

In the meantime, the central question remains: if the Clerk of the Privy Council is not focusing on getting the Canadian federal public service to perform better, who is? Why is it that well-known, necessary reforms called for by reports to the Prime Minister are ignored, and how come the top bureaucrat can take refuge in the elusive fairy tale that the Canadian federal public service is not inefficient and ineffective but simply highly stressed?

The Supreme Court's crippling epistemology

It is not only the politicians and senior bureaucrats who would appear to have fallen prey to the Don Quixote syndrome. Even the Supreme Court of Canada would appear to have lost its moorings, and fallen *cul par dessus tête* in a series of recent judgments.

I will use only *Saskatchewan Federation of Labour v. Saskatchewan 2015 SCC 4* (a judgment rendered on January 30, 2015) to illustrate the way in which the majority in this case (5-2) has been entirely swamped by the Don Quixote syndrome in choosing to give predominance to the right to strike of public sector employees over the right of citizens to essential services.

Instead of recognizing the primacy of essential services in the case where the public sector has a monopoly, the Supreme Court of Canada has occluded completely this obligation of the public sector, and chosen to focus entirely on a questionable extension of the right of association to mean the right to strike. This is pure sophistry.

This sleight of hand has been accomplished by the majority through inventing a right to strike under Section 2(d) of the Charter, thereby creating a constitutional right to strike. As explained very well by the minority in this case (Rothstein and

Robert), the majority has transformed a policy choice that the majority deems worthy into constitutional imperatives.

On the basis of this ideological bias of the majority, it has departed from a convention that had been prudently protected by the courts in the world of labour relations – i.e., to refuse to inject constitutional protection to one of the parties. In this case, the majority has injected such protection for labour by choosing to regard the right to strike as "an indispensable component of collective bargaining." As the minority argues, this is way out of line with recent jurisprudence. Especially in the public sector where citizens are taken as hostages in a strike situation where the public sector is a monopoly, this unreasonable extension is constraining unduly the right of elected officials to protect their citizens from essential services being curtailed by strike action from public employees.

The Supreme Court of Canada in this case is an ass.

The majority position has unduly extended the notion of collective bargaining, has taken distance from protecting the process and access to the process of collective bargaining by choosing whimsically to constitutionalize the right to strike. It has determined that the right to strike of public sector employees (i.e., the right of taking citizens as hostages by denying them access to essential services – as defined by their duly elected officials – does take precedence over the right of citizens to have access to essential services). The lack of strident reaction to this abuse of power of the Supreme Court in not interpreting the law (as is its duty to do), but rather in creating new law in a toxic way (as a result of ideological bias) – is difficult to understand.

What is the point of having a notwithstanding clause to stop the carrying out of unreasonable decisions arrived at by the Supreme Court, if it is not used in such a situation?

Common law is not meant to allow the judges to use their personal biases to determine how conflict-ridden situations between parties are going to be resolved. The fact that the political world appears to be forced to bow to the judiciary when its decision is so glaringly, ideologically thwarted is difficult to understand, but may be revealing an unwarranted deference to the courts.

The fact that the intelligentsia and the media have been so silent on the subject is troublesome. Some more outspoken than me might speak of a betrayal of the intellectuals.

Conclusion

These illustrations of Don Quixotisms that have elicited little or no response are cause for concern. They reveal the great cost of the demise of critical thinking in public affairs in doxacracy Canada – where what matters is less what a factum reveals, but about different shades of opinions inspired more or less by one gospel or the other.

The point has been made by Paquet that critical thinking has declined to the point where failure to confront has become a national disease (Paquet 2014). Canadians indeed are polite to a fault, and gentle but, as André Trocmé suggests – "who begins with gentleness. He shall finish in insipidity and cowardice" – not very encouraging!

References

Coyne, Andrew. 2014. "Battle over Inequality looks like Phoney War," *Ottawa Citizen*, September 25, C7.

Coyne, Andrew. 2015. "The Middle Class Myth, " *Ottawa Citizen*, May 6, C5.

Eyries, Alexandre. 2013. *La communication politique ou le mentir-vrai*. Paris, FR: L'Harmattat.

Hubbard, Ruth and Gilles Paquet. 2010. *The Black Hole of Public Administration*. Ottawa, ON: The University of Ottawa Press.

Hubbard, Ruth and Gilles Paquet. 2014. *Probing the Bureaucratic Mind: About Canadian Federal Executives*. Ottawa, ON: Invenire.

Hubbard, Ruth and Gilles Paquet. 2015. *Irregular Governance: A plea for bold organizational experimentation*. Ottawa, ON: Invenire.

Leibenstein, Harvey. 1978. *General X-efficiency Theory and Economic Development*. Oxford, UK: Oxford University Press.

Onfray, Michel. 2014. *Le réel n'a pas lieu – Le principe de Don Quichotte*. Paris, FR: Les Éditions Autrement.

Paquet, Gilles. 2014. *Unusual Suspects: Essays on Social Learning Disabilities*. Ottawa, ON: Invenire.

Sibley, Robert. 2013. "Young men can be turned to good or evil," *Ottawa Citizen*, April 29, http://www2.canada.com/ottawacitizen/news/archives/story.html?id=67b9004d-2cda-4c97-874b-fd8946e51led6&p=2 [accessed May 2, 2014].

CHAPTER 6

Columnists vs Academics: A Value-adding Flip in Public Affairs?

Introduction

In the world of public affairs, two different tribes have been competing for the attention of the citizens seeking help from the media to decipher complex public affairs issues: columnists and academics. These are only very lightly overlapping sets: some academics are regular columnists like William Watson, but there are very few. For a long time there was little competition between these groups. Columnists were generalists who dealt with thorny issues from the vantage point of a lay person with much experience of a broad sort. They were writing for the day, for instant consumption, and had no time for extensive research and no taste for scholastic rigour. Academics, on the other hand, were asked to comment in pointed ways about more specific issues on which they had done some in-depth research. They took pride in their rigour and professionalism.

This sort of division of labour would appear to work well. While the expectations from columnists were relatively low and depended much on the wisdom of the particular individual involved, the academics, on the other hand, were expected to provide high-quality reports on matters that only experts could be expected to handle deftly.

In the old days, neither columnists nor academics were regarded as necessarily ideology-free. Indeed, one would expect ideological slants that were quite different when a columnist operated from the *Toronto Star* rather than the *National Post* (or from *La Presse* rather than *Le Devoir*), but columnists wore their colours rather proudly on their sleeve, and each one could be trusted to issue his bulls with his particular perspective in mind. One could count on their professionalism to ensure that whatever point of view they purported to represent, they would marshal their argument in as forthright and honest a way as possible. Professionalism was the guarantee the reader could expect to act as setting a sense of limits.

Academics contributing views based on technical expertise could be ideologically motivated, but they were expected to suppress such leanings somewhat in their analyses, to try explicitly to take distance in their style of communication from the sort of abusive language that would often flow from the pen of columnists. The reader felt also protected from abusive arguments by the fact that other experts would scrutinize unwarranted expert statements, and denounce errant academics who would have been tempted to sneak in some sophistry. The academic writer entering the broad public scene was kept in check by his other expert colleagues and was likely to remain prudent.

Those were the old days.

This division of labour has more or less vanished. Columnists have remained jacks-of-all-trades, but they are now much better trained and their analyses can be much more sophisticated. They are currently most often demonstrating an effort at constantly buttressing their arguments by careful research, and mindfulness for the complexities of the context in public affairs. Academics, on the other hand, have begun to stray farther and farther away from their field of expertise in affording statements and comments, to issue opinions, declarations and bulls on all sorts of subjects without much serious research to back them up, and more and more often in the form of sermons and rants that would appear to be fuelled entirely by more or less well hidden ideology, partisan slurs, or unsubstantiated arguments. These are no longer expert-based quality views. As a result, the general quality of the work of columnists has increased, while the general quality of the contributions of academics has become more problematic.

An additional slippage of consequence has been that academics, presenting themselves as public intellectuals, have systematically, abusively and pompously tried to parley their expertise and authority in Field A as providing expertise and authority for pronouncements in all sorts of unrelated Fields: B, C, D, ... : serious physical scientists making foolish statements in policy files about which they would appear to be grossly ignorant; sociologists denouncing policies entirely on the basis of their compassionate beliefs without any serious supporting analysis, etc.

This has been especially troublesome because there would appear to be no safeguard mechanisms any longer when academics utter sheer nonsense in areas they know little about. For the columnists, there is always the safeguard in good currency – professional ethics – and some official body that may be called upon to chastise delinquent journalists. However weak such a safeguard may be, it is there. On the other hand, there is no such thing for truant academics. One cannot count any longer on other academics to systematically provide a rebuttal of the ideological or incompetent rants of colleagues: collegiality would appear to have generated a general pact of non-aggression that has all but sanitized public forums from any of the detox action that one could count on in the past.

My testable hypothesis

This recent drift has undermined a celebrated urban legend: the one that held that columnists were light-weight and fleeting commentators of current events (easily swayed by fads in good currency and ideologies of the day), while academics could be counted on to provide a much more substantive and evidence-based diet to readers.

Most persons somewhat attentive to what is provided by newspapers and media that have hosted side by side reports from their regular staff of columnists and a variety of op-ed pieces by luminaries from academe, have come to the conclusion that columnists have tended to become a much more reliable and serious source of evidence-based information and critical analysis than a great majority of academics prone to generate off-the-cuff rants and unsubstantiated ideological harangues.

While my proposition is based on a limited, if attentive, press review, and a serious comparative study of the quality of these two types of contributions would appear to be badly needed before any final verdict is arrived at, I would like to suggest a working hypothesis based on fairly regular scanning of dailies in French and English in Canada, that might read as follows:

the intuitively appealing view that the bulls from academe on public affairs issues are much more analytically solid, evidence-based, and enlightening than the daily contributions of mere columnists would NOT appear to be vindicated by an examination of the fruits from those different trees. Why such a flip?

This may be ascribable to a number of reasons.

First, professional columnists have a reputation to sustain. They cannot utter any piece of nonsense without retribution. Academics have made their reputation elsewhere, and when they venture into the media, they have nothing to lose. Therefore one would expect more care from the former and more carelessness from the latter.

Second, for the professional columnist, in the beginning is the issue: the columnist reacts to complex and debatable issues that come his/her way. He has no choice but to enter the fray to help clarify it. Academics only enter the fray when some of their firm beliefs are challenged. They write to make a point, to challenge an argument, to denounce wrongdoing. Consequently, one may expect the footloose academic of the present (the one that chooses to enter the fray in areas where he is not an expert) to be more ideologically and emotionally motivated. This does not ensure mindfulness and due diligence.

Third, the columnist is a writer. His capacity to express himself clearly and serenely is part of his toolbox. Academics are not usually good writers, and when writing under the influence of anger or spite, they are less likely to be able to exercise restraint and to focus on persuasive arguments. Consequently, it is more likely that academics will overreact than columnists who would rather put their priority on making the argument smarter, more effective, more clever.

Be it as it may, my experience over the years has been that the contributions of academics to the media have often been trite, impressionistic, ideological and pompous, while the daily contribution of good columnists have been much more thoughtful, evidence-based and enlightening.

This is obviously a general impression that should not be used to exonerate the odd fool parading as a columnist. Columnists have also written nonsense, and manufactured non-issues with much damage inflicted on Canadian society (I am thinking of the journalist who invented the HRDC billion dollar boondoggle) and academics like William Watson or Jack Mintz who have kept to their field of expertise have not spewed opinions on us, but have developed arguments of consequence that have contributed to illuminating issues. So there has been professionalism and unprofessionalism in both camps. However, in general, there seems to be a difference between the relatively constant professionalism of columnists, and the ever present unprofessionalism of academics when they burst out in the op-ed pages.

So, even if occasionally the citizen can be badly served by both tribes, my contention is that if one were to analyze the contents of the offerings of columnists on the one hand, and the offering of academics on the other – in the public affairs scene in Canada – one would find that columnists would win hands down in terms of analytical quality, basic research and balanced appreciation of complex issues.

A recent tournament

Let me illustrate my point with two pieces published recently about the Lac Mégantic train derailment strategy: one by Andrew Coyne in the *National Post* on July 24, 2013, and another by Rodolphe de Koninck in *Le Devoir* on July 25, 2013.

The interest of these pieces is that they are easily accessible on the Web, so the reader can read both pieces at leisure – in a matter of minutes – and ascertain for him/herself whether my view is warranted. Coyne is a columnist on Canadian public affairs; de Koninck holds a Canada Research Chair on Asian Studies at the Université de Montréal.

As can be easily checked by reviewing the offerings, Coyne carefully analyzes this unique event. He examines the confluence of factors that led to the accident, and ascertains that nothing like it is ever likely to happen again. He also cuts to ribbons the knee-jerked reactions of a variety of political and governmental officials, intent only on appearing to do something and thereby placating hound-dogs from the editorial pulpits and the political opposition parties. He underlines that one should be careful in ascribing blame mindlessly, and suggests prudence before reacting to this accident by inundating this sector with undue additional regulatory burden. The paper is well documented, is based on the results of many studies in Canada and in Europe, and forces the reader to reflect thoughtfully on the issue, and not only emote and feel compassion for those who suffered from this tragedy.

Compare this with the rant by Professor de Koninck who, from the strength of his Asian studies competences, transforms himself into a new Zola, and writes a letter to Prime Minister Harper under the title *J'accuse*. There is no need for documentation here or even for any critical thinking: the culprit is the PM and deregulation, and ultra-liberalism and super-profits (mentioned three times). Harper is accused of having [*fait*] *régresser le Canada sur le plan de la civilisation* – nothing less! This sort of rant would yield an F in any high school essay, but becomes the gospel according to academe. In yesteryears, another academic might have found it imperative to denounce such nonsense, but such critical thinking is no longer in good currency in our collegial world in Canada.

Had a columnist generated this sort of nonsense, one would have challenged his judgment. But there is scant possibility to chastise the nonsense that chaired academics can commit. Professionalism is a dirty word in large sections of academe: the focus is not on academic professionalism and responsibility but only on academic freedom – and licence for academics as a new clergy to utter any nonsense without ever having to suffer any opprobrium, except in the mind of the lay reader who is not impressed, but such views are not taken into account at times of promotion or grant renewal.

Coda

At a time when, rightly, academics are encouraged to enter the public forum, and partake in debates about public affairs, it may not be unimportant to remind them of their burden of office: the need to contribute to the public debates in a responsible and professional way. This would appear to call for academics to exercise much self-restraint in uttering nonsense about matters they do not know much about; to recognize the difference between an argument that deserves airing, and an ideological rant that might best remain in the privacy of the home; to apply a Wittgenstein test of value-adding to contribution to public debates (if you have nothing to say, say nothing), instead of being guided by the self-righteous arrogance and lack of judgment of those academics who regard any of their offering as by definition value-adding.

In the absence of gate-keepers in the press that would protect us from the offerings of mindless academics, and of any capacity within the academy to expose the histrionics of their members, there seems to be no other way to detox our public affairs debates except to develop an agile finger capable of hitting the DELETE button at maximum speed, and to apply it as robustly to academic contributors and as we have come to do with columnists – based on a Red, Yellow and Blue appreciation – leading to fast, slow and no action with the delete button.

References

Coyne, Andrew. 2013. "No proof of safety crisis on Canada's rails after Megantic train derailment," *National Post*, July 24.

de Koninck, Rodolphe. 2013. "Explosion à Lac-Mégantic: j'accuse," *Le Devoir*, July 25.

CHAPTER 7

Laments of
Two Fundamentalists

"If you only have a hammer, everything looks like a nail."

– ANON

"La transparence ... qui est à la vérité ce que la nudité est à l'amour."

– Jean Lacouture

Introduction

Over the last year or so, two players on the Ottawa scene, Brent Rathgeber, an elected member of the Canadian House of Commons and Kevin Page, a former Parliamentary Budget Officer in the Canadian federal government, have each produced a book in which the first one declared the Canadian government "irresponsible" and the latter declared it "unaccountable." In so doing, they joined a chorus of academics and columnists who, over the last few years, have denounced the behaviour of the Harper government as "reprehensible" (Rathgeber 2014; Page 2015).

These two books have been written from the fundamentalist perspective, respectively, by a parliamentarian obsessed by the accountability of all detailed governmental actions to the elected legislatures, and by a super-bureaucrat mesmerized by numerology, transparency and his own self-esteem (Paquet 2014).

Some of those ideas are not heretical. One may reasonably argue in favour of more checks and balances, more accountability to elected officials, of more and better measurements, and of more transparency. But these ideas become toxic when they become mythified as all-important, dominant, *absolute principles*, instead of being regarded as matters having to be traded-off with the efficiency, effectiveness, smartness and wisdom of government activities, taking into account the circumstances and the nature of the political game at play.

When more and better measurements become a whiff of quantophrenia and a source of sclerosis of the policy process; when accountability to elected legislatures cannibalizes the whole notion of accountability and becomes a source of paralysis; and when optimal transparency becomes a drive to panopticon – a reductive representation of our real democratic regime ensues that is used to obsessively promote a few guideposts to the exclusion of a large variety of crucial dimensions that are consubstantial in our democracy.

The assumptions that only what can be measured matters, that the affairs of the state can be conducted in Macy's windows, and that obstructionism and the tyranny of the minorities are always enlightened are undue simplifications of our political system. This sort of hyper-focalization on a few dimensions of complex wicked problems, and the obsessive and blind pursuit of some rigid targets that one is led to promote to the role of sole policy guides, need not be the panacea that naïve mythologists suggest.

The particular status or expertise of any inquirer always colours somewhat his view of the world, and inflicts a distorting twist to the inquiry. However, serious inquirers go to much trouble to identify those biases, and to temper them in order to ensure that the inquiry can legitimately claim to "fairly present" the issue at hand. Some professional orders even invite their members (the accountants) to use this sort of language as a way to officialize their documents, and to identify thereby their code of conduct. However, when an inquirer becomes so imbued with zeal that it makes his/her particular perspective the only relevant one, he becomes a zealot, and the inquiry may easily degenerate into an exercise tainted by pneumopathology (as inquirers sink into a fantasy-world of self-righteousness) (Sibley 2013). The outcome is no longer an enlightening analysis but a tract.

The two books I am about to discuss may be said to have fallen into this category, but to different degrees.

However, these two tracts are exemplary enough of a genre in good currency to deserve some critical attention. They reveal different brands of frustration, but most importantly the limitations of "absolutist reductive cosmologies," and the dangers of allowing a truncated vision of the world – which is another name for ideology – to become hegemonic. The stories and recommendations that flow from such univocal works are condemned to be somewhat biased and truly partial.

In the rest of the paper, first, I present a critical assessment of the form and substance of the argument proposed by each author as marred by the fundamentalisms underlining the mental prisons of elected officials and the tunnel vision of technocrats. Second, I suggest that these tracts, lacking the dialectical quality one would expect from seasoned and experienced officials, should be accompanied by a robust *caveat emptor* for the unsuspecting reader. Yet even tracts contain some lessons about what might be done to improve our political regime.

Two fundamentalist laments

Brett Rathgeber as legal fundamentalist, obsessed by checks and balances and permanent answerability to elected officials

The form of the argumentation

Rathgeber does not indulge in melodrama and histrionics. His book clearly states that, after having been a Conservative MP since 2008, he resigned from the Conservative caucus in 2013 because of its lack of commitment to transparency and open government (Rathgeber 2014: 21) – something that would appear to mean relentless challenges and efforts to check the acceptability of all decisions of the executive at all possible levels.

The book proceeds in six steps:
- first, to establish his basic assumptions: as a Conservative who believes in small government, and as a lawyer who counts on rules to ensure responsible government;

- second, to trace the historical development of the crucial feature of our governing system – responsible government – i.e., the rules that establish that a government must have the support of the elected members of the Legislature or Parliament, otherwise it must resign;
- third, to show that as a result of the drift from the 'welfare state' to the 'entitlement state' (where everyone feels entitled to a handout courtesy of other people), Parliament's ability to hold government to account has declined significantly, and fiscal accountability has all but died;
- fourth, to scrutinize the role of the different features of Canadian governance that might have some responsibility for the present accountability debacle, and therefore should be contained (federalism, Parliament, Cabinet, political parties, the prime minister (PM) and the prime minister's office (PMO), the bureaucracy, the media, the failing access to information legislation, the judiciary);
- fifth, to synthesize what has happened to responsible government as a result of all this; and
- sixth, to propose some reforms.

The fourth and fifth segments above (*Ibid.*: 54-213) are a careful analysis of the ways in which these different arrangements or actors, contributed by their insouciance to the debacle and of the ensuing disaster, according to Rathgeber.

The substance of the argument

While Rathgeber details the failures of the checks and balance system at all levels, his attacks are on the many glitches of the multi-faceted Canadian political system rather than on individuals. Rathgeber focuses on the failures of the political process: anything that enfeebles the deliberative process, defuses accountability, and declaws the checks and balances process is attacked. This is done to excess: anything that allows escaping from rigid rules and short-circuits the sabotage tactics of a disingenuous Opposition, or that is the result of better managing a very heterogeneous civil society is bazookaed with the same force as reprehensible practices or tactics explicitly designed by rogue executives to avoid the hardship of accountability to elected officials in Parliament.

This is where Rathgeber's fundamentalism as a lawyer enamored with absolutes becomes objectionable.

For Rathgeber, federal-provincial, cost-shared programs compromise perfect accountability, and therefore are regarded not as a useful hybrid institution but as a toxic feature. Anything like omnibus bills that might be said to obscure accountability by not putting front and centre the particular details of specific procedures or particular proposals is regarded as indefensible. The same may be said about party discipline or caucus conventions that limit the total freedom of elected officials to openly oppose their party policies. He is even more aggrieved by the PM's authority and the omnipotence of the PMO that he sees as impediments to the hegemony of elected officials as free electrons.

In the same spirit (despite his fully recognizing the extraordinary potential for abuses), Rathgeber regards the bureaucracy, the media and the courts as mainly, if not solely, groups charged with holding the executive (the government) to account, and would appear to defend their licence to be disloyal, to be agents of disinformation, and to intervene destructively in the social order, as long as they act to check government action – seemingly without much consideration for the costs on other fronts of their misguided ways.

Rathgeber bases his concern on a complete trust in the purity and wisdom of elected officials, and a complete distrust of the executive.

This leads him, first, to fight any impediment on the power of the elected officials, and to support the maximum amount of impediments and constraints on the executive 'in principle'.

This fundamentalist posture leads him first, as a lawyer, to denounce any hybrid arrangement that might generate imprecision and complexity in the lines of accountability. This taste for formalization and clarity also leads him, second, to such a commitment to doing the thing right (i.e., according to rules as accountability does) that he objects to all forms of subsidiary arrangements like political parties, caucus, Cabinet, etc. that may require trading off accountability in order to ensure that one is doing the right thing, engagement, innovation, etc. because those would restrain the full and sole authority of elected officials. Thirdly, this posture leads Rathgeber to support unconditionally the maximum autonomy of bureaucracy, media and courts because he sees their vocation as strictly to counter the executive.

To the extent that these three propositions do not hold, or hold only under certain conditions, the absolutism of Rathgeber is unwarranted.

For instance, it leads Rathgeber to celebrate the work of Kevin Page solely because he was challenging the executive. One would be more at ease about this position if one were more certain that the posture of the Parliamentary Budget Officer (PBO) was warranted. Rathgeber is not as particular as I am on this front.

In the same way, the act of faith in the media and the courts would appear to be the consequence of much naïvety. While his stance may be the result of a blind loyalty of a lawyer to other lawyers in the case of the courts, it takes an extraordinary amount of willful blindness for anyone to refuse to see the extent to which courts and bureaucrats may err, and the extent to which the media are too often agents of disinformation in Canada as elsewhere (O'Neill 2002; Poivre d'Arvor and Zemmour 2000; Paquet 2012).

In summing up his argument, Rathgeber points *not* to the prime minister but to a systemic rot that will not be cured by firing the prime minster, but by undergoing a systemic reform.

In fact, the beauty of the Rathgeber tract is that, as a good lawyer, Rathgeber, in summing up his argument, starts with an explicit recognition that, as a practical man, he must clearly state that there is no magic bullet (*Ibid.*: 230) and that whatever argument might be put forward with any possibility of persuading, must be marshalled at the tangible and practical levels, and not merely at a rhetorical level.

In that sense, the assortment of reforms proposed as a first step on the way to broader and more ambitious reforms to our democracy, in the last chapter of the book, may sound to readers as a bit too focused on the plumbing rules of Parliament. Maybe this is because these changes are easier to initiate and implement. But it may also be that, fundamentally, Brent Rathgeber is neither an ideologue nor a dyed-in-the-wool fundamentalist really, but a wise and practical man: someone who would appear to wisely agree with the old jazz ballad – "the difficult we'll do right now, the impossible may take a little while."

Kevin Page as supremacist technocrat obsessed by transparency and the 'right numbers'

The form of the argumentation

It is surprising that a former super-bureaucrat who claims to "know better," in most circumstances about most things, than either elected officials or enlisted active bureaucrats, has chosen:

- to use the memoir genre to convey his message; and
- to use a ghostwriter (best known for his ghostwriting of Bobby Orr's memoirs) to melodramatize his offering.

As a result, from a person who portrays himself as a myth-slaying expert whose studies, we are told, marshal hard evidence to counter the less rigorous endeavours of bureaucrats and the anecdotes of elected officials, we are treated to a book written in the first person that has – at times – a Harlequin Romance flavour … of a dark sort, obviously!

The prologue would appear to set the tone with a High-Noonish account of a scene when Kevin Page allows the readers to enter his inner mind on May 3, 2012, as he is about to make a statement to the Standing Committee on Public Accounts. He shares with the readers his contempt of the Conservative backbenchers in attendance "lined up shoulder to shoulder, like so many Roman centurions with shields up and ready to serve their Caesar. They weren't in that room because of their gift for independent thought. Rather they were in attendance because of a call for loyalty" (Page 2015: 3).

In the next scene, a few pages later – a scene that could have been scripted by Clint Eastwood – the close-up is on Kevin Page who, after his presentation, meets a group of journalists outside the committee meeting. Page replays for his readers his internal monologue as he reflects on how to answer the question of a journalist in the scrum, who wants to know if the government wanted to mislead Canadians about the cost of the F-35s. In a sort of vision, Page sees the journalist as representing all Canadians, ruminates about this "touchy question … with a lot of political implications" … surmises that Canadians "deserved a direct answer for a change"… "Then, suddenly, I just didn't really give a damn anymore. As I turned back toward the scrum, I blurted out my answer. 'Yes,' I said" (*Ibid.*: 5-6).

Unfortunately, these theatrics are a fair harbinger of the rest of the book: Kevin Page/Bruce Wayne presents himself as the super-bureaucrat/superman at the centre of a dynamic team that fought the dark forces of Penguin in Gotham City. He shows that despite modest beginnings and tragic family circumstances (chapter 2), he took the challenge of an "institution set to fail," and was able to produce the "right numbers" – something that the whole of Ottawa bureaucracy and House of Commons was clearly unable and unwilling to do before he came on the scene.

Page does not say much about his superior methods for forecasting. For, as opposed to the Auditor General who works *ex post* in the manner of a coroner, the PBO works *ex ante* and has to decipher the future with all its uncertainties and avalanches. He only hints at the fact that his dynamic team "worked in a manner completely different" (*Ibid.*: 52) and "if the government of Canada would not hand over reliable information for us to use, we would draw our conclusions based on the analogies we might derive from outside database sources" (*Ibid.*: 53).

Persiflage about Prime Minister Harper, in connection with all sorts of aspects of his government's activities, imbibes the whole book: from statements about his intent to deceive, to his poor judgment in running his prime ministerial affairs (*Ibid.*: 55), to an explicit invitation to change government with the October election of 2015 (*Ibid.*: 7). Indeed, despite explicit denial about it, the tone running through the book proves incontrovertibly that the game against the government was much more important than the mission to "fairly present" issues to Parliament.

One could sense a quiver of joy in the PBO's office when an NDP member of the House of Commons conveniently asked them to estimate the costs of the engagement in the war in Afghanistan. One of the members of the dynamic team walked into Page's office "smiled and said, 'This is the one we've been waiting for'" (*Ibid.*: 59).

The substance of the argumentation

This book is not a serious attempt by Kevin Page to demonstrate technically to third parties how the PBO was able to expose the lousy work the federal bureaucracy and government officials were doing. The book only surfs on many *causes célèbres* for the popular press, and in no way does the book analyze in depth the differences of opinion between the government officials and the PBO, nor does it document technically the superiority of the PBO's methods.

Kevin Page only tells stories about these *causes* célèbres: we are told that the PBO dug deeper, used more modern techniques, found ways to use "analogies" where the real data were not available. And we are told that all sorts of external authorities from the US Congress to the IMF have given their blessings to the dynamic team around the PBO. But no hard evidence is provided that would allow third parties to gauge how and why the PBO 'forecasts' were more 'truth' than the so-called 'lies' of the bureaucracy and the government officials.

Even relatively simple projects get entangled in cost overruns because circumstances change. When it comes to a war or to a many-country project to develop a new type of aircraft, the degree of relevant uncertainty is phenomenal, and learning by doing is often the only reasonable way to proceed. Cost estimates have to be monitored and must be adjusted to circumstances. Ascribing all cost differentials to incompetence and deceit amounts to systematic calumny.

Whenever some details are provided, and a more extensive notion of costs is used than what would appear to have been used by the government officials, it is not always clear if the earlier estimates of the government officials were part of a sliding plan that was meant to evolve as operations proceed, or if entering the file at a later stage, the PBO was only trying to artificially show how wrong the government officials were, because the PBO was reporting at a later stage in the development of the file.

Moreover, there is a systematic claim throughout the book that all the cost forecasts were not only the result of technical incompetence, but part of a strategy of deceit on the part of the Harper government – a claim that reeks of conspiracy and paranoia, and is repeated through the book.

In other cases, like ascertaining if the country is in recession or not, one would expect a reasonable PBO to understand the strategic nature of such an assessment when it is put forward by the government. Governments have to exercise a great deal of prudence in not trumpeting Cassandra-like messages for fear of provoking self-fulfilling prophecies. When the PBO chooses to ignore these unintended consequences, and insists on announcing a recession on the basis of a technical definition of its choice to challenge the prudent statement of the government officials, can this not be regarded as somewhat irresponsible? "Unsettling or rash lack of concern" is the definition of criminal negligence in the Criminal Code.

One could go on. With so many of the cases on which Kevin Page surfs, what is reprehensible is not so much that the PBO disagrees with the government officials, but the fact that he presents his version as the 'truth', and theirs as 'deliberate and purposeful lies'. This leitmotif is stated up front, on the cover of the book.

The basis of this conspiratorial argument appears to this reader, depending on the specific page, to be unfounded, gratuitous, temerarious, contemptuous, spiteful, mean-spirited or a mix of the above. The Harper government and senior bureaucrats ... indeed the whole public service, is maligned.

Even for one who has been very critical of the federal technocracy, the damning is overdone. This is especially offensive when, in parallel and by comparison, Kevin Page inflicts on the reader a continuous flow of self-congratulatory comments by the author about the resourcefulness and infallibility of his dynamic team (including everyone mentioned by first name with their *bons mots* archived for posterity).

Later in the book, Page will even suggest, as he pronounces his successor incompetent, that only a miscarriage of the process of selection of his successor can explain the fact that one member of his glorious entourage has not been anointed to continue the crusading work of his magnificent bunch.

Some lessons from comparative tract reading

Both Brent Rathgeber and Kevin Page have pointed to some problems in our political regimes, and have reported on their inquiry about the sources and causes of these failures.

First, both books have adopted quite different styles. Page has used theatrics and overstatements without much evidence or references adduced to make his case. Rathgeber has produced a carefully documented and balanced book – maybe sprinkled with some naïve assumptions and some excessive statements from time to time, but firmly anchored in good research and on the first-hand experience with the lifeworld of politics.

Second, the two books have identified quite different anchors in their search for repairs. Rathgeber has been betting fundamentally, *à la* Dewey, that the solution for the ills of democracy is more democracy. So the core of his response is to give more and more power to elected officials. Page's choice is a bet on super-technocracy. He has shown nothing but contempt for elected officials and bureaucrats, and proposed that only a super-bureaucracy capable of providing technical answers to political questions would work.

Third, Rathgeber has established his preference for clear and precise answers, but concluded that there was no magic bullet. The way out of the present disastrous situation is a long process of practical repairs to the political apparatus, starting with modest tweaking with the hope that more profound reforms will become possible later. Rather Page has built a technocratic magic bullet: the utopian view that better financial information would command the agreement of all parties and trigger technically superior policies.

Fourth, Page has constructed his argument on generating the "right numbers" and factored out concerns about any extra-financial dimension, with the consequence that there was no interest or space in his approach to debate the trade-offs among financial accuracy and other relevant dimensions. Rathgeber has incorporated the right numbers as one of many dimensions that the elected officials have to take into account in arriving at a decision, and has been satisfied to search for what one would regard as roughly right.

Fifth, Rathgeber has adopted an optimistic outlook about the overall operations of the democratic regime: from complete trust in the wisdom of elected officials to complete trust that media, bureaucracy and courts are going to perfectly play their role as guardians of the public good by constraining the executive. Page has taken a rather pessimistic view that both elected officials and ordinary bureaucrats (even senior ones) are wantons more likely to be self-serving, and that only super-bureaucrats are likely to act as completely unbiased and disinterested parties in the search for the public good.

Sixth, Page has adopted a very personalized view of a very small number of actors, and has not hesitated to use persiflage and to speculate temerariously about their foibles and their malevolence – to the point of naming those politicians to whom the problems were ascribable, and suggesting that getting rid of them might be the solution. Rathgeber has adopted a system's approach, and a broad view of the democratic regime that included the mega-community, has focused on systemic repairs and redesign as a way out of the present predicament, and has throughout not used personal accusations and *procès d'intention*.

Seventh, there has been a significant difference between the two ways of marshalling their arguments and proving them. In the case of Page, everything is seen through the lens of his *persona*, and nothing is adduced except on the basis of selective here-says and impressions. Rathgeber has carefully documented all of his assertions, and nuanced considerably his position as the book progressed.

Eight, in terms of conclusions, Rathgeber has proposed a long list of repairs that would improve significantly the Canadian political regime. Page would appear to have little more to suggest than electing a government that would allow his team to continue its work, and to inject a more technocratic twist to Canadian governance.

Finally, Page has proposed little more than a personalized morality play. Rathgeber has produced a manual that might be a most useful starting point for a reflection on what should be the next step in Canadian democratic reform.

Conclusion

Canada does not have a long tradition of politicians and super-bureaucrats entering the forum with a book to explain who they are and what they think. Each electoral campaign has a crop of books supposedly written by political figures, but no one takes those self-promoting offerings any more seriously than the vapid press releases of their parties or the confessions of Kim Kardashian.

So it is worth reading carefully the offerings of heretical members of Parliament who are not trying to run for higher office or of super-bureaucrats who have been offered extraordinary positions in our democratic regime.

Other readers may draw different conclusions than I have from the reading of these two books, but I feel that their relative intellectual contribution is likely to be quite different.

I came out of Rathgeber's book with a full appreciation of his quality of mind, and much to reflect on. Rathgeber's book, despite some excesses, is a very thoughtful piece of writing that reminds one of the thoughtful books of J. Patrick Boyer in yesteryears. It should become compulsory reading for any candidate for election to the House of Commons, and for any Canadian interested in the improvement of our democratic regime.

I came out of Kevin Page's book empty. Its analytical content and the value of its recommendations are unbearably light. Despite the genre chosen by the author or his ghostwriter, the reader might have expected a more sober and helpful book. If Kevin Page had decided to write his own book with his own voice, and taken distance from the boosterism of his dynamic team, we might have had quite a different book – one that would have helped all of us, by reporting more genuinely on his successes and failures, to better understand the difficult trade-offs that a Parliamentary Budget Officer may not always be able to negotiate perfectly. This would have contributed to ensuring the perenniality of the PBO function by wise advice to his successor instead of fizzling out in a feat of self-congratulation and pompous announcement of *après moi le deluge* – as if it was not well known by all the serious readers that cemeteries are full of irreplaceable people!

References

O'Neill, Onora. 2002. *A Question of Trust*. Cambridge, UK: Cambridge University Press.

Page, Kevin (with Vern Stenlund). 2015. *Unaccountable – Truth and Lies on Parliament Hill*. Toronto, ON: Penguin.

Paquet, Gilles 2012. "Médias, imprécations et désinformation," *www.optimumonline.ca*, 42(1): 41-18.

Paquet, Gilles. 2014. "Super-bureaucrats as *enfants di siècle*," *www. optimumonline.ca*, 41(2): 4-14.

Poivre d'Arvor, Patrick and Eric Zemmour. 2000. *Les rats de garde*. Paris, FR: Stock.

Rathgeber, Brent. 2014. *Irresponsible Government – The Decline of Parliamentary Democracy in Canada*. Toronto, ON: Dundurn.

Sibley, Robert. 2013. "Young men can be turned to good or evil," *Ottawa Citizen*, April 29.

CHAPTER 8

The Demonization of
Stephen Harper

"une idée fausse, mais claire et précise,
aura toujours plus de puissance dans le monde
qu'une idée vraie mais complexe"

– Alexis de Tocqueville

Introduction

No Canadian citizen needs to agree with Stephen Harper's government policy stance on all issues of import. Disagreement may exist among citizens and groups in a democracy. Normally this would lead to lively conversations about the pros and cons of particular policy stands, in the way it happened in Canada at the time of the negotiations about the free trade agreement with the United States or about the GST. These issues were hotly debated, often in ways that revealed the dishonesty and the disingenuity of many of the parties involved, but nobody felt the urge to suggest that the proposed policies should be ascribed to Brian Mulroney's personal malevolence, and that he should be personally blamed for them.

Things are now quite different from what they were 25 years ago. Much of the annoyance about some policies or stands of the Canadian government over the recent decade would appear to be regarded by a number of Canadians (bureaucrats, journalists, academics, etc.) as the toxic personal responsibility of one man – Stephen Harper. This has not resulted in a critical discussion of

Harper's ideas, but in a sort of demonization of Stephen Harper as a person. This has grown viral in the Ottawa area, and in the majority of the media reports emerging from Ottawa. It is also common currency on Radio-Canada airwaves that have played out *ad nauseam* the consubstantial incompatibility between Harper's mindset and *l'esprit du Québec*.

This has grown to such an extent in certain social circles in Ottawa that the very mention of the name of Stephen Harper raises the temperature in the room and triggers explicit expressions of personal dislike and contempt. So whatever the nature of the issue discussed – be it austerity measures, poor treatment of some veterans, immigration policy, etc. – even usually reasonable and prudent persons are heard either ascribing the blame to Stephen Harper personally, or at least not daring to question such sentiments when they are evoked in their presence. Few dare to ask denunciators to explain why a particular policy stance is so despised, or how it is that this particular policy can legitimately be regarded as Stephen Harper's brainchild. Once such a denunciation is articulated, no one around the water fountain would appear to be willing to challenge it except at his own peril.

This phenomenon is all the more puzzling because of the very peculiarity of what emerges when such denunciations are truly challenged – an experiment I have personally provoked on numerous occasions. The conversation immediately fizzles, and takes a bizarre turn: it generates mainly either an anecdote, or a reference to a rumour, or some gossip about a well-placed official who has been heard saying something implicating Harper in some shenanigans, or a diatribe about the profound evilness of the man – all this often quite unrelated to the topic of the conversation being originally carried out.

Colleagues have reported to me that this phenomenon is not necessarily at play everywhere else in the country. True, some media in Quebec are singing from the same hymn book as the Ottawa tribe, and Ontario's Premier Wynne has been known to synchronize her incantations with the Ottawa tribe also, but this is not necessarily the case in the rest of the country.

This is a matter that has fascinated me for quite a while, and has led me to do some ethnographic work to understand why and how this personal animus has developed, and has contaminated the National Capital Region's *ethos*. As my probing proceeded, I have come to be persuaded that much of it may be ascribed to a mutation of the Westminster system that has modified the balance between advice-giving and implementation work in the role of the senior federal bureaucracy.

There may be differences of opinions as to the source and cause of this mutation. My own view is that it has been the result of a clash of cosmologies between an elected government that is intent on elected officials having the legitimate last word in the debates with the technocracy, and a clutch of mandarins (retired or in active duty) who, with some help from accomplices in the media, and from some academics and some disgruntled ex-bureaucrats, have taken refuge in academe, have come to argue that their weight in the final determination of what to do should be greater than it is.

This conflict of cosmologies has produced a *conflictive equilibrium* in which each group (politicians and bureaucrats) knows that it cannot rid the system of the other, and that it will have to invent some form of compromise, but neither group quite knows how to get there. The dynamic of this conflictive equilibrium has led to unfortunate slippages on the road toward a viable compromise, of which the demonization of Stephen Harper is one.

The peculiar mindset of some influential senior federal bureaucrats

Retired senior federal public servants stand as an interesting *révélateur* of the true mindset of the senior Canadian federal public service. With retirement comes the possibility of speaking up, after years of extramural discretion on matters of partisan politics. It is not that active senior public servants have no view on these matters, but in a system that is supposed to have a professional, non-partisan, public service, such views are expected to be toned down (if not suppressed) at least externally, when federal public servants are on active duty.

However, when senior federal public servants formally retire these days, many do not really retire. On the basis of their former status, they seek employment in a variety of positions outside the federal public service: lobbyists for industry, return to private practice for lawyers who might procure access to government officials, refugee in academe, etc. From such new perches, they have a much greater licence to speak on any matters they feel strongly about – whether these views are competent and informed, or not.

The wise ones remain quite discrete in retirement, for they feel they have a *devoir de réserve*. But most are not that wise. They rather sense that their special status as 'certified mandarins' in the federal public service, even if it is only for a moment, stands as a proof, in their own minds at least, that they can be presumed to be better informed and wiser than most. This status is perceived as carrying with it a responsibility to remain on guard for us, lesser Canadians, even in their new civilian life.

Indeed, this special status has often been the major asset they have displayed to persuade their newly acquired bosses of their value-adding capabilities. Such special status is undoubtedly real when it comes to the personal links mandarins have retained with senior public servants still in active duties – and their ability to parlay such intelligence into advantages in their new positions – privileged access that can be used by universities, law firms, lobby firms, etc. for their own benefits.

But such mundane advantages are usually not the main asset that retired mandarins claim to possess. They most often feel that their tenure and experience as mandarins have definitely established them as persons of superior quality, whose storytelling and judgment have greater intrinsic value than those of ordinary citizens on any matter they choose to address.

So certain former clerks of the Privy Council, not especially known for their great wisdom when in active duty, but rather more for their craftiness and disingenuity, have had no hesitation, in retirement, in trotting themselves out of their new academic homes into the public forum to denounce actions of the government now in place, on the sole basis of their supposed former moral authority being sufficient for their views to be regarded as consequential if not canonical.

One can certainly point to some former senior federal civil servants who have, in retirement, demonstrated their extraordinary intellectual resourcefulness by impressive endeavours: pathbreaking books, enlightening papers, imaginative initiatives, etc. But most have not shined in that way. They have simply parlayed their former overblown status into financially profitable sinecures in organizations naïve enough to believe that their 'greatness' would be value-adding somewhat in the new setting.

Such matters however are only of interest to the chroniclers in the social pages of the Ottawa daily newspapers. What is much more interesting is the storytelling of those retired mandarins.

Conservatorship

Many of those retired federal government mandarins of recent vintage have developed, from their experience in public administration, a sense that their primary function as mandarins was to protect, maintain and preserve the administrative institutions in a manner consistent with constitutional processes, traditions and beliefs. The notion of 'administrative conservatorship' has shaped the manner in which many of the senior career executives in the federal public service have come to define their roles: "balancing the inherent tension in the political system between the need to *serve* and the need to *preserve*" (Terry 2003: 29).

As Hubbard and Paquet have suggested in the introduction to their book, this worldview has fed a most unhealthy tendency for the mandarins to lionize the role of the bureaucracy as guardian of the fundamental principles of democracy, and to coax the bureaucratic clergy into acquiring a determining role in the definition of what has to be preserved (Hubbard and Paquet 2015).

This sort of hijacking has been anointed by a plurality of public administration academics, who share with these mandarins a great suspicion for the elected officials. This movement has guided the bureaucracy's strategy in defining what needed to be preserved – i.e., most things that helped the bureaucracy maintain its own power base and putative dominium.

Such an attitude has translated into many senior federal public servants developing a conviction that they are better guardians of basic values of our democracy than elected officials. While this attitude had to be somewhat tamed while they were on active duty, it has become fully unleashed in retirement. So what was only a toxic train of thought in earlier times has transmogrified into a most aggressive *modus operandi* for many retired mandarins. This has even led some to cast the bureaucratic-political interface as a war zone in which bureaucrats have to 'fight' politicians, and where any cooperative *rapprochement* with politicians is condemned as 'promiscuity' (Heintzman 2014).

This has naturally generated a flow of self-righteous condemnation of the Harper government policies by many newly unencumbered, retired, senior officials, and has thereby provided immense moral support for those senior public servants still in active duty – former colleagues and friends – to heighten their own passive (or semi-active) opposition to the elected government from within. As a result, the corridor of what has come to be regarded as "tolerable disloyalty from within" would appear to have widened considerably (Paquet 2014: chapter 4).

It is now common in early 2015 for the Harper government to be accused by retired mandarins of inventing its policy stands on the sole basis of anecdotes (or worse, ideology), *in lieu* of following the wise and prudent advice of the senior bureaucrats whose policy advice is based, so we are told, solely on evidence and sound research (Griffith 2013; Paquet 2013).

Much of the storytelling of retired mandarins (and *sotto voce* from senior bureaucrats within) has been about the Harper government being illegitimate because it is not being compliant with the advice of the bureaucracy – or even interested in it. But since the storytelling, aimed at attacking government activities head on, has often proved too elusive and vague to be effective when directed to the mushy entity called 'government', demonizing Stephen Harper as the person embodying the virus of bad governance, (i.e., governance that is not in keeping with the wishes of bureaucrats imbibed by administrative conservatorship) has become the new *modus operandi*.

A minority of retired mandarins have chosen to indict not the elected officials but the bureaucracy itself for much of what is going awry (Clark and Swain 2005). But this is a small minority. A much larger portion of the group has opted for storytelling, denouncing the elected officials, and demonizing Stephen Harper, in particular, as responsible for everything they do not like, for not operating in ways compliant with the doctrine of administrative conservatorship, and therefore, so they say, not acting in the best interest of the country.

This denunciation of Stephen Harper both from without and within the federal public service by many senior bureaucrats has been carried out in the name of the pursuit of higher ideals that the elected officials are considered incapable of even understanding. And a significant portion of the media and of academe in public administration has worked hard to ensure that this message would be appropriately reverberated – sometimes for ideological reasons, but also sometimes as a result of some pique ascribable to the lack of reverence elected officials have recently shown for them.

The gumption of elected officials

Elected officials do not go through the ordeal of being elected not to act, when elected, on what they have promised to do. For them it is a matter of honour and survival. When René Lévesque was first elected as Quebec's premier, he insisted on raising the minimum wage to one of the highest levels in North America despite the stern advice of experts that it would kill tens of thousands of jobs in Quebec. His sole argument was that he had promised he would do it. He suffered the consequences.

Federal political parties are elected on more or less explicit platforms, based on their assessment of the situation facing them, but also on some beliefs about how the world works, and how one can best resolve the problems posed by these circumstances. Most political parties are forced by a fuller appreciation of the circumstances, when in power, to modify somewhat their viewpoint and their plans. This has been the case for the Harper government like all others.

Whenever a new government is elected after having been in Opposition for more than a decade, it inherits a public service recruited and promoted by the former government, and habituated to its priorities. Even though in a Westminster system, the public service is supposed to be independent and non-partisan, it would be naïve to believe that the bureaucracy the newly elected government is inheriting is not tainted somewhat by its earlier experience. Some distrust is therefore inevitable. A few mishaps or misunderstandings in the early days of the new incoming government can only get this distrust to crystallize, especially since the new government is most intent, in those early days, to deliver on its promises.

It is difficult to reconstruct precisely the way in which the dialectics between elected officials and senior bureaucrats evolve in this early phase of tense cohabitation when the Harper government was elected, to gauge who might be more responsible for any escalation of distrust, but it is not surprising if it occurs. Suffice it to say that the confrontation between a new government, inspired by new beliefs, and somewhat suspicious that a number of senior bureaucrats might not share those beliefs, and a largely loyal senior bureaucracy but comprised of a plurality of mandarins finding it difficult to adjust to new imperatives, has generated the basis for a conflictive equilibrium, and, through the catalytic role of mishaps, some toxic dynamics.

A toxic dynamic

The process of contagion of the emergent view that (1) senior bureaucrats know best, and (2) the elected officials are not universally served well by all senior officials in all issue domains – have quickly led to dual urban myths about the disloyalty of the senior bureaucrats and about the systemic disinterest of elected officials in the advice of the mandarins. This has coalesced into some differences in the interpretation of the Westminster system when it comes to the optimal relative balance of advice-giving and implementation work in the duties of the senior bureaucracy: the elected officials insistent on bureaucracy giving priority to 'serve' in the implementation of the policies put forward by elected officials, and the senior bureaucrats insisting more on their contribution as advisors in the name of administrative conservatorship, in order to 'preserve' some of the features of the existing system – whatever elected officials may wish.

A combination of mechanisms and forces – some helpful, some not – have been at work.

Stories have replaced explanations

As Lant Pritchett would put it, people are not very good at thinking about systems problems (like whole of government problems), because, in their daily lives, they only need to be experts as agents to get by (Pritchett 2013: 41). So when faced with complex systemic issues that are difficult to understand, it is quite natural for people to create stories involving only individuals to explain complex systemic issues. So, the emphasis of storytelling has shifted from explaining to narrating. This is what Fox News does so well (Salmon 2008).

Narrating focuses on the use of rhetorical devices, and is directed to imagination. It is based on a logic of persuasion, and on fictions, personal representations, etc. that are the result as much of ideologies as of facts and objective realities. Narrating is a construction designed to persuade an audience of the canonicity of one representation of what is going on in the presence of alternative and contradictory representations.

If a particular representation/story is to prevail, it needs the complicity of a good portion of the media as an echo box for the story. Yet stories about systems are quite difficult to relay because they are of necessity complex. Stories about people are more easily relayed and absorbed, however surreal they may be. A personal story, relayed by columnists as echoes of what they claim to have been observing at close range, or corroborated by so-called unidentified but reliable sources, is more gripping and carries better than a complex, disembodied story about flawed systems (Boudon 2005: 167ff). A story about Harper carries better than a story about the cosmology of the Conservative party.

The power of persiflage

The storytelling of some mandarins (retired and in active duty) – and relayed by a significant segment of the media – has seemingly succeeded in surreptitiously shaping *un état d'esprit* in which the demonization of Stephane Harper plays a dominant role. However, this has not taken the form of an explicit clinical indictment. Rather it has largely materialized in the form of persiflage: based on hints, *double entendre*, satirical implication, or simple assertion – allowing the audience to infer often what has not been very explicitly stated. While this suffices for a point of view to crystallize despite its elusiveness, a counter-point of view is very difficult to effectively mount both because of the very vagueness of this supposed canonical view, and because of the vociferous self-righteousness, and damning denials of the disingenuous *persifleurs* when they are exposed.

Rabid *persifleurs* take offence at being accused of calumny, and demand that their innuendoes be demonstrably proven libellous in a court of law – a matter that is difficult and risky, because innuendoes by definition are elusive, and yet can be lethal. Innuendoes, like rumour and gossip, spread without the need of being articulated in a disprovable form, and when they fuel the language of persuasion of ideologically-driven interest groups, or of self-righteous mandarins who share the *weltanschauung* of former governments, very often the only thing left at the end of the debates are the innuendos (Boudon 2004; Eberstadt 2012).

The contagion of innuendoes triggered by storytelling unfolds in waves like public opinion, and carries the support of the unsuspecting – many of whom would be incapable of arguing the case they are pronouncing on, but are swayed sufficiently by the information bit they receive, to repeat it uncritically – each of these repeated bits adding to the believability of the item.

Unreflexive contagion

Such contagion is particularly potent a vehicle in a Canadian society that is marred by a *malaise*, striking it with much cognitive dissonance and inertia caused by weakened critical thinking, rampant political correctness, failure to confront and a proclivity for unreasonable accommodation (Higham and Paquet 2013) – all features that exacerbate the vulnerability of being swayed by rumours, gossip and fantasies, especially in the absence of the requisite degree of critical thinking in academe and the media.

Contagion can be a blind and destructive force when it is unreflexive and unchecked. This is the logic of mobs, financial cascades, herd mentality and group think.

The demonization of Harper by self-righteous mandarins, wounded journalists and ideologically-minded academics has spread like wildfire in progressive circles. For them, a personalized attack on Harper has allowed their multifaceted critical stance of the Conservative government – about the questioning of the entitlement epidemic, the pursuit of austere policies, the attack on their progressive cosmology, etc. – to gain both focus and traction. Demonizing Stephen Harper has amounted to identifying the axis of evil, fighting the dragon that is questioning the primacy of their social-democratic ideals – however rationally indefensible these ideals may be in these disenchanted times.

A confederacy of romantic or ideological groups – but also of crass interest groups like public sector unions – have also found the anti-Harper campaign gratifying and soul-satisfying – because it allowed them to personalize their fights without having to articulate any coherent counter-proposals. How much easier is a debate when you do not need to make your case but only to point to a culprit responsible for all evils.

The lack of effective counter-storytelling

The success of any contagion is not exclusively ascribable to the blind acceptance of the message by uncritical minds; it also depends on the unavailability of alternative stories to those swayed by the contagious wave. The poverty of the counter-storytellling to this contagious wave by the Conservative party or government has allowed the contagion to go unchecked (Coyne 2014).

The Harper government has presumed that humans live by numbers and figures and systems analysis alone. This is delusional. The views, representations, attitudes and behaviours of citizens depend also very much on an appreciative system that is built on stories and storytelling. It is true that some storytelling may be toxic and contagious, but identifying it as such does not suffice to kill its impact. It is incumbent for those not mesmerized by this sort of hogwash to find ways to expose the weak foundations of the stories in good currency by providing alternative stories that may be better grounded, and more enlightening and persuasive.

On both fronts, the Harper government, in place over the last decade, may have been negligent.

First it has allowed its critical thinking edge to get eroded. It has allowed many fairy tales to be spread without robust rebuttal and sharp critical scrutiny being brought to bear on them. This has left the citizenry more vulnerable and less well immunized against snake-oil salesmen. More needs to be invested in developing substantial mechanisms to sanitize the various forums where the ill-founded stories are told: sophistry deconstructed, false arguments exposed, and group think neutralized (Sunstein and Hastie 2015).

Second, the Harper government has not generated imaginative counter-storytelling capable of providing citizens with alternative stories, informing more intelligent, comprehensive and enlightening representations and communication of what is going on, and of the reasons why traditional views and policies need to be reframed. The refusal by the Conservative government to spend sufficient time on inspiring storytelling has too often allowed the citizenry to conclude that Conservatives had no interesting and gripping stories to tell (Paquet 2015).

The way to counter toxic storytelling is not to refuse to indulge in storytelling but to provide more authentic storytelling. Refusing to do so, and cowering into a state of refusal to communicate to the citizens, except in terms of facts and figures, has left the Conservative government vulnerable.

A Liberal Party underground

Many of these mechanisms might not have worked so well without the existence of an extensive network of organizations and institutions with deep sympathies with the Liberal Party, populated by Liberal *aficionados* in key positions, willing to provide a home for retired mandarins, and a temporary working place for political personnel while the party is out of power.

This institutional refuge for a fifth-column has enabled this *maquis* of *aficionados* to serve as a most effective dissemination machine for the corrosive messages about the new government in the guise of semi-independent and supposedly non-partisan connectors capable of relaying the canonical storytelling throughout the system.

The role of this fifth column in universities and in the political communication community should not be underestimated. This is only a subsidiary force in the bigger scheme of things, but an immensely effective one (1) in providing a steady supply of confirmatory messages to support the venomous persiflage emanating from some retired mandarins, academics and media persons, and (2) in maintaining financially alive squadrons of *aficionados* ready to jump back into active party duties when necessary.

A new orthodoxy

This toxic dynamic has generated over the last quarter of a century a new orthodoxy that has taken time to fully crystallize, but that has evolved into a fine form of late, and has left us with a transformed Westminster system.

The Chretien government of the 1990s was probably the architect of one of the most centralized governmental apparatuses of recent times at the federal level in Ottawa. By the end of the 1990s, academics (Savoie 1999) and journalists (Simpson 2001) had identified this trend perceptively.

There were forces pressing toward decentralization imposed by the new turbulent context, but the Chretien government was only dragged most reluctantly in that direction and by the end of the 1990s, it was still imbibed by the virus of hyper-centralization.

In 1999, I remember that, in my participation in the debates preceding the Social Union Agreement, that "the Prime Minister sounded like Louis XIV when he mused in public that sometime on Monday he felt like giving the provinces more money, and then Tuesday he did not" (Paquet 1999: 79). Those were the days when the Liberal Party did not feel it had to apologize for its hyper-centralization.

The next decade saw additional pressure to relax the process of centralization within the federation, but, also, *and much more importantly*, to relax the central control of elected officials over the technocracy at the federal level.

The debates about governance challenged the Big G government philosophy a bit during the first decade of the 21st century, but it focused much more on a re-alignment along the political-bureaucratic frontier than on the federal-provincial lines. The full weight of Larry Terry's work about the rebalancing of power between elected officials and technocrats was felt. This is also the direction in which Donald Savoie and his colleagues were moving in the work they did for the Gomery Commission.

But it is only of late (Heintzman 2014) that the new orthodoxy has acquired its canonical form: a form in which the authority of elected officials was squarely put into question, and the cognitive and moral superiority of the technocracy affirmed quasi-bombastically.

This new orthodoxy would purport to grant to the mandarins a more significant role in the power equation, as guardians of always capricious and irresponsible elected officials. It is music to the ears of mandarins (retired and in active duty) who have been denouncing Stephen Harper's political maneuverings. Indeed, it grants them the moral authority to do so as guardians of our democracy.

Conclusion

In the task of constructing alternative and better stories, experts in public administration and mandarins must have input, but it will have to be contained as long as a plurality of them would appear determined to hijack the power for the technocracy. This is the dark side of the process of demonization of Stephen Harper: many are fighting Harper because he has done much to wrestle power away from the technocrats, and to bring it back forcefully to the elected officials.

On the one hand, advice and dissent from experts and mandarins may be useful when it is meant to improve the governance by elected officials. When bureaucratic pressure reaches the point where the very person of the Prime Minister is under attack, because the mandarins are losing their power, it becomes unbearable. This is a lesson that some earlier governments have failed to learn, often at their own peril. But given the new level of toxicity of the attacks by technocrats on the elected officials, in recent times, it may be important to take action to contain that venomous influence. Ignoring those retired mandarins barking at government initiatives may appear to be taking the high road for the government in place, but it may also be naïve, and encourage further disloyalty.

On the other hand, if this world of friction at the political-bureaucratic interface were to lead a large number of loyal senior bureaucrats to withdraw into a cocoon, and to fail in informing and advising helpfully elected officials as a result of voluntary servitude, elected officials would not be well served either.

If the only choice for senior public service officials was ever only between traitor or eunuch, the citizenry would be in the worst of all worlds. It may lead future governments to politicize much more than they should the higher echelons of the public service, to combat the new toxic orthodoxy, and this may turn out to be, in the final analysis, to the detriment of the citizenry at large.

References

Boudon, Raymond. 2004. *Pourquoi les intellectuels n'aiment pas le libéralisme*. Paris, FR: Odile Jacob.

Boudon, Raymond. 2005. *Tocqueville aujourd'hui*. Paris, FR: Odile Jacob.

Clark, Ian D. and Harry Swain. 2005. "Distinguishing the real from the surreal in management reform: suggestions for beleaguered administrators in the government of Canada," *Canadian Public Administration*, 48(4): 453-476.

Coyne, Andrew. 2014. "In Canada's contest of ideas, the left is winning," *National Post*, December 30.

Eberstadt, Nicholas. 2012. *A Nation of Takers – America's Entilement Epidemic*. West Conshohocken, PA: Templeton Press.

Griffith, Andrew. 2013. *Policy Arrogance or Innocent Bias – Resetting Citizenship and Multiculturalism*. Ottawa, ON: Anar Press.

Heintzman, Ralph. 2014. *Renewal of the Federal Public Service: Toward a Charter of Public Service*. Ottawa, ON: Canada 2020.

Higham, Robin and Gilles Paquet. 2013. "Reflections on the Canadian *malaise*," *www.optimumonline.ca*, 43(2): 1-12 (reprinted in Gilles Paquet. 2014. *Unusual Suspects:Essays on Social Learning Disabilities*. Ottawa, ON: Invenire, p. 133-156).

Hubbard, Ruth and Gilles Paquet. 2015. *Irregular Governance: A Plea for Bold Organizational Experimentation*. Ottawa, ON: Invenire.

Paquet, Gilles. 1999. "Innovations in Governance in Canada," *Optimum*, 29(2/3): 71-81.

Paquet, Gilles. 2013. "The Political-Bureaucratic Interface: A Comment on Andrew Griffith`s Expedition," *www.optimumonline. ca*, 43(4): 61-74.

Paquet, Gilles. 2014. *Unusual Suspects: Essays on Social Learning Disabilities*. Ottawa, ON: Invenire.

Paquet, Gilles. 2015. *Communication politique : analyse médiologique,* (mimeo 128p).

Pritchett, Lant. 2013. *The Rebirth of Education.* Washington, DC: Center of Global Development.

Salmon, Christian. 2008. *Storytelling – La machine à fabriquer des histoires et à formate les esprits.* Paris, FR: La Découverte.

Savoie, Donald. 1999. *Governing from the Centre.* Toronto, ON: The University of Toronto Press.

Simpson, Jeffrey. 2001. *The Friendly Dictatorship.* Toronto, ON: McClelland & Stewart.

Sunstein, Cass R. and Reid Hastie. 2015. *Wiser – Getting beyond groupthink to make groups smarter.* Boston, MA: Harvard Business Review Press.

Terry, Larry D. 2003. *Leadership of Public Bureaucracies – The Administrator as Conservator.* Armonk, NY: M.E. Sharpe.

CHAPTER 9

The Long Form Census Psychosis as *Révélateur* of Governance Failure

In the annals of public administration lunacy, the long census form psychosis that hit Canada in the summer of 2010 will probably warrant only a minor footnote. There will be a simple note about the kerfuffle generated by the Government of Canada's decision to make voluntary rather than compulsory the filling up of the long form of the Census questionnaire in 2011. This long form has in recent censuses been a staple of the census-taking ritual – being sent to a plurality of censees. The new ritual would call for this longer questionnaire to be sent to a larger percentage of censees, but they would have the choice of filling it up or not, as opposed to being legally forced to do so as they were in the past.

Canada's chattering class has discovered the foundation of a Shakespearean drama in this issue. At a time when other countries were abandoning census-taking altogether decades ago, and others like Britain are thinking of doing the same, in Canada the maintenance of the *status quo ante* became the rally cry of a number of groups when the government proposed a modification to the ritual.

Two sets of questions

(1) A first set of questions is raised by the proposed procedural modification: (a) how much information should the state be allowed to extract forcefully from the citizen? and (b) what criteria should be used in arriving at the decision of what can

and cannot be legitimately forcibly extracted from the citizen, and whose responsibility should it be to make such a decision?

In a democratic world in which forcible violation of privacy is firmly resisted, it would appear to be clear that what can be coercively extracted from the citizen is only such information that is absolutely necessary for the state to effectively conduct its business of promoting the collective interest.

The criteria to be used should flow from an appraisal of the trade-off between convenience and expediency on the one hand, and privacy considerations on the other. What should be coercively required from the citizen is only (1) the information that would appear to be essential for the state to operate effectively and cannot be effectively obtained in any other less intrusive way; and (2) when it is established that the social benefits clearly outweigh malefits or privacy concerns.

In a democracy, such determination is the responsibility of elected officials, taking into account the technical advice of the expert bureaucrats, after full consideration of the alternative ways in which such information can be obtained in a less intrusive manner. If approximately the same information can be obtained from alternative sources, coercive methods should not be used.

(2) A second set of questions has to do with conflicts between elected officials and bureaucrats when they disagree about such census matters. If, for reasons of priority to privacy, elected officials want to introduce changes in the census process (e.g., making filling in the long form voluntary), and if bureaucrats regard this as undesirable for a variety of technical reasons (e.g., sampling bias, less reliability for calculation matters of national interest, loss of continuous data series, and the like), one may ask how the disagreement is to be resolved reasonably.

One would expect in any sound public administration regime that there would be negotiations, and, if matters did not get resolved, that mediation and arbitration involving the Clerk of the Privy Council (or his appointee) would of necessity kick in. The outcome would be an exercise in scheming virtuously, i.e., a process of reconciliation of the differences of opinion in a manner that would meet both the fundamental objectives of the government as much as possible, while meeting the objections of the technocrats to the greatest extent possible. This would constitute a reasonable fail-safe mechanism. This would appear to be beyond our governance reach in Canada.

The setting

To make the issues as clear as possible, one might imagine a variety of situations:

Situation I   Information A is essential for the state to do its work, and
A is not available to the state by any other practical means.

Situation II   Information A is essential for the state to do its work, and
A is obtainable in some form by other practical means.

Situation III   Information A is argued to be useful to stakeholders, and
A is not obtainable by the state or stakeholders by other practical means; and benefits (private and social) for all parties from having A are clearly regarded by many if not all as higher than the privacy costs regarded as acceptable.

Situation IV   Information A is argued to be useful by some stakeholders;
A may not be obtainable by the stakeholders by other practical means; and benefits (private and social) for all parties from having A are regarded by many if not all as clearly lower than the privacy costs regarded as acceptable.

Situation V   Information A is argued to be useful to stakeholders, and
A may be obtainable for the stakeholders by other practical means.

One may reasonably argue that in the case of situation I, coercive extraction of information by the state is warranted, and that in the case of situations II, IV and V, it is not. Situation III is problematic: the case for coercive extraction of information depends meaningfully on the relative appreciation of benefits and costs in each case.

Special problems in a federation

One may expect a certain degree of contentiousness about the different situations in a federation since there exist many governments that are using the data collected, and they may not all have the same degree of critical need for the information or the same degree of respect or lack of respect for the right of the citizen not to be coerced unless it is absolutely necessary. Negotiations are required.

For example, some information may be more crucially required by one provincial/territorial government than another, and one such government may be more or less privacy-sensitive than another. This may entail strong differences of opinion among governments, not only about the information they themselves require, but also about the sort of information their constituents claim they are entitled to.

Asking the citizens to voluntarily transmit such information may or may not fully satisfy governmental users who have been used to the information being legally and coercively extracted from citizens in the past, because the voluntarily supplied information may not (in their estimation) be of the same quality (i.e., not be as accurate and reliable as what they are used to).

These matters may not be easy to resolve, and there can be legitimate differences of opinion about acceptable and unacceptable trade-offs among different governmental stakeholders. For instance, non-state-stakeholders may argue for intrusive access in order to secure information for their own purposes, regardless of citizen sensitivity. This may or may not be regarded as legitimate by the government, and certainly would not qualify automatically as information that can legitimately be coercively extracted from the citizen by the state.

In the same manner, one elected government may choose to exercise the coercive action aggressively and routinely, while another may choose to use it only with the greatest of care – depending on its philosophy and its respect or lack of respect for the right of citizens not to be coerced unduly unless it is absolutely necessary.

Whatever the case, one would expect, in a modern democracy, equipped with a professional public service, that there would be fail-safe mechanisms in place to handle these contentious issues, and that in most circumstances (if not all), a resolution of these differences of opinion would materialize.

In cases of acute or major differences of view, a mediation and arbitration process would be expected to generate a viable and mutually tolerable (if not fully satisfactory) solution that would recognize the legitimacy of both families of concern (convenience and privacy), and would find creative ways out of such dilemmas.

In the case in point, one might speculate that an acknowledgement of the legitimacy of the concerns of the different governments, and an acknowledgement of the soundness of some concerns of the technocrats and meaningful stakeholders, would have translated into the sort of decision process announced (through a press release) by the Cabinet Office Minister, Francis Maude, in the United Kingdom on July 10, 2010. On that occasion, the Government of the United Kingdom announced that, despite its concerns about the census process as it is carried out:

(a) it would proceed with the 2011 census because it was too late to tinker with it;

(b) it would also examine alternative ways of gathering the required statistics (other than the census) that would produce data that are more accurate and timely in a less costly and intrusive way over the next while;

(c) it would work with experts and stakeholders in generating methods that would be less inefficient and intrusive;

(d) but it also served notice that the 2011 census could be the last of its kind.

The extent to which the traditional ways could be replaced by modern computerization capacities of statisticians to interrogate data bases (1) in ways that were not possible when information was stored in filing cabinets, and (2) in ways that would better keep pace with the accelerating pace of societal change (e.g., immigration, etc.) has been underlined aptly in an editorial of *The Economist* (July 17, 2010).

It would appear clear from experiences elsewhere that, despite the laments of historians and of some statisticians, there are efficient ways to replace much of the anachronistic and increasingly inaccurate head counts generated by the traditional ritual.

The modification of the census process in Canada

Canada did not use the prudent UK approach.

The government obviously had concerns about the census process, but it chose to modify it immediately and unilaterally, and it decided that the modification would be implemented in the census of 2011, without any broad consultation. On a matter that involved so many disparate interests (public and private), it was obviously a risky decision – some less generous might call it a mistake.

Moreover, it would appear that the decision was taken without an extensive expert evaluation of the usefulness to governments and other stakeholders of all the information collected in the long form, or of the extent to which, in the case of all the questions of the long form, alternative means existed to generate from other sources approximately something like the same information.

The presentation of the rationale for the proposed change by the government has been confused and is most inarticulate. At times, it has seemingly been argued that the key concern was the fact that the long form was too intrusive, and that the coercive power of the state should not be used to extract this information under the threat of prison. At the same time, the responses given to those who have suggested that voluntary responses would generate unreliable information have been clumsy and haphazard.

Anyone aware of debates in other countries about the usefulness of the ritual census knows that there are reasonably persuasive answers to many of the questions raised by opponents to any change. But the preceptoral work of the Canadian government was botched.

To the extent that polls are reliable, the citizenry would appear to be split on whether the proposed modification should proceed or not. This is not surprising in a world where privacy concerns are ever more played out, and where Canada even has a Privacy Commissioner to act as watchdog; but where, ironically, at the same time, so many Canadians are choosing to share the most intimate details of their lives on Facebook.

One may reasonably conclude that the process that has led to the decision to modify the census has been clumsy and flawed.

Whether the bungled manner in which the current government has dealt with the need to rethink the census ritual warrants the flurry of attacks it received is less interesting a question than the extent to which this episode might serve as a *révélateur* of the paucity of the public discourse in Canada, and of the incredible degree of ineffectiveness of the machinery of government in dealing with issues that might require fail-safe mechanisms when the elected officials and the bureaucracy are at loggerheads.

The long form psychosis as *révélateur*

This technical decision has become the occasion of an inordinate flare-up of anger at the government, and the lightning rod for a wave of declarations by a vast array of public actors denouncing the government in vitriolic terms. Most importantly, however, with few exceptions, both the reporting and the pronouncements have been short on explanation and search for solutions, and long on denunciation, ascribing the worst possible ideological motivation to the government.

Manicheism and fundamentalism

Statistics Canada carries out a multitude of surveys of all sorts, and is not relying solely on data generated by the census. In Canada, as in other countries, the fact that the census may be a costly and inefficient method of data collection, that the results collected every 10 years are quickly out of date, that there might be ways to provide better information, more frequently and more cheaply by using a variety of existing administrative databases, etc. – have been the source of many conversations.

The vast literature dealing with these issues has not received much attention in the Canadian media over the last while, and when it was mentioned, it was in the margin of page x while front page stories and editorials were feeding the frenzy about something unwholesome being perpetrated on the country.

Indeed, the paucity of serious reporting, the extent of disingenuity, and the sheer manicheism (yes or no?) of much that was written would appear to indicate that one cannot count any longer on the mainstream media for serious investigative analysis of complex issues. More revealing perhaps, what has been put on the table in the last few weeks is an array of pronouncements by persons claiming some authority to speak on these matters, but very little that would suggest ways to reconcile the different points of view.

For instance, there was little serious discussion about the true importance (or lack of it) of the information collected for the purposes of public policy, of the extent to which all of the 50 questions of the long form are indeed necessary, and of the extent to which some reasonable proxies are available from other sources for some or all of the information collected. The public has instead been treated to anecdotes and hyperbole, and the long form was promoted to the level of an icon.

Interest groups have broadcasted their preferences for retaining the *status quo*: those vested interests who claimed to rely on numbers collected on the long form for making their case, or those who earn a living retailing for innumerate clients whatever data are collected in this form. Their claim – that the information collected in the long form should be regarded as a public good, and deliverable in perpetuity in the particular form in use until now, is an entitlement and not only a convenience – was largely unscrutinized and unchallenged, and remains so.

The former Chief Statistician, Ivan Fellegi, declared in the media that the long form is truly indispensable, and pronounced that had he been asked to tinker with it, he would have resigned. Journalists and academics have allowed themselves to speculate and pontificate about the sinister meaning of the government move. And even former clerks of the Privy Council like Mel Cappe and Alex Himelfarb, rising from retirement, felt compelled to defend and celebrate the long form, and the courage of the Chief Statistician who has chosen to resist the governement's diktats on this matter.

Michael Ignatieff also felt compelled to add his voice to the choir (*pour ne pas être en reste*), but felt that he had to shift up the shrillness of the tone one full octave: he pronounced the government guilty of obscurantism, and of defending ignorance; *Le Devoir* won the prize for the most over-the-top statement when it declared that it saw the event as the dawn of an era of *"nouvelle noirceur*"; and the Chamber of Commerce and the provincial governments have bemoaned the fact that their right to all the information they can get (accurate or not, useable or not), and in the form they have been accustomed to is an entitlement that cannot be merrily rescinded or tinkered with.

There has been, neither from the government nor from these epistles, no suggestion about how to reconcile the diverse points of view, even though, *sotto voce* and in private, all parties would appear to recognize the validity of the concerns of their opponents: in the public forum, the matter was cast in terms of absolutes. As a result, there has been nothing but a hardening of the position on both sides as the controversy deepened.

Governance failure revealed

One may reasonably suggest that this theological debate was both toxic and unnecessary. It revealed a fundamental governance failure: a complete lack of appropriate and workable fail-safe mechanisms to deal with situations when elected officials and technocrats find themselves at odds in seemingly-irreconcilable ways.

In the absence of a Canadian Jonathan Swift, capable of exposing the bizarreries of the day, the best we can do is to underline some concerns brought forth by this episode:

- the poor ability of the government to play its necessary preceptoral role in explaining clearly and persuasively a move intended to improve the data collection process while protecting privacy;
- the lack of capacity and will by journalists to help correct this government failure and their propensity to fall into irresponsible theatrics instead of educating the public;
- the failure of academics to propose anything but trite conspiracy theories instead of suggesting better ways to balance the legitimate concerns about information access and privacy; but
- most importantly, the failure of the machinery of government to have in place reasonable ways of dealing with genuine deep differences of opinion very early on as they develop, and of engineering imaginative and intelligent resolution of conflicts at the bureaucratic-political interface when

political wishes and technical constraints call for them; it is clear that the National Statistics Council reasonably-sounding compromise that was tabled late in July 2010 came too late – at a time when the controversy had already led to a hardening of the positions.

Yet this sort of governance failure at the federal level, revealed by this crisis is not new.

Some will recall the medical isotope crisis generated by the conflict arising from the difference of opinion between the President of the Canadian Nuclear Safety Commission and the Government of Canada in 2007. This led to a stoppage of the nuclear reactor that produced half the medical isotopes in the world for a number of weeks until the House of Commons brought forth an override decision.

One could reasonably ask why, at the time, the Clerk of the Privy Council, Kevin Lynch, did not see fit to intervene to prevent that crisis by acting as a mediator and the generator of a compromise solution. Fundamentalism was allowed to prevail, and the costs of this disaster will continue to be important for Canada for a long time.

Today, one may ask why the Clerk of the Privy Council, Wayne Wouters, has not seen fit to intervene effectively in the long form issue in a timely way, and why he has allowed this contentious issue to deteriorate into an irreversible clash of fundamentalisms and a psychodrama in Ottawa.

In both the cases of the medical isotopes and of the long form of the census, the government of the day has been at loggerheads with an arm's length agency in the whole (Canadian Nuclear Safety Commission) or in part (Statistics Canada) by law but also by tradition. In both cases, the relationships between government officials and such arm's length agencies are fraught with difficulties and are quite sensitive. In both cases, the Clerk allowed the situation to deteriorate and did not find ways to engineer a compromise solution. In both cases, Canada has suffered from the lack of effective fail-safe mechanisms in the machinery of its federal government.

This is reprehensible and must be corrected.

Conclusion

It would appear that the machinery of government in other countries is in a less terrible state than in Canada in this regard, and that public management operates more imaginatively: *les partenaires obligés* seem to have found ways to reconcile the different cosmologies of elected officials and bureaucrats. Moreover, they have shown that they are able to creatively resolve emerging crises. Indeed they are in the process in the United Kingdom of jointly inventing new ways to get the information they really need more cheaply and less intrusively, while in Canada we wallow in toxic psychodramas.

It is high time to review the tension zones at the interface between elected officials and technocrats, and to design the fail-safe mechanisms we obviously need. But it is perhaps also time to reflect anew on the burden of office of the Clerk of the Privy Council.

PART III
Toxic Trends

CHAPTER 10

About the New Rhetoric
of Promiscuity

"Croire plus vraie son idée que ce que le réel montre."

– Michel Onfray

Introduction

It is hardly surprising that, in our *société du spectacle* (Debord 1967) and in our *civilisation du spectacle* (Vargas Llosa 2015), rhetorical devices such as calumnious labeling have acquired a new prominence even in academic papers and communications claiming to be austere. These devices are most often intellectual shortcuts, intuitive pumps meant to propose a striking metaphor in lieu of a satisfactory explanation.

Over the last while, the word *promiscuity* has crept into the papers of a good number of Canadian public administration specialists from coast to coast (Aucoin, Heintzman, Rasmussen, Lindquist, among others) to characterize activities at the political-bureaucratic interface. Since the word promiscuity connotes notions of licentiousness, wantonness, immorality and sluttishness, the intent of those using this word is not innocent. It wishes to convey the message that these activities, whatever they are, should be regarded as reprehensible *per se*, under all circumstances. Most often the word is uttered with little of substance offered to explain why such a derogatory label should be attached to actions, persons and institutions. Ralph Heintzman has been one of the few who has tried to argue the case (Heintzman 2014, 2016) but, I would suggest, not persuasively.[9]

My reflections on these recent papers of Ralph Heintzman have led me to the conclusion that not only the use of the word promiscuity may not have been warranted, but that there might be some merit in drawing attention to some blind spots in the Heintzman argument that may have led him to fall prey to the Don Quixote principle according to which *"l'idée qui dit le monde est plus vraie que le monde dit par cette idée"* (Onfray 2014: 10-11).

Heintzman's analysis unfolds deliberately in a rather aseptic, ethereal and stylized context, even though his indictment pertains to the very specific circumstances of the Clerk of the Privy Council, for promiscuity with political power in the Clerk's handling of a particular request by the Parliamentary Budget Officer (PBO) for information about the 2012 Canadian budget implementation departmental spending plans.

My contention is that the circumstances of this affair were not aseptic and ethereal, but toxic and that the decision to indict emerged from:

(1) an unfortunate occlusion of the broad counter-democracy movement that has led the technocracy to usurp more and more of the effective power across Western democracies (Rosanvallon 2006);

(2) an unduly simplistic characterization of the public policy process as a bow-and-arrow exercise *à la* deliverology;

(3) a very stylized appreciation of the dynamic of the budget implementation process in real time with its required ongoing strategic adaptation to evolving contingencies in order to reach broad goals at minimal cost to the citizen; and

(4) a refusal to take into account the political economy dynamic of this particular policy environment in which the PBO might not have acted as a dispassionate and fair super-bureaucrat, intent on helping Parliament to find its ways in the budgetary maze, but acted as a crusader on the warpath, somewhat instrumentalized by the opposition parties, and

---

[9] My comments are presented *without prejudice* as a reflection on two recent pieces of writing by Ralph Heintzman which have made use of promiscuity as a rhetorical device. Nothing said here is meant to impugn in any way other works by Heintzman that I have found enlightening.

vindictively committed first and foremost (in his own language) to exposing the deliberate lies of government officials and of the bureaucracy.

If my reading of the case has merit, independent observers might be led, on the basis of a less constrained analysis, to be much more temperate than Heintzman has been in his conclusions.

In the next paragraphs, I hint at the fabric of our 'new world' in which the technocracy has come to play an ever more crucial role in the generation of a counter-democracy movement that is challenging the democratic process. Then, I draw attention to the unduly desiccated notion of public policy that seems to cast a distorting shadow on Heintzman's analysis. I further draw attention to the somewhat mechanical image of the budget process of the PBO, before underlining its overt, anti-Harper government attitude – a matter that is entirely and inexplicably occluded in Heintzman's analysis.

From my perspective, these blind spots have allowed Heintzman to give a free rein to his platonician inclination to accept that *"l'idée qui dit le monde* [or that he has of the world] *est plus vraie que le monde dit par cette idée"* (*Ibid.*) to prevail.

As a result, I am led to:

- question Heintzman's indictment of the Clerk of the Privy Council for promiscuity;
- argue that if the Clerk had chosen to bow in a servile manner to the wishes of a PBO on the warpath, it might have been a dereliction of the Clerk's burden of office – taking the risk of allowing a mean-spirited and ideologically-inspired PBO to imperil unduly the budget implementation process; and
- express concern about the sort of 'neutering' or even 'emasculation' of the role of the Clerk – an *homme-passerelle* (Bruckner 1994: 62) whose burden of office is to bridge the different worlds and to be the artisan of effective reconciliation and collaboration at the political-bureaucratic interface.

In the last section, I argue vehemently against the firewall between politics and public administration that Heintzman defends, and suggest that there is a case to be made for taking into account politics explicitly in public administration.

The rise of counter-democracy

The basic principle at the foundation of democracy is the legitimation of power by the people. This is accomplished via the electoral process. But the daily life of democracies between elections offers many an occasion for the citizens to express discontent about the way legitimate political powers are used. In recent times, with the permeation of governmental presence in all sectors of activities, a heightened level of questioning of the legitimacy of the elected authorities has come to the fore. Indeed, the mistrust has grown exponentially with the flowering of the 'democracy of opinions' (doxacracy, opiniocratie) that has allowed populist outbursts, with the complicity of the media, to get mountebanks and deceitful groups to carry the day less as a result of reasoned arguments or on the basis of their genuine governing capabilities than as a result of *poussées de fièvre*, blind passions, rhetorical artifices, and the contagious forces of *pouvoir social à la* Tocqueville (Boudon 2005).

This new instability of the democratic process has created new possibilities for various counter-movements to emerge: counter-democratic forces bent on constraining the democratic process (Rosanvallon 2006), counter-societal forces challenging the foundations of civil society (Sue 2016), etc.

In certain instances, this has brought forth some positive vigilance, and has thereby fundamentally reinforced the democratic process by providing certain safeguards or *garde-fous*. But, in other cases, it has also generated negative vigilance, and the instituting of a plurality of toxic surveillance agencies that have often coalesced into a crippling technocratic apparatus, whose sole vocation would appear to be to prevent democratically elected governments from doing their legitimate jobs in the name of some ideals bloated, by these agencies, into absolutes like progressivism, egalitarianism, or the like.

Negative vigilance has generated impediments to effective governance. This has brought forth a new generation of single-purpose super-bureaucracies or agents of Parliament, commissions, judicial or quasi-judicial contraptions that have unfortunately succeeded both in promoting themselves as founts of wisdom and infallibility, and in hoodwinking an unsuspecting public into believing that they have greater legitimacy than elected officials.

Indeed, many of them have come to abuse such usurped status with pit-bullesque aggressiveness – not being satisfied with monitoring government activities in search of exactions, but engaging in second-guessing the choices being made by elected governments in real time, and thereby usurping the role of governors.

For instance, the PBO, prompted by the opposition parties, came to request *ex ante* from elected governments what some would regard as unreasonably accurate numbers about ongoing evolving processes like the war in Afghanistan or the 2012 budget implementation workforce reduction process in the federal public service – basing their request on a rather mechanical and deterministic notion of budgeting, but also on a claim of clergy-like status of the PBO as an agency claiming to be able to interpret the meaning of such data better than the government. Mostly, these requests appear to be based on the presumption that governance is a precise science, and that governance processes can always be deconstructed at no cost into precise and deterministic mechanical slices. Governance experts know better: governance is an imprecise science, and such deconstruction may produce bogus results, and have toxic impacts (Paquet 2008a, 2013a, 2014).

This slow drift from democracy to a regime run by the technocracy and the courts is objectionable for many reasons, but it would appear to have been welcomed by public administration academics and by those who are purporting to rethink the future of the Canadian public service. Their distrust and/or poor understanding of politics led them to assume *holus bolus* that this drift is not only desirable in general, but that the health of our democracy might, in such a new world, be reasonably gauged by the servile deference of senior federal public servants to the zealotry of the super-bureaucrats and the tunnel-vision of the courts.

Heintzman has shown deference for this technocratic apparatus: he has even suggested on the occasion of the conflict between the Clerk and the PBO that, in case of doubt, the appropriate behaviour of senior bureaucrats should be to "favour a generous interpretation" of the mandates of all those super-bureaucracies marching in with their aggressive mandate creep (Heintzman 2016: 9).

A desiccated notion of public policy formation[10]

Until the 1990s, it was still tolerated in certain circles to caricature the public policy formation process in a rather simple-minded way: to presume that the task at hand was always already well-defined, and that the range of alternative delivery instruments was well-specified. Consequently, the sole remaining task was to ensure that the most technically efficient/economic stratagem be selected.

This perspective trivialized the real-life complexity of the public policy formation process: policy problems are rather usually ill-defined; policy issues are most often not well understood and cannot be collapsed into well-structured program tasks; and the range of plausible alternative delivery schemes may not be well specified at all *ex ante*, but emerge through social learning. In a more modern parlance, the public policy formation process poses 'wicked policy problems' (Paquet 2013b): goals are either not fully known or are very ambiguous; means-ends relationships are highly uncertain and poorly understood; and the only meaningful way to proceed is to initiate an inquiry process, and to ascertain what dynamic social learning process is likely to generate the emergence of the most effective way to deal with the evolving concerns.

This more complex view underlines the artificiality of the mechanical separation of the policy process into supposedly independent segments – policy-making, program design, and service delivery – and the danger of insisting on basing advice on a mid-time, instant photograph of the process.

Any significant change in each phase of the policy formation process is bound to have significant impacts on other phases in this integrally, interconnected process and is likely to interfere with the continuous feedback among them that is central to the whole social learning process. Moreover, facile, simplistic or malevolent interpretations of the results of the policy process at intermediate stages may be grossly misleading.

[10] This section draws freely from Paquet 1997.

Failing to understand these central features of the policy process was the major source of the failure of the alternative service delivery initiative, and of other versions of this philosophy of intervention at the end of the last century. This has not discouraged the urge to segment the public policy process in recent times, and the efforts to collapse the whole process into a sole problem of service delivery. The current version of this undue simplification is marketed under the label of 'deliverology', and is bound to go the same way as the earlier versions of this snake oil because it is anchored in the same mistaken and ill-inspired fragmentation of the policy funnel into segments that are not meaningfully separable.

The reason the deliverology mythology has risen from the ashes of earlier initiatives of the same ilk is ascribable to a fundamental misunderstanding of the dynamic social learning process by a number of tenors of the public administration tribe, who have fallen prey to the dogma of separability of the public policy formation funnel. Peter Aucoin was probably one of the most incorrigible of these (Aucoin 1995, 1996).[11]

This disfiguration of the public policy process has allowed many to assume that the process can be mechanically segmented like a sausage, by presuming that the integration of the different phases can always be sutured through explicit contracts. Such misrepresentation of the policy process also legitimized hyper-focusing on gauging the service delivery process as a way to evaluate the whole public policy process. I have shown the unwisdom of such views in an article entitled, "Alternative Program Delivery: Transforming the Practices of Governance" (Paquet 1997).

Ralph Heinzman as a scholar has had sympathies for Aucoin's *problematique*, and a significant portion of his career has been engaged in developing measurements for the efficiency of service delivery. This may explain why he appears to be not the least concerned with carefully scrutinizing the ways in which the PBO interventions might or might not disturb the dynamic social

---

[11] This does not mean that the policy funnel cannot ever be segmented in any way, as Heintzman has aptly done in suggesting elsewhere that management boards could be created to take care of routine processes like human resources and finance.

learning underpinning the policy process. One may presume that, in his mind, a modularized policy funnel *à la* Aucoin is entirely workable and effective: each segment inhabiting more or less a separate facility, having separate rationales and rules, and disturbances in certain phases not inhibiting the dynamic social learning process.

Consequently, Heintzman appears to:

- have taken an Aucoin view of the policy funnel;
- see no real dangers in phases of the public policy process being unduly interfered with; and
- see nothing reprehensible in the PBO probing the service delivery phase of the budget implementation process with a view to gauging whether it would be successful, without having to take into account the whole process, and the whole context constraining the dynamic social learning.

A broader and more all-encompassing perspective of the whole public policy process might have commanded a somewhat different view, and might have led to different sensitivities about disturbances in the implementation process preventing the normal process of adaptation through social learning to proceed – especially if the disturber were less interested in being helpful in this process than in exposing wrongdoing.

For instance, can a snapshot at mid-course of temporary and evolving accounting results on workforce reduction be a basis for providing advice to Parliament on the soundness of the whole budget implementation process any more than a posse being sent to Afghanistan to look at the accounting in the war zone can help Parliament pass judgment on the overall financial effort entailed by the war in Afghanistan? One may record juicy stories and surmise quite contestable guesses on the basis of these singularly narrow forays, and generate grist for quite contestable government criticisms, but how much credible information is likely to be produced to help Parliament make its macro-decisions?

The PBO as an anti-government super-bureaucrat

If one assumes as an act of faith that any particular super-bureaucrat is entirely free of any bias, there may be little reason to believe that an agent of Parliament would deliberately search for juicy stories with a view of casting disrepute on elected officials and its bureaucracy. But it is difficult in 2016 to cling to the assumption that Kevin Page was unbiased, given his freely revealed confessions of 2015.

Since nobody seems to overview the behaviour of super-bureaucrats, agents of Parliament, Supreme Court judges, etc., out of kindness, Heintzman may have generously concluded that the 'character' of such super-bureaucrats might reasonably *not* have to be taken into account in interpreting the extent to which everybody else in the federal public sector needs to deal with their requests. Yet, would it not be a matter of due diligence to make sure that such holiness is fact, not fiction. Blind trust or 'generous trust' might be an acceptable attitude in the abstract, but 'vigilant trust' might be a preferable stand in the real world.

It remains that presuming that the process of nomination of every super-bureaucrat (whatever may be known about them and whatever their behaviour may have revealed) is the result of a process of immaculate conception may be a bit naïve, and most certainly quite risky. Entertaining the view that a particular Supreme Court judge might be somewhat biased in favour of certain interest groups in Canada may be *verboten dans certains milieux bien-pensants* in Canada, does this mean that due diligence about the existence of a biased attitude should be regarded as something *verboten* also on the part of an academic examining contentious political/bureaucratic or judicial issues?

Some members of the academic gentility of the public administration tribe have conveniently chosen to avoid the issue by adhering dogmatically to the myth that the neutrality, impartiality and superior reliability, if not infallibility, of the super-bureaucrats is a given.

As an observer of that scene over the years, I have found that such a myth does not fit my experience of the real world. Super-bureaucrats, like justices in our courts even at the highest level, never divest themselves completely of their biases when they are elevated to these positions. Some make enormous efforts to be as impartial as possible, and they must be praised for it. But others often allow the inclinations that they have developed over their lifetimes before the appointment to guide their endeavours in their new position. Indeed, some so-called progressives regard those mental prisons as a badge of honour. While it might be unreasonable to generalize that all super-bureaucrats are not neutral, it would equally be incredibly naïve to assume that they are *per se* neutral.

In the case of the agent of Parliament playing a key part in the morality play examined by Heintzman in his 2016 paper – the PBO Kevin Page – one has two reasons to be particularly vigilant – his contentiousness, and the window to his inner soul opened by his co-written memoirs (Page 2015).

I will not review this book of memoirs here: it has been done in chapter 7 of this volume. As it is shown there, Page is a supremacist super-bureaucrat, full of contempt for the members of Parliament (*Ibid.*: 2), the Prime Minister (PM) (*Ibid.*: 15 and *passim*), and the senior bureaucrats. He saw his job not as helping Parliament to navigate wisely through the shoals of public finances, but as exposing, in his language, the deliberate and purposeful lies of the bureaucracy and the government officials.

His memoirs are full of persiflage about the PM, and vitriol for both elected officials and senior bureaucrats. This is hardly the image of a dispassionate super-bureaucrat capable of or interested in a fair analysis: Page saw himself as a crusader in a morality play, and there is no reason to believe that this is an attitude he only developed after his retirement.

Even though Heintzman would appear to share both Page's low regard for Harper and his government as "the first to adopt a deliberate policy of weakening responsible government in Canada" – a throw-away comment offered in the very front section of the 2016 paper – this is hardly sufficient for him to occlude the potential toxicity of Page's approach to his job, and to ignore the way in which this might be said to have contaminated the whole PBO/PMO situation in which he was.

The crusading and vindictive nature of the PBO is a matter that one may expect to distort the texture of the chessboard in the interface between the Clerk and the PBO somewhat. It would be unreasonable to expect that it would not influence the nature of the reactions of the Clerk of the Privy Council to Page's requests.

Is it fair then for Heintzman's readers – as a result of his silence about such things – to be left with the view that Page is an honest broker from whom any request should only be regarded as fully warranted without any scintilla of a doubt? Have we all already forgotten about the dire consequences of some unfortunate, ill-considered statements by the Auditor-General about the sponsorship affairs, and the disastrous impacts they had (Hubbard and Paquet 2007)?

The matter has been made all the more awkward by the *deux poids deux mesures* attitude of Heintzman *vis-à-vis* the two main protagonists in the PBO/PCO affair: total inattention was given the PBO's publicly demonstrated attitude and erring ways, while the Clerk's writings were submitted to hyper-careful textual interpretation (probing at times intentions more than actions, bordering *par moments* on *procès d'intention*).

Again, one can only be logically led to think that a more even-handed approach might have forced a reframing of the circumstances of the episode under study, and might not have led to the same suggestions for handling the problems observed at the political-bureaucratic interface.

All of this brings us back to the central question of the legitimate definition of the mandate of the PBO.

On the interpretation of the mandate of the PBO: Heintzman's surprising gamble, Page's fundamentalism, Wouters' *gaucheries*, and the Clerk's burden of office

Let us start with three general considerations.

First, as might be said in the case of any large public organization, it is equally fundamentalist and *intégriste* to claim either a right to complete confidentiality by government, or a duty of complete transparency and disclosure as certain groups would suggest. In the first case, opacity would lead to public ignorance and, over time, to the emergence of exponential distrust; and in the second case, operating in Macy's window would render the effective operations of governance immensely difficult if not impossible (Bennis 1976).

Second, one should expect more openness when the request comes from a fair and neutral agent, and more limited openness when it comes from some explicitly hostile or seemingly unfair agency.

Third, as to who might be in a better position to determine what is the optimal degree of transparency that should be required in certain circumstances, *a priori* and *ceteris paribus,* one might be tempted to opine that the Clerk of the Privy Council might be better equipped to do the job than the head of a single-purpose audit or quasi-audit agency like the PBO.

However, as we will see, these seemingly innocuous statements have proved contentious.

Heintzman's surprising gamble

Like parliamentarian Brent Rathgeber, Heintzman would appear, at first, to argue simply and fundamentally for as much transparency and open government as possible (Rathgeber 2014). But under closer scrutiny, his diagnosis and his inclinations do not appear to converge fully with Rathgeber's.

The differences are twofold.

First, Rathgeber has provided an analysis of the many factors that have generated the reduction of the ability of the Parliament of Canada to hold the government accountable over the years (of which Prime Minister Harper's *modus operandi* is only one – the others being the entitlement state, the workings of Cabinet, the bureaucracy, the media, the failure of access to information legislation, etc. – all factors that Rathgeber examines in his book). Heintzman's analysis is seemingly *plus courte*: blaming Harper.

Second, Rathgeber indicts the very imperfect Canadian model of democracy, and welcomes any useful bricolage that might repair its many types of deficiencies. Indeed, he proposes an array of reforms to deal with the different factors he has identified. Heintzman, on the other hand, would appear to have chosen to work at the level of an ideal-type of democracy, and to be willing to settle for nothing else but an approximation of the ideal-type of transparency and accountability – seemingly something he senses would require the removal of Harper.

By focusing somewhat exclusively on what he regards as the toxic impact of the Harper government, and spiriting away other sources of concern, and any concern with the context (i.e., a hostile PBO), it is possible for Heintzman to hyper-focalize on an interesting but relatively small part of the problem around the so-called independence of the Clerk, when a more comprehensive perspective might be required.

For instance, government executives need to maintain as much flexibility as possible in the budget implementation phase. They might therefore quite reasonably hesitate before providing public estimates of spending reductions that would have to be revised significantly as a result of plan adaptations, especially:

(1) given the strategic sensitivity of such information at a time when the opposition parties and the unions are fighting austerity initiatives tooth and nail (whatever the long run consequences) and cannot be expected to act in anything but the most partisan way; and

(2) given a responsibility to manage the process with maximum flexibility and minimal damage to the citizens, using all favourable circumstances and contingencies, but faced with the probability of much damage to these anticipated plans if the provisional and incomplete results were to be used mischievously by the PBO, thereby preventing the government from proceeding as planned.

The crucial issue at the centre of Heintzman's 2016 paper is whether the request for additional information about the detailed spending plans of federal departments in the budget implementation plan of the Harper government should have been regarded as warranted in 2012 given the circumstances? A secondary question has to do with who was most legitimately qualified to decide in such a case. Those matters are not discussed by Heintzman: he felt *ab ovo* that the PBO as super-bureaucrat was the one party whose view should prevail. He then proceeds to indict the Clerk of the Privy Council, another technocratic agent, for having behaved in a reprehensible way in opposing the wishes of the PBO, and having chosen to obfuscate and equivocate about it.

Given the roguish nature of the attitude of the PBO, would it not have been preferable and more reasonable to ask the following questions:

1) Was it reasonable or not for the Clerk of the Privy Council, as the person most fully informed about the evolving budget implementation process and its circumstances, to ascertain what part of ongoing operations involved should be revealed to the PBO?

2) In what details should information be handed to the PBO, if any at all, for the Office to be able to perform

its mandated job – while protecting the sensitive and delicate public finance operation from being sabotaged or derailed by the actions of a PBO explicitly hostile to the government in place?

3) On the balance of evidence, in what way is one to better ensure that an acceptable sort of transparency is achieved: relying on a hyper-activist and anti-government agent like the PBO to self-redefine its mandate to fit its dubious intentions, or relying on the Clerk of the Privy Council to arbitrate?

Page's fundamentalism ignored by Heintzman

One of the Heintzman's blind spots in his handling of the 2012 controversy between the PBO and the Clerk has been his insistence on looking at the PBO as if it were in the ideal-type world, Heintzman postulates, instead of looking at the world as it is. The issue here is not to build a case on a *procès d'intention* but to build on explicit statements by the PBO. I have referred earlier to Page's memoirs which I feel are making a strong case about the intents of the PBO and his *modus operandi*. The memoirs came out in 2015, so it may be said that Heintzman (2014) did not have access to it. This might explain why he was able to make an act of faith in the neutrality of the PBO. But this is not a tenable position for his 2016 paper.

Another related blind spot is the simplistic view of the budget implementation process that is carried by the PBO, and allowed to stay unchallenged by Heintzman, whose long career in the public service would have made him aware of the much greater fluidity and imprecision of that process.

The process of reducing public expenditures with minimal damage to the citizenry is not a simple matter of deterministic mechanics imposed on each department, but an ensemble of actions aimed at reaching various moving targets through the use of all emerging opportunities, depending on circumstances and contingencies.

Disclosing provisional and incomplete information midway through the process may reveal very little about the ways in which overall public expenditures will ultimately materialize, but may allow such information to be used as an instrument of disinformation by a fundamentalism-driven PBO.

Heintzman fully trusted the PBO and would appear to be paranoid about the Clerk's relations with the government. It is not clear how one could argue persuasively that either of these assumptions could be regarded as warranted.

What would appear plausible by examining the evidence is that Heintzman's assumptions, both of which are immensely questionable, are not as questionable one as the other:

- the case for Wouters's promiscuity with the Harper government is entirely based on Heintzman's very thin notion of the burden of office of the Clerk that would appear at odds with anything like a reasonable notion of the burden of office of the Clerk in modern times. Heintzman's desiccated notion of the role of the Clerk is indeed the basis for his indictment of Wouters;
- Heintzman's blindness in the face of Page's fundamentalism is impossible to understand. We have already said enough about the frame of mind of the PBO super-bureaucracy and its 'gotcha' philosophy. It flagrantly percolated when NDP Paul Dewar requested that the PBO investigate the costs of the war in Afghanistan: Page shamelessly recounts the celebratory jubilation of his staff reportedly stating "This is the one we have been waiting for!" (Page 2015: 59).

Wouters' gaucheries *and the Clerk's burden of office caricatured by Heintzman*

The summary condemnation of the Clerk of the Privy Council, after a skilled textual analysis of a Clerk's letter responding unfavourably to the request of the PBO, might be even more difficult to understand than the blind faith in the PBO granted by Heintzman from the start. In this second case, the sanitization and trivialization of the role of the Clerk that is marshalled to indict the Clerk would appear to be very consequential: such trivialization might endanger Canada's governance, and be quite risky if it were a view of the Clerk to become accepted.[12]

It is true that Heintzman's textual analysis reveals that there is a certain degree of penumbra about whether the Clerk speaks at times for the bureaucracy or for the government or for himself. But this is only bothersome because of the highly and reductive corset in which Heintzman circumscribes the notion of the burden of office of the Clerk. Heintzman's speculations about the different ways in which the Clerk could be wrong only hold if the stylized view of the Clerk *à la* Heintzman is to be regarded as the canonical and only acceptable view.

In fact, Heintzman's notion of the burden of office of the Clerk is neither canonical nor acceptable.

Nobody would deny that the Clerk was particularly *gauche* in defending his position. He was obviously not aware that his letter would be subjected to close textual analysis. He should have known better when dealing with the hostile PBO and his allies. These *gaucheries* have allowed Heintzman to have a field day, and to make fun of him. But Heintzman went further and overboard by suggesting that he had thereby impugned his integrity. What Heinzman has done is to put a bullet hole through a straw dog.

In a paper co-authored with Ruth Hubbard, I have provided a panoramic view of the evolving role of clerks of the Privy Council from the 1860s to the first decade of the 21st century. In this paper, we follow the evolution of the broader Canadian socio-economic-political context over time; we identify the ways the governance challenges evolved and gauged the ways in which the role of the Clerk of the Privy Council was transformed (Hubbard and Paquet 2008).

While in the early days, the Clerk was mainly a registrar, later his role evolved into that of a maven, a connector and an *entremetteur* in the best sense of the word.

---

[12] The experience with the Canadian Nuclear Safety Commission and other single-purpose entities in a multiplex world has been a cautionary tale (Hubbard and Paquet 2009, 2015: chapter 4). One may recall that the fundamentalism of the Commissioner generated a world crisis in the production of medical isotopes that might have been resolved by an intervention of the Clerk, but was not as a result of a doctrine of incapacitation of this function. This illustrated the cost of imposing impotence on the Clerk of the Privy Council as *personne-passerelle*.

The elusiveness of the Clerk's role – who is the locus of neither *imperium* (absolute power) nor *potestas* (real power) – does not deny that he has significant *auctoritas* "based on an impersonal capacity to augment, safeguard, and add value to what exists, which is embodied in the person charged with that role" (*Ibid.*: 116).

In recent time, especially when the environment has been turbulent, the Clerk has aptly played the role of coordinator, integrator, steward and crisis manager, using his/her *auctoritas*. Whatever emanates from a person with *auctoritas* is less than an order but more than simple advice, and it has become an important capability as turbulence increased, and as coordination, integration and stewardship challenges have become more challenging and also more crucial.

It is only through a disfiguration of the role of the Clerk that Heintzman would appear to be able to rationalize his view that the Clerk of the Privy Council could never have any legitimate reason to use his *auctoritas* to ensure that the request of a hostile PBO would not be met. For Heintzman, the Clerk has none of the substance or legitimacy of a central actor on the Canadian federal scene. This is a fundamentalist position anchored in philosophical principles that one may welcome in a desiccated, ideal-type model of democracy, but would not meet the standard of common sense and reasonableness in the messy world of real-world democracy in Canada.

Heintzman would appear to suggest that his phantomatic Clerk can only be out of bounds:

- if he explicitly agreed on his own (for the benefit of sound public administration) with the views of the government about the extent of the mandate of the PBO: he would then act as a messenger boy and a puppet; or
- if he interprets, on his own, the mandate of the PBO not to be as "generous" as Heintzman would like (i.e., the PBO request to probe the evolving operations of budget implementation is denied because it might do damage to the public administration of Canada): he would then be accused of *ultra vires* action.

The fact that the Clerk of the Privy Council chose to respond to the appeal of his decision by Kevin Page at first (to avoid confrontation with the PBO, I presume) by claiming that he could not provide the information because of side arrangements with the unions, and later (after the unions had argued that this need not be the case), by claiming that he did not agree that the mandate of the PBO extended to the budget implementation plans, may suggest that he was *gauche*. He was *gauche* indeed. But this is hardly sufficient to argue that he was thereby deliberately undermining the foundations of democracy.

It may not be so much Wouters' *gaucheries* in responding to Kevin Page that disqualified him in the mind of Heintzman, but the fact that the Clerk has, in Heintzman's opinion, no *auctoritas* at all.

For Heintzman, it would make no sense for Wayne Wouters to launch an argument that good governance requires some secrecy. For him, the optimal amount of transparency cannot be in all matters and at all times anything but the maximum amount of transparency – even though the opposite would make sense for Bennis (1976) or Lacouture (2005) or many of us.

In the post-Gomery world, transparency had become such an hegemonic value, and agents of Parliament were temporarily idolized. It would have taken an unusual amount of gumption on the part of Wayne Wouters to take the stand that the optimal amount of transparency is not the maximum amount of transparency. That may explain his equivocation.

A less impractical doctrine than Heintzman's would recognize the legitimate possibility for a Clerk who wishes to live up to the duties defined by his burden of office:

- to take action to limit the nefarious impact of a hostile PBO on the budget implementation operations, and
- to choose not to be "generous" (as Heintzman suggests he should be) in interpreting the PBO's mandate, and not to provide a helpful hand to such a partisan PBO in certain circumstances.

Heintzman not allowing these possibilities might be regarded by independent observers as being unduly narrow-minded.

One of the important lessons from this dual exercise in dwarfing the texture of democracy to its formal or even conventional usages, and in dwarfing the role of the Clerk to a shadow of itself is to remind all of us of the cost of such conservatorship. We have made the case against this sort of mental prison in the introduction of *Irregular Governance: A Plea for Bold Organizational Experimentation* (Hubbard and Paquet 2015).

In our chimeric world, empathetic imagination and multiplex bricolage are *de rigueur*

Heintzman has dealt with democracy in a grand, stylized and abstract manner. In this world, there is little place for base realities. He is dealing with an ideal type of democracy: one where each part has a precise role, and messiness is unwelcome. The boundary between political values and public service is never to be crossed. Yet collaboration is essential in democracy, and collaboration entails messiness, so the political-bureaucratic interface is bound to be muddied.

Heintzman does not like messiness, and his efforts to avoid messiness have taken the form of imagining both a fire wall between politics and public administration, and a charter of public service that would regulate neatly and constitutionally this interface. This sort of Cartesian neatness may appear on the surface to create a superior organizational form, but it is a fantasy. In the world of governance, imprecision is the rule, strategies may be originally crafted but of necessity they evolve, and in the end they 'emerge' in a form and with results that are very imperfectly anticipated. In the panoply of designs being experimented with, the attractiveness of moral contracts is their elusiveness and their continually evolving nature. They firmly resist any effort to constitutionalize or freeze them.

The Heintzman cosmology creating a mythical boundary between political values and public service never to be crossed is another way to present the case for anti-politics in public administration – a most unnatural entity, a sort of *être de raison*. The real world of public administration is a chimera – part goat, part lion, part serpent – where these components cohabit in a single animal. Trying to keep these components artificially apart is bound to generate analyses that fail: in the real world, one must be able to take into account politics in public administration or be condemned to live in fantasy land.

The case is made persuasively by Michael W. Spicer. Spicer argues that governance is inherently political. While social sciences may offer the artillery of instrumental rationality and determinism, this is not sufficient. Ultimately, the spirit of value relativism has to come to the fore, and one has to recognize that the multiplicity of values and concepts of the good needs to be reconciled. For public administration, this can only come from politics: the best that can be expected is some evolving approximation of fairness in resolving conflicts. There is neither need nor possibility for a deep moral consensus, only a willingness to resolve differences by politics and not force (Spicer 2010: 89).

Practical moral reasoning is not like self-contained geometry or formal logic. It is much more like law: it is not rational in the sense of formal mathematical deduction. Both moral and legal reasoning are sensitive to many values simultaneously, and, in specific concrete situations, this may even generate unreasonable conclusions or protect incompatible ones (Perelman 1980).

This sort of reasoning is mainly analogical reasoning – reasoning by example, reasoning from case to case – a proposition describing a first case is made into a rule, and then applied to other similar situations. "The arguments can never be proven demonstrably to be correct or incorrect" (Aronovich 1997: 81). Arguments are made on the basis of plausible analogies, and such arguments in politics are open to contestation (Spicer 2010: 99).

Public administrators are, in this sense, like lawyers and judges. Analogical reasoning may suffice to base a legal decision, but "legal reasoning alone cannot provide a sufficient guide for moral action in public administration ... moral reasoning calls for a greater degree of imagination than is typically found in legal reasoning" (*Ibid.*: 100-01). Robert Goodin would translate this requirement to mean that members of a public administration unit, in reasoning about public issues, should self-consciously imagine a discourse on these issues among different people, taking different positions – a process of "empathetic imagining" sort of making others imaginatively present (Goodin 2000; Spicer 2010: 101).

All this can only be generated by injecting politics into public administration.

Conclusion

The PCO/PBO case examined by Heintzman has therefore been illuminating in an unusual way.

It has not provided a clean fable on which one could build a case for a Le Corbusier minimalism in the architecture of government – like the idea of a charter of public service, and a stylized and rigid code to ensure that bureaucrats are never instrumentalized by politicians. It is not that Ralph Heintzman has not tried his best to make that case. It is both that reality as square pegs do not fit well into round holes, and that such constructs may be expected to end up paving the way to a consecration of an ever greater role for the technocracy and the super-bureaucracy in our democracies – something that can only make our society more anti-democratic.

It has rather provided a 'cautionary' tale, reminding us of all of the difficulties of collaboration, of the centrality of messiness, and the need to cope with the *incontournabilité* of real politics – a world that is fundamentally baroque (Paquet 2008b), and reminds one much more of Frank Gehry than of Charles-Edouard Jeanneret-Gris *dit* Le Corbusier.

In the Heintzman ideal-type world of constitutional gears, there is no place for a rogue PBO, for *pouvoir social à la* Tocqueville, carrying opinion waves that may be senseless but are quite difficult to counter, and for the intelligentsia being captured in the maelstrom. Convenient erasures of details from the broad canvas are hardly noticeable: the cute truthinesses of the Chretien era, the convenient amnesia (pace the friendly dictatorship) that accompanied them, and the demonization of Stephen Harper as a form of enlightenment.

In the real world, what are central are the details that contaminate the crime scene, and the impossibility of excising inconvenient memories.

The details of the PMO/PBO saga have had to do with circumstances calling for the design of innovative strategies, and the bricolage of workable arrangements in dealing with something as elusive as the Wouters' burden of office and Page vindictiveness. This is troublesome for those who think that political science holds the key to problems of public administration – it drives them mad.

As Fukuyama has starkly stated, there is no science of public administration – it is a black hole – good solutions have to be local, context-specific (Fukuyama 2004: 44-45). They require the design of effective bricolage.

In this maelstrom, the political-bureaucratic interface is always in motion, and it would be a Promethean challenge to codify it. It must rather be conceived as an evolving nexus of games of competition and collaboration in which there may be some taboos, but where creative imagination is more important than rigid dos and donts. An ethics of duties presented in a code may provide a basis for discussion, but it is unlikely to generate anything sufficiently robust and solid. Too much would depend on rhetoric, disinformation and deception.

What has to evolve is moral capital that would underpin inclinations and dispositions, and would lead to action being taken by individuals and groups as echoes of some capital of virtue (Paquet 2016).

Making this terrain playable would entail as serious a screening of politicians and bureaucrats as Toyota imposes on the screening of its operatives, some sense of the sort of qualifications required to be ready for these roles, some evolving moral contracts to embody always temporary working rules, and some mechanisms through which the moral capital would develop.

As Candice Bergen used to say in a neat television commercial way back when, "it is that simple and that complex!"

References

Aronovich, Hilliard. 1997. "The Political Importance of Analogical Arguments," *Political Studies*, 45: 78-92.

Aucoin, Peter. 1995. "Canadian Public Management Reform: A Comparative Westminster Perspective" (mimeo).

Aucoin, Peter. 1996. *The New Public Management: Canada in Comparative* Perspective. Montreal, QC: IRPP.

Bennis, Warren. 1976. "Have we gone overboard on the right to know?" *Saturday Review*, June 3, p. 18-21.

Boudon, Raymond. 2005. *Tocqueville, Aujourd'hui*. Paris, FR: Odile Jacob.

Bruckner, Pascal. 1994. *Le vertige de Babel*. Paris, FR: Arléa.

Debord, Guy. 1967. *La société du spectacle*. Paris, FR: Buchet-Chastel.

Fukuyama, Francis. 2004. *State-Building*. Ithaca, NY: Cornell University Press.

Goodin, Robert E. 2000. "Democratic Deliberation Within," *Philosophy and Public Affairs*, 29: 81-109.

Heintzman, Ralph. 2014. *Renewal of the Federal Public Service: Toward a Charter of Public Service*. Ottawa, ON: Canada 2020.

Heintzman, Ralph. 2016. "Border-crossing: The PBO, PCO and the boundary of the public service," *Canadian Public Administration*, 59(3): 357-381.

Hubbard Ruth and Gilles Paquet. 2007. *Gomery Blinders and Canadian Federalism*. Ottawa, ON: The University of Ottawa Press.

Hubbard, Ruth and Gilles Paquet. 2008. "Clerk as *révélateur*: A panoramic view" in P. Dutil (ed.). *Searching for Leadership – Secretaries to Cabinet in Canada*. Toronto, ON: University of Toronto Press, p. 85-120.

Hubbard, Ruth and Gilles Paquet. 2009. "Design Challenges for the Strategic State: Bricolage and Sabotage" in A.M. Maslove (ed.). *How Ottawa Spends 2009-2010*. Montreal, QC: McGill-Queen's University Press, p. 89-114.

Hubbard, Ruth and Gilles Paquet. 2015. *Irregular Governance: A Plea for Bold Organizational Experimentation*. Ottawa, ON: Invenire.

Lacouture, Jean. 2005. *Éloge de secret*. Brussels, BE: Éditions Labor.

Onfray, Michel. 2014. *Le réel n'a pas eu lieu – Le principe de Don Quichotte*. Paris, FR: Autrement.

Page, Kevin (with Vern Stenlund). 2015. *Unaccountable – Truth and lies on Parliament Hill*. Toronto, ON: Penguin.

Paquet, Gilles. 1997. "Alternative Program Delivery: Transforming the Practices of Governance" in R. Ford and D.R. Zussman (eds.). *Alternative Service Delivery: Sharing Governance in Canada.* Toronto, ON: IPAC/KPMG, p. 31-58.

Paquet, Gilles. 2008a. "Super-bureaucrats and Counter-democracy," *Canadian Government Executive,* 14(6): 4p.

Paquet, Gilles. 2008b. *The New Go-Governance: A Baroque Approach.* Ottawa, ON: The University of Ottawa Press.

Paquet, Gilles. 2013a. "La gouvernance, science de l'imprécis," *Organisations et Territoires,* 21(3): 5-17.

Paquet, Gilles. 2013b. *Tackling Wicked Policy Problems: Equality, Diversity and Sustainability.* Ottawa, ON: Invenire.

Paquet, Gilles. 2014. "Superbureaucrats as *enfants du siècle,*" *www.optimumonline.ca,* 44(2): 4-14.

Paquet, Gilles. 2016. "Tramps in mud time: the public sector ethical process in an age of entitlements, deception and sophistry." Paper presented at a conference jointly sponsored by the Office of the Conflict Commissioner of Ontario, the Osgoode Hall Law School and the University of Toronto Law School on September 29-30, 2016 at Bennett Lecture Hall, University of Toronto Law School.

Perelman, Chaïm. 1980. *Justice, Law and Argument – Essays on Moral and Legal Reasoning.* Boston, MA: Reidel.

Rathgeber, Brent. 2014. *Irresponsible Government – The Decline of Parliamentary Democracy in Canada.* Toronto, ON: Dundurn.

Rosanvallon, Pierre. 2006. *La contre-démocratie – La politique à l'heure de la défiance.* Paris, FR: Seuil.

Spicer, Michael W. 2010. *In Defense of Politics – A Value Pluralist Perspective.* Tuscaloosa, AL: The University of Alabama Press.

Sue, Roger. 2016. *La contre-société.* Paris, FR: Les Liens qui Libèrent.

Vargas Llosa, Mario. 2015. *La civilisation du spectacle.* Paris, FR: Gallimard.

CHAPTER 11

Disinformative, Ideological and Oikophobic: On a Piece of Storytelling by Quixotic John Ibbitson[13]

"For every complex problem, there is an answer that is
clear, simple and wrong."

– H.L. Mencken

This is a critical appraisal of the arguments that are at the core of Darrell Bricker`s and John Ibbitson`s *The Big Shift – The Seismic Change in Canadian Politics, Business, and Culture and What It Means for Our Future* (2013).

One may ask why a critical review three years after the date of publication. The answer is simple: we became aware of this book only in July of 2016, and we were shocked by the fact that its unusual bravado was inversely proportional to its intellectual contribution to current debates – to the point of qualifying as an inordinate intellectual *pétard*.

One may also ask why John Ibbitson is singled out in this note. The answer is also simple: the most objectionable aspects of the book – and the only ones on which we dwell in this note – are clearly Ibbitson's contribution, since they are an echo of the same argument made more guardedly by Ibbitson in an earlier book he single-authored – *The Polite Revolution* (2005). It is not reasonable to chastise Bricker by association.

---

[13] This chapter was co-authored with Gary Caldwell.

Finally, is there a need for this belated appraisal?

Some would say no. Its main prediction about Harper's win in 2015 has already been blown out of the water, and Ibbitson's Quixotic characterization of Canada – based on Don Quixote's presumption that *"l'idée qui dit le monde est plus vraie que le monde dit par cette idée"* (Onfray 2014: 10-11) – would suggest that the book should be left unperturbed.

Unfortunately, bad books filled with blatantly unwarranted assumptions, flawed analyses and ill-founded conclusions – based mainly on an author's mental prisons – are as toxic as bad meatloaf, and have a tendency to resurface in the forum through the babblings of unsuspecting readers, who will uncritically repeat some parts of the message, and thereby cause the continuation of the process of disinformation. Silence in the face of this amounts to complicity.

This chapter proceeds in three stages. First, we roughly summarize the contents of the book in order to provide the reader with its general flavour, and some context for the central portions that we vigorously contest. Second, we indict Ibbitson on three counts that appear to us most toxic:

1) his unwarranted celebration of indiscriminate mass immigration and multiculturalism, and his betrayal of the burden of office of a good journalist which is 'not to disinform';

2) his unduly thin notions of citizenship and nation; and

3) his reprehensible oikophobia (amnesia combined with repudiation of the past), and his denunciation of the notion of 'common public culture'.

These indictments – for shoddy journalism and disinformation on the first count, for ideological blindness on the second count, and for paranoia on the third count – amount to a severe damning of the book's core. Third, we speculate, in closing, on what might explain this sort of paranoid argumentation, and we suggest elements for a cure.

An overview of *The Big Shift*

The document is:

- a selective but useful assemblage of data about the 'Big Shift' in Canada's socio-demographic fabric in the recent decades;
- some polling data and statistics, mixed with statements of "beliefs" (served raw) that drive the argument throughout the book; the reader is force-fed dogmas (e.g., there is no such thing as a Canadian nation and never was (Bricker and Ibbitson 2013: 15)) without a scintilla of a supportive argument;
- a bold science-fictional scenario, considered irreversible, conjecturing that the 'Big Shift' has triggered the displacement of the so-called 'Central Canadian elites' who believed that "no party could win a majority government without substantial support from Quebec" (*Ibid.*: 49), they have been replaced by a new coalition of suburban Ontario voters and Western voters that has now seized power over the political landscape. All this to be followed by the superbold declaration that "the Laurentian elites may never again be in charge" (*Ibid.*: 30);
- a flurry of eclectic disquisitions purporting to 'document' circumstantially the science-fictional view sketched above; this is usually gingered up by throw-away sensational opinions of the authors in the form of 'conclusions' – e.g., about the geriatrics of the sovereigntist movement in Quebec (including an insulting and gratuitously sexist remark about Louise Beaudoin as the "coquette" of the movement) or the impending extinction of the Quebec Liberal Party, foretold in 2013 (*Ibid.*: 65) – which the Quebec elections in 2014 revealed to be a fantasy;
- finally, woven through this storytelling, the major proposition suggesting that "open-immigration immigration combined with multicultural tolerance" – what the authors regard as "the finest achievement of the Laurentian elites" but one that "also helped do them in" (*Ibid.*: 16) – is the source/cause of this 'Big Shift';

- together with a true Ibbitsonian excursus (*Ibid.*: 227-236) in which, having somewhat dissolved the notions of citizenship and nation, Ibbitson subjects the reader to a *morceau de bravoure* where (1) he vehemently attacks some of those who have grave doubts about the wisdom of the massive indiscriminate immigration and the multiculturalism imposture by repeating louder what he knows to be falsities about the supposedly positive impact on economic growth and compensation for the aging population of these initiatives, before (2) allowing his true oikophobic colours to break out in a tirade about what he finds abhorrent and offensive (*Ibid.*: 233-234) in the argument of Paquet (and Caldwell) – the need to pay attention to the erosion of 'common public culture', and to what he calls the "dubious standard of citizenship."

The central point of Ibbitson`s baroque pamphlet buried inside the book is that Ibbitson believes that "policies of high immigration and multicultural diversity are tremendously good for Canada" and "whether for good or ill, they are *entrenched and unstoppable*" (our emphasis) (*Ibid.*: 236). From our point of view, this is a matter for concern, not celebration.

Ibbitson suggests that these policies have generated an irreversible shift of power to a new hegemony of voters in suburban Ontario and the West – based on a perspective cleansed of the fiction of a bilingual country among other things (*Ibid.*: 59). These sorts of 'cleansed futuribles' are based on a very thin notion of citizenship, an erasure/denial of the reality of the notion of nation except in its tribal sense, and a sentiment of oikophobia, paradoxically accompanied by a Panglossian overture to diversity.

The authors state they want to initiate a debate (*Ibid.*: 277). However, Ibbitson's blindness and deafness to opposing views, his radical fundamental cultural and moral relativism, and a denial that there is such a thing as a set of prevailing mores, which determine how we communicate with one another or *sociality* (except for the hegemony of English and a utopian universalism), constitute rather important ideological blinders and more than a whiff of bad faith. Consequently, whoever is searching for the magic of dialogue might have to find a different forum.

Three indictments

Unwarranted celebration of mass immigration and multiculturalism

Nobody is blinder than one who does not want to see. This book needs the twin engines of mass immigration and multiculturalism as *dei ex machina* for the 'Big Shift' scenario to unfold. Consequently, these two phenomena are uncritically embraced as positive forces, and their negative, silent, societal, erosive impacts are deliberately and irresponsibly ignored.

Both phenomena have been critically appraised by a large number of credible experts (Economic Council of Canada 1991; Collacott 2003), however Ibbitson does not pretend to ensure due diligence in his discussion of those matters. Paquet has written two books on this issue (Paquet 2008, 2012); Ibbitson claims to have read only one chapter of the second book (Paquet 2012: chapter 1). Yet, of this chapter, Ibbitson would appear to have remembered only a small portion of the material. His willful blindness ensured that he would pay no attention to the portion of this chapter that demolishes quite persuasively the vacuity of his foundational myths (about mass indiscriminate immigration generating substantial economic growth, or compensating for the ageing of the Canadian population, and about multiculturalism eroding Canada's sociality). Ibbitson parrots mythical untruths on these matters.

The lack of critical thinking is of the same order of magnitude in the discussion of the impact of the state-promoted multiculturalism as ideological programming about cultural relativism, about the insane idea of equality of cultures, about the domino effect of the Charter commitment to the "preservation and enhancement of the multicultural heritage of Canadians." Combined with the echo effect of mass indiscriminate immigration, the multicultural propaganda has eroded Canada's self-image, its identity, and silently redefined the Canadian common culture. The refusal to be concerned about the common public culture – its references, norms and social codes – (indeed, finding the idea of any concern about it to be abhorrent) reveals an insouciance and irresponsibility about even the ways in which public institutions are unwittingly being transformed.[14]

In summary, our argument suggests that:

1) there can be no denial that the current Canadian immigration regime supports massive and indiscriminate immigration;

2) there is also something puzzling/fishy about the so-called 'pan-Canadian consensus' that is said to have 'materialized' between the mid-1990s and the mid-2000s (from a position where two-thirds of Canadians polled consistently found immigration levels to be *too high*, to a position where two-thirds of Canadians polled disagreed with this statement). This reversal of position at times when immigration flows were dramatically higher, and newcomers were experiencing increasing difficulties of integration, may reasonably be said to be an echo effect of the deepening multiculturalist propaganda (as Andrew Cohen suggests, "if enough people tell you this, you come to believe it" (Cohen 2007: 158)).

Ibbitson refuses to consider any possibility of the brainwashing of the Canadian population by its elites. Supposedly, because it is a Marxist notion, this phenomenon cannot exist in Canada! He cannot even envisage that the public could have been deceived by its elites. "We must have much greater faith in the collective wisdom of the body politic. The Laurentian elites *guided* (our emphasis) the country ... because they knew the bounds of what the public would tolerate. ... Multiculturalism was and is an inspired approach to fashioning a society based on tolerance and

---

[14] These matters are always difficult to gauge but careful observers of the Canadian scene have noted that transformation (Cohen 2007: chapter 5). For a more general discussion of such transformations, see Akerlof and Kranton 2010. Recent events around the Shafia affair (Afghan-Canadian parents condemned for honour killing in the death of their three daughters) have also led commentators to speculate on the fact that public officials would appear to have been slow and numb in reacting to the call for help of the Shafia sisters in Montreal, when the same sort of family violence in a *Québecois de souche* family would have most certainly triggered more intrusive and robust action. It is legitimate to ask whether cultural relativism has already permeated the *manière de voir* of officialdom, and whether it has led to a degree of tolerance in the name of 'cultural difference' that could be responsible for criminal tolerance (Blatchford 2011; Martineau 2011).

diversity. Canadians have embraced the policy because it works, not because it has been drilled to accept ... . Paquet should give people some credit for knowing their own minds" (Bricker and Ibbitson 2013: 234).

Now this is a particularly interesting intellectual somersault.

The Laurentian elites were supposedly able to deceive not only all Canadians for decades, but even to deceive themselves into "doing themselves in" by allowing mass indiscriminate immigration from the 1990s on. But on a matter probably more complex – multiculturalism – the Canadian public becomes wise and Ibbitson can write (without a smile) that the Laurentian elites (on this matter) "guided the country... through consensus" (*Ibid.*: 234) – whatever this means.

So sometimes Canadians are gullible and manipulated by the Laurentian elites into swallowing "the fiction of a bilingual country," and sometimes they are wise and inspired in the face of the multicultural policy. Canadians are "guided" by their elite in one case, and not guided in the other, and only Ibbitson knows how to tell the difference? One would like to know why two-thirds of Canadians felt that there were too many immigrants when the inflow was modest in the 1980s and the same proportion felt that there are *not* too many when the immigration flows more than doubled in the late 1990s? If this is not multicultural propaganda, how has this happened organically? Is it more credible to assume that their wisdom "grew" organically, or to presume that Canadians have been "misguided" by their elite into changing their minds? And if Ibbitson has any reason to believe in the former explanation, why has he not said anything at all about it in his book? And how can he be so contemptuous of those who are conjecturing that some "misguidance" has been present in both cases?

Citizenship and nation

The failure of Ibbitson's analysis is, in part, a willful blindness ascribable to ideological biases when he whimsically determines cases where the public was bamboozled or not. But a big part of it is also ascribable to two mental prisons that reveal a strong preference for a very thin democracy.

Democracy is not reducible to the mechanics of Constitution, the rule of law, and elections. So the notion of citizenship is more than an engagement to respect the law, and it is not exhausted by the notion of a rational pact.

As Chantal Millon-Delsol would put it, behind the formal agreements or accords, there are three important elements that contribute to shaping it:

- there must be an *affective support* (a people does not connect to an entity that does not reflect the image of its convictions and of the possibilities of living by them); behind rights and obligations, there must be an idea of the common good;
- citizenship must connote a *locus of belonging*: one cannot identify with organizations and institutions without feeling that he/she belongs there, that certain principles are shared that constitute some basic reference points; and
- citizenship requires certain structures in which the members will recognize themselves, some common principles, some *"certitudes intérieures"* without which any *agir-ensemble* is somewhat problematic (Millon Delson 1993: 270-71; Paquet 1994).

Citizenship must match the socio-political texture of the world it is trying to re-articulate. In a world of limited and multiple identities, one must accept the idea of *multiple citizenships* – more or less tangled or nested – echoing *"le résultat d'une démarche interactive et créatrice ... une persona que l'on force au fur et à mesure que l'on vit et pense au milieu de concitoyens... un système de différences partagées que ses membres reconnaissent"* (Drummond 1980-81).

This world appears to be too complicated for Ibbitson. For him, citizenship is a "dubious standard" to begin with that can only be meaningfully defined in legal terms (Charter, constitution, rule of law). In the Ibbitson world, there is no underground to citizenship: his only concern is the legalistic plumbing. A citizen is any person who abides by the law of the land. This is a sanitized, minimalist, and very thin notion of citizenship, one designed to ensure maximum negative freedom and maximum inclusiveness, but entailing minimal engagement in the process, no responsibility, no place for positive freedom, for activism. In fact, in the Ibbitsonian world, there is no need, nor place for sociality. The individual is a disconnected nomad existing in a social vacuum: sociality is nothing but a constraint on negative freedom. Ibbitson regards anything added to the minimal/legal notion of citizenship as unwarranted, questionable, and as a nuisance.

When it comes to the notion of nation, for Ibbitson it is a form of sociality impregnated with ethnicity and tribalism. The nuisance level becomes even more taxing than in the case of the sanitized notion of citizenship. It would appear to necessarily refer to a *deep or hard group* (i.e., referring to skin, gender, language, mores, ways of living, etc.) – to a sociality where otherness is part of the identity (Van Gunsteren 1998). These ligatures are clearly making inclusion more difficult: for a person entirely devoted to negative freedom, the very notion of nation is incompatible with the minimalist notion of citizenship and maximum negative freedom. Only erasure of the nation will do.

Ibbitson regards the notion of ethnic and tribal nation appropriate for Quebec – and expresses pity for its fate, but in the case of the rest of Canada (ROC), he responds by a *cri du coeur* — *the Rest of Canada* is not a nation nor has it ever been (Bricker and Ibbitson 2013: 15). This is meant to restrict the notion of nation to its ethnic/tribal version – something Canada has never pretended to be.

As Frank H. Underhill explains, the "new nationality" – the words used in the Speech from the Throne at the first session of the first Parliament of the new Dominion of Canada in November 1867 to define the new reality of Canada – was anything but this sort of ethnic/tribal enclave. From its very moment of birth, it wished to transcend communities divided by language, race or religion.

Underhill defined a nation as "a body of men [obviously in the generic sense of men and women] who have done great things together in the past, and who hope to do great things together in the future. What makes them into a nation is not necessarily community of race, language, and religion, though they are powerful forces when they are present, it is their common history and traditions, their experience of living together, their having done great things together in the past, and their determination to continue doing great things together in the future" (Underhill 2008: 124).

It is only through an ideological use of eviscerated notions of citizenship and nation that Ibbitson can spirit these notions away. To the extent that the foundations of the nation are not its physical anthropological roots (and Ibbitson reduces it to those very characteristics), he completely misses the point that *nation* connotes solidarity. This presumes a common past, a common memory, but it is tangibly expressed by daily consent and a clear desire to continue a common experience. This is Ernest Renan's sense of nation when he calls a nation *"un plébiscite de tous les jours"* (Finkielkraut 1987: 48). This is also the sense of nation for Underhill.

In that sense, to say as Ibbitson does, that Canada has never been a nation makes no sense.

Oikophobia and the tirade against common public culture

These toxic maneuvers of denial are exposed when Ibbitson denounces the notion of 'common public culture' later in the book (Bricker and Ibbitson 2013: 227ff). This attack was not only senseless, but also formulated in a most imprudent and impudent manner: it was an emotional outburst in which he aggressively intended to savage an idea, without either having taken a modicum of care to inform himself about it, or a modicum of precaution to ensure that he really understood what this idea was all about.

At the time of Ibbitson's writing, an extensive discussion of the notion was available in both of Caldwell's books (2001, 2012) and in Paquet's (2012). Ibbitson did not bother to look into it. He simply reacted unreasonably and emotionally because of a third mental prison: oikophobia.

Ibbitson would not only appear to abominate memory and sacralize amnesia, but also to abominate *"la maison natale"* – whatever his community has brought to him, vowing to get rid of all that has been accomplished as social learning over the centuries by that community (Finkielkraut 2013: 104). Oikophobia is not only amnesia, but hatred and repudiation of the past.

Oikophobia is a state of mind, Roger Scruton argues. He defines it as the repudiation of inheritance and home, a propensity to denigrate culture, customs and institutions (Scruton 2008: chapter 8). We already know from his treatment of citizenship and nation that Ibbitson is offended by anything that might threaten to limit negative freedom in any way, and that he attaches no import whatsoever to positive freedom, or to engagement.

The antonym of repudiation of the past is not sacralisation of the past, but the critical appreciation of the past so as to ensure that the good is not discarded with the bad and the ugly. Both Caldwell and Paquet have been most careful about defining the common public culture as an evolving set of reference points allowing viable *vivre-ensemble*, and have suggested that there may be some elements of this set of values and customs that are not worth preserving, but that there may be other elements not only worth preserving but also worth fighting for.

Ibbitson reaches a climax of *fermeture d'esprit* when he identifies the past with one label – "Christian and white" (Bricker and Ibbitson 2013: 235). That is immensely reductive. Moreover, when reacting emotionally to the very notion of common public culture (without having probed the meaning of these words), he does not hesitate to conjecture that it might "limit the right of immigrants to vote" (*Ibid.*: 236). Not only is Ibbitson ideologically amnesiac and oikophobic, but his denunciation of tradition – of Canadians having done great things together even – verges on the mindless. He not only disagrees with efforts to preserve certain values Canada has developed over time that have helped it in doing great things, but he "abhors" the very idea of so doing (*Ibid.*: 233). In the same way, we would conjecture, he seems to abhor "the fiction of being a bilingual country" (*Ibid.*: 59). Truly, Ibbitson would appear to drift here into what Robert Sibley would call a pneumopathological state – the state of "those `living' as it were in a fantasy world of self-righteousness" (Sibley 2013).

To gauge the *démesure* between the attack on the notion of common public culture and what had been proposed by Caldwell and Paquet (in works that Ibbitson had chosen not to read) allow us to reproduce several paragraphs from Paquet, 2012 (96-100 passim):

> *When newcomers request the privilege of joining the host society, they have to accept the idea that they are entering a complex and delicate set of arrangements that cannot be disturbed without consequences. Some of these arrangements may ostensibly be visible, but may not constitute something*

that is particularly cherished. Cohabitation of different ways of life may then be regarded as quite acceptable, and even, in a relatively short time, become part of the refurbished common public culture. Others may be cherished for reasons that are not clear to the newcomer, and quickly become a source of tension when they are challenged. Indeed, some may be icons representing fundamental aspects of a way of life that the host society regards as quintessential and not negotiable.

It would be great if all this baroque ensemble of conventions were clearly and unequivocally defined, and if the degree of non-negotiability of each one was well known to all. It would also be great if the newcomer were to join the host society unburdened by any cultural baggage of his/her own. Such is not the world we live in.

There is much that is latent and unspoken in the host society's common public culture, and any newcomer carries with him/ her many conventions originating from another society where the common public culture may be quite different.

The only reasonable basis for viable accommodation between these different common public cultures is for the newcomer to ascertain as fully as possible the nature of the common public culture of the host society, and to determine if he/she can accommodate it. If, for instance, a newcomer were to join a host society while firmly believing and stating clearly that he/she considers (1) the members of the host society as 'dogs' unworthy of any consideration, and (2) that their usages and mores are globally depraved and to be opposed in toto, one might reasonably suggest that this is a bad fit, and that the newcomer should consider joining another sort of club.

However, it should also be clear from our earlier discussion that not all aspects of the common public culture of the host society are equally non-negotiable. The reality of 'reasonable accommodation' is the determination of the extent to which the newcomer will have to adapt to the different sets of arrangements in good currency in the host society: either totally, in good part, or not necessarily.

But it should also be clear that, if the newcomer wants the privilege of joining the host society, he/she has to agree to shoulder most of the accommodation to the common public culture in the host society. This is the view held by 70 percent of Canadians, but not the view arrived at by the officialdom of the Bouchard-Taylor Commission in Quebec. Rather, the commission has suggested that the bulk of the accommodation has to be shouldered by the host society. This explains why the Commission Report was summarily shelved: it was in too sharp a contradiction with the views of the citizenry.

Consequently, one needs to start with the host society's common public culture as ground zero, as the starting point for negotiations between the host society and the newcomers.

...

Nowhere is there a clear mapping of the terrain where accommodation can or cannot be negotiated. Gary Caldwell has prudently surveyed the terrain, but has been reluctant to determine whether crucial tangible borders might exist between what is negotiable and not negotiable. Yet this is an issue that requires immediate attention because, even if in the longer run this may change, it is not possible to engage newcomers in a meaningful conversation unless one is able at the very least to identify a plausible list of some of the items that would appear, in the short run, to be non-negotiable.

A complete review of the whole array of conventions (covering the whole range from etiquette to freedoms, rights, responsibilities, to principles and beliefs) might be both tedious and fraught with immense difficulties, at least until one has clarified some foundational basic principles and essential beliefs that would appear to underpin the common public culture.

As a preliminary step, I have taken the bold move of producing a minimal list (drawing much from the lists proposed by Caldwell) under each of the two more fundamental rubrics he has used, in order to present a plausible set of principles or beliefs about which a broad consensus might be generated.

Basic principles	Essential beliefs
Representative democracy	*Freedom of choice*
Separation of church from state	*Equality of opportunity*
Rule of law	*Equality of men and women*
Responsibility for one's actions	*Collaboration*
Duty to help those in need	*Fraternity*

These lists are not presented as self-evident, but as examples of principles and beliefs that might be of help in determining what is and is not negotiable in the moral contracts with the newcomers. It should be clear that while, in practice, one may fail to live up to these principles and beliefs, they would appear to correspond to a plausible set that might approximate a sort of hard core of the common public culture that may be defendable.

This sample of principles and beliefs is itself open to debate, and should indeed be debated in due course. But for the immediate purpose of discussion, let us assume that until these sets have been disputed and dislodged from such a position (representing the defendable outcome of a long, common experience that has led a community to develop such an anchor), they may be regarded as temporary reference *points in determining what is not negotiable."*

Nothing in the above statement of 2012 would seem to be offensive or abhorrent. It is only from Ibbitson's ideological prison that it might appear so. Consequently, the very toxicity of Ibbitson's oikophobia is bound to force the reader to ask whether such aggressiveness is warranted, or whether it is unreasonable and paranoid – and whether it calls for a robust book review or a psychoanalytic *séance*.

Understanding John Ibbitson

Ibbitson has been responsible for sound and enlightening political commentaries for decades, so it is impossible to discard the sort of work produced in this recent book without searching for an explanation of its arguments.

Take one

The most reasonable explanation is that Ibbitson – a relatively conservative journalist – has been carried away by the mistaken idea of the 'Big Shift' as the source of a "seismic" discontinuity in the future of Canada, when it is actually something less fundamental. This might have led him to force the evidence a bit too conveniently into a mold.

That might have led him to a naïve acceptance of mass indiscriminate immigration to promote growth and correct the aging of the Canadian population (Bricker and Ibbitson 2013: toned down on page 233) and to accept the utopianism of the multicultural imposture that sees diversity as a primary good that has only positive effects. Ibbitson admits that the Laurentian elites have been done in by the unintended consequences of these movements (*Ibid.:* 16), and that these movements are "unstoppable" (*Ibid.*: 236), as a result of the more than 20 percent of Canadians born outside the country who vote for governments that will perpetuate massive immigration and of those who do venerate diversity without recognizing that optimal diversity may not be maximum diversity.

Now that the election in the fall of 2015 has forced a recalibration of the 'Big Shift' hypothesis, Ibbitson may also wish to recalibrate some views that he has too uncritically swallowed *dans le feu de l'action*, especially given the disastrous results of the mass immigration + multiculturalism policies in so many countries in the world. He may even be willing to envisage that Canada is no exception after all, that these policies have been deleterious in Canada too, and that we might well be close to the end of the era of mass indiscriminate immigration, and the search for maximal diversity.

Ibbitson, the rational journalist, may have already begun work on his next book, acknowledging the excesses of *The Big Shift*, and documenting the sort of epiphany that would bring Canada back to its earlier immigration policy – one based on absorptive capacity, and leading to a declawing of the excesses of the multiculturalism policy. Already consultations with immigrant groups have revealed that they support a more temperate approach to mass indiscriminate immigration in the future (Paquet 2012: 50).

Take two

When confronted with the alternative scenario conjectured by Paquet, who envisages indiscriminate mass immigration and multiculturalism imposing excessive diversity and the equality of cultures as potentially "eradicating the notion of a Canadian public culture, [to] dissolving Canada's cultural traits into a vast soup and [to] shaping Canadians into shapeless selves" (Paquet quoted by Bricker and Ibbitson 2013: 233), Ibbitson has recoiled and rightly so. On page 235, Ibbitson is clear: he "do[es] not contend that modern Canada is valueless" but he is afraid of them, and he cannot fathom that the vast soup scenario is in the realm of possibilities, and that Canadian values are being eroded by massive indiscriminate immigration (*Ibid.*: 235-6).

As a result, despite the experiences of mass immigration and multiculturalism in European countries that have led to disasters of different orders of magnitude, Ibbitson regards Canada as the *exception* in this family of countries. So for him, the likes of Caldwell and Paquet as Cassandra's ... whose pessimistic views should be discarded ... even though he knows well that Cassandra was always right in her predictions.

Ibbitson should read Roger Scruton's *How to be a conservative* (2014). This marvelous book reminds true conservatives – a group to which Ibbitson, Caldwell and Paquet belong – of having the duty to seek truth everywhere, including in the very places which may appear inconvenient.

References

Akerlof, George A. and Rachel E. Kranton. 2010. *Identity Economics*. Princeton, NJ: Princeton University Press.

Blatchford, Christie. 2011. "Trial shows system numb to abuse," *Ottawa Citizen*, November 25.

Bricker, Darrel and John Ibbitson. 2013. *The Big Shift – The Seismic Change in Canadian Politics, Business, and Culture and What It Means for Our Future.* Toronto, ON: HarperCollins.

Caldwell, Gary. 2001. *La culture publique commune.* Québec, QC: Éditions Nota Bene.

Caldwell, Gary. 2012. *Canadian Public Culture – The Rules of the Game in Canadian Public Life and Their Justification.* Ste-Edwidge-de-Clifton, QC: Fermentation Press.

Cohen, Andrew. 2007. *The Unfinished Canadian.* Toronto, ON: McClelland & Stewart.

Collacott, Martin. 2003. *Canada's Immigration Policy – The Need for Major Reforms.* Vancouver, BC: The Fraser Institute.

Drummond, Lee. 1980-81. "Analyse sémiotique de l'ethnicité au Québec," *Question de culture,* no. 2, p. 139-153.

Economic Council of Canada. 1991. *New Faces in the Crowd.* Ottawa, ON: Supply & Services.

Finkielkraut, Alain. 1987. *La défaite de la pensée.* Paris, FR: Gallimard.

Finkielkraut, Alain. 2013. *L'identité malheureuse.* Paris, FR: Stock.

Ibbitson, John. 2005. *The Polite Revolution – Perfecting the Canadian Dream.* Toronto, ON: McClelland & Stewart.

Martineau, Richard. 2011. "Une tragédie évitable?" *Le Journal de Montréal,* November 26.

Millon-Delsol, Chantal. 1993. *L'irrévérence – Essai sur l'esprit européen.* Paris, FR: Mame.

Onfray, Michel. 2004. *Le réel n'a pas eu lieu – Le principe de Don Quichotte.* Paris, FR: Autrement.

Paquet, Gilles. 1994. "La citoyenneté dans la société d'information : une réalité transversale et paradoxale," *Transactions of the Royal Society of Canada,* Sixth Series, Volume V, p. 59-78.

Paquet, Gilles. 2008. *Deep Cultural Diversity: A Governance Challenge.* Ottawa, ON: The University of Ottawa Press.

Paquet, Gilles. 2012. *Moderato Cantabile – Toward a Principled Governance of Canada's Immigration Regime*. Ottawa, ON: Invenire.

Scruton, Roger. 2008. *England and the Need for Nations*. London, UK: Civitas.

Scruton, Roger. 2014. *How to be a conservative*. London, UK: Bloomsbury.

Sibley, Robert. 2013. "Young men can be turned into good or evil," *Ottawa Citizen*, April 29.

Underhil, Frank H. 2008. *The Image of Confederation* [3rd Massey Lecture originally published by House of Anansi Press in 1963] reprinted in Bernie Lucht (ed.). *More Lost Massey Lectures*. Toronto, ON: House of Anansi Press, p. 121-207.

Van Gunsteren, Herman R. 1998. *A Theory of Citizenship – Organizing Plurality in Contemporary Democracies*. Boulder, CO: Westview Press.

CHAPTER 12

The Obscenity of Hyper-toleration

"... la dictature effective de l'illusion dans la société moderne ..."

– Guy Debord

Toleration is an act of tolerance, and 'tolerance' is a sort of forbearance and indulgence in judging other persons' opinions or customs or propositions. This capacity to concede and endure, despite a profound *malaise* – and most certainly not to react negatively or defensively to views or proposals at odds with what one would regard as reasonable – is often praised as a sign of politeness and civility. Indeed, this attitude of submitting or of being inclined to submit is even regarded in some quarters as a virtue for it makes for easier social intercourse.

However, there is a downside to toleration when it means bowing in a submissive and intimidated way in the face of unreasonable proposals. In such a case, toleration becomes an act of intellectual cowardice, a sort of weakness of will, a form of *soumission*. Thereby, it is an attitude allowing imposture to remain unexposed. This sort of behaviour deserves to be chastised as a reprehensible lack of critical thinking and courage.

In times of moral relativism, and political correctness (Paquet 2014: chapters 1 and 5), reprehensible toleration has tended to spread like wildfire, sophistry to prevail unchallenged, and sacred cows to remain unslaughtered. Intellectual exchange being tainted, the degree of nonsense allowed to survive and to be propagated has reached an obscene level – a level of indecency and offensiveness that has debased public discourse and has led, among other things, to pathologies of governance and significant welfare losses.

Who is responsible?

This toxicity has now reached endemic proportions in the discourse of many academics (philosophers, political scientists and sociologists) in Canada. These tribes have been deeply permeated by the 'progressive ethos' that developed in the post-World War II era – a movement anchored in compassion rather than reason, built on politically-invented social wishes of all sorts, a cumulative ratcheting of these nominal wishes into entitlements, an excessive deference to the precedence of compassion-cum-ideology-ordained in policy development, an abandonment of critical evaluation when do-gooding is at issue – all this leading to an endemic failure to confront inefficiency and waste in public administration (Paquet and Wilson 2016).

This 'progressive ethos' has fuelled all sorts of schemes rooted in ideology that have been supported and propagandized by the *pouvoir social* – in the sense of the word used by Tocqueville – embodied in mechanisms of manufacturing and diffusion of public opinion. Many of these half-baked ideas have been transformed into dogmas that have come to be so firmly rooted in the public mind that even political power has been intimidated and discreetly censored into criminal silence – when politicians and bureaucrats were not part of the machinery promoting these aberrations (Boudon 2005).

One of the most toxic outcomes of this 'progressive ethos' may have been a general attenuation of logic and reason in public discourse. The media and the intelligentsia, doing the heavy-lifting in the pursuits of these highfalutin ideals, have allowed themselves to routinely ignore the basic reality of the situations they were dealing with, and to self-righteously engage in defending feel-good policies in the most irresponsible ways: persiflage has replaced analysis; *mentir-vrai*, disingenuity and disinformation have been in common currency, and the most contrived 'opinions' have been presented as conventional wisdom. Our modern societies have been mauled by the 'pneumopathological' – the state of "those who are morally insane, 'living' as it were, in a fantasy-world of self-righteousness" (Sibley 2013).

These imaginary representations of the world, manufactured by the intelligentsia and propagated by the media, have come to be regarded as more real than the world they are trying to depict and understand (Onfray 2014). Efficiency has come to be denounced as a cult (Stein 2001), and waste to be regarded almost as 'virtuous' in public opinion, as long as it could be interpreted as the price to pay for the compassionate comforting of some interest group or other.

The main conduit of the degradation of critical thinking has obviously been the media. The intellectual standards in good currency in most public affairs reporting and debates have become immensely questionable at best. This is particularly ironic that, at a time when journalists vehemently demand special status, consideration and protection in our societies, they are generally failing so miserably in their role as the fourth estate.

But the source of this degradation of critical thinking is most importantly flowing from the betrayal of a major segment of the intelligentsia. These intellectuals debase the currency of public discourse by allowing groundless opinions, disinformation, ideologies and deceitful mirages to remain unchallenged and propagated. Indeed they lend them their shallow authority. Their reprehensible toleration of *molle pensée* has immunized such twaddle from critical challenge. Cynics even suggest that modern democracies are degenerating into 'doxacracies' – a world in which governance is entirely fuelled by fluffs of groundless opinions. Academics are too often significant culprits (Gingras 2017).

Three impostures among many

The intellectuals, who have been preaching accommodation and tolerance in the face of disingenuity, deception and sophistries meant to deny or unduly minimize significant threats to the social and cultural orders, have been responsible for irreversible damage. Such sins of omission need to be exposed.

In this section, I examine in a summary way a few recent unchallenged impostures, I expose the ruses of their perpetrators, and I underline the criminal degree of toleration by observers and publics that have so ensured the effective propagation of such deceits:

- in the case of Charles Taylor and *aficionados*, the slumping into oikophobia that has led to the denial of a Canadian common public culture, and therefore to the occlusion of the need to be concerned with the forces that might erode it;
- in the case of Keith Banting and associates, the assumption of Canada as a mysterious exception, as a *dispositif* to sanitize into innocuousness the toxic decision of mixing indiscriminate mass immigration-cum-the ideology of multiculturalism; and
- in the case of Roger Bernard and his jurist acolytes, inventing an unwritten principle in the Canadian Constitution that would guarantee the maintenance in perpetuity of any privilege once granted by governments to any minority group as the foundation of SOS Montfort-type crusades.

Oikophobia: Charles Taylor and his aficionados

The cosmology of Charles Taylor

Charles Taylor is a professor of philosophy at McGill and a former NDP candidate – regarded as a true 'progressive thinker'. Taylor startled his colleagues in 1989 with the pronouncement he made at the time of the Rushdie controversy – the UK writer, Salman Rushdie, had been served a death sentence by Ayatollah Khomeini for insulting Islam's prophet in his book, *Satanic Verses*. Most academics defended the freedom of expression of Rushdie, but Taylor did not. He stated that there is no universal definition of freedom of expression, and came to the conclusion that Rushdie was simply an insensitive Western unbeliever who should have known better than to insult other people's prophets. Therefore, he found himself unable to squarely denounce the death sentence pronounced by the Ayatollah (Taylor 1989).

Occasions for Taylor to finesse his cosmology came forth in subsequent writings (Taylor 1992, 1994). In these pieces, he sharpened the asymmetric view of his cultural sensitivity. While he expressed empathy for minority groups in the Canadian context like Aboriginals, Quebeckers, and newcomers from other cultures, it became clear that he did not have the same sensitivity about the culture of the Euro-Canadians or of Westerners in general. In his world of massive multinational migration, the "members [of modern societies] live the life of diaspora, whose center is elsewhere. In these circumstances, there is something awkward about replying simply 'This is how we do things here'" (Taylor 1994: 63, quoted in Duchesne 2016: 17).

As Ricardo Duchesne sharply rebutted: what is really awkward and pathological is "demanding that the founders of Canada reply that the way we do things here is to promote the cultures of others while essentially denying the existence and legitimacy of their own folkways" (Duchesne 2016: 17).

In 2008, Taylor co-chaired, with Gérard Bouchard, a public commission on reasonable accommodations in Quebec between *citoyens de souche* and newcomers. The presumption on which this commission was created was that there were trade-offs to be struck in such accommodation between the adjustments required from old and new Canadians. Unsurprisingly, the report of the commission conveyed the general message that the bulk of the adjustment would have to be made by the host country accommodating the cultural ways of the newcomers, not the other way around. But there seemed also to be a scintilla of concern for the cultural sensitivity of Euro-Canadians to the extent that the Bouchard-Taylor Commission would suggest restrictions that newcomers might expect on religion-related garb (niquab, thchador, etc. for instance) for authority figures like judges or police officers in the public service of Quebec.

However, this latter point did not sit well with Taylor at the time. Charles Taylor first revealed this view in a 2013 interview (Taylor 2013), and then more sharply in 2017 in an op-ed piece in *La Presse* (Taylor 2017a): he informed the citizenry that he had changed his mind on the question of religious garb restrictions for authority figures like judges or police officers in the public service of Quebec. Taylor even volunteered that he did not truly support the restrictions implied by the sort of dress code prescribed by the commission in the first place, but that, in 2008, he felt that "not imposing them would have shocked public opinion." He now feels that this recommendation has stigmatized Muslims, and fed the rise of islamophobia. In explaining his change of mind, Taylor would only say that he now feels that Quebeckers have become more 'tolerant', and that they are ready to accept that freedom of expression of the newcomers should be the dominant value.

Indeed, in an interview on Radio-Canada, on February 9, 2017, he added that when the Bouchard-Taylor Commission asked newcomers why they had come to Canada, the first reason given was "freedom". This expectation of the newcomers was presented by Taylor as what should be regarded as the absolute imperative (Taylor 2017b).

So, in summary, in Taylor's view, Rushdie (a Western writer) should have been more sensitive and should not have insulted the prophet, and we (Westerners) should not be so insensitive as to impose any restrictions on the disciples of the prophet who may choose to migrate to Canada. If it sounds as if the non-Western newcomers should be allowed to do anything they want as long as it is not explicitly against the law (even if they come from ill-liberal cultures, and whatever the intended or unintended societal and cultural consequences might be of their bringing with them to Canada mores from their native lands) – it is because this is exactly what it means.

There is little attention paid in Taylor's reasoning to the 'common public culture of Canada as the host country', to its heritage, and to the legitimacy of imposing on newcomers constraints in order to be able to maintain the host country's own culture or language. The culture of the newcomer has to be accommodated, but there would appear to be no legitimate 'progressive' rationale for Canada, as the host country, imposing any constraint on newcomers who wish to join the Canadian community when they choose to import cultural mores or traits from their originating country that might endanger or weaken the common public culture of the host country.

For Taylor, it would appear that cultural recognition and cultural rights are only legitimate in Canada for minorities – defined by him in the Canadian context as Aboriginals, Quebeckers and immigrants – for it is not fair to expect them to give up their cultural ancestries and to be expected to assimilate. On the other hand, claiming that immigrants might endanger or weaken the dominant culture of the host country is not admissible, according to Taylor, for it could only lead to intensified discrimination against the minorities.

The rationale for disqualifying Euro-Canadians from having any such claim – i.e., to request that their 'culture' be recognized and protected to the same degree as the culture of newcomers – brings the conversation into murky territory. According to Taylor, Euro-Canadians have been the conquerors who, since 1492, have projected an image of minorities as inferior; moreover, they have no authentic traditions or ethnic heritage, so they cannot legitimately claim to have a cultural identity that matters to them (Duchesne 2016: 11ff). From there, it is only a short step to say that for the rest of Canadians (excluding Aboriginals, Quebeckers and immigrants), claiming an identity or a culture is a bogus and racist stance.

One may legitimately ask why Canadians – who are not Aboriginals, nor Quebeckers, nor immigrants – would ever have accepted this 'intellectual *entourloupette*' denying the existence of a Canadian culture. The issue is never persuasively addressed by Taylor and his *aficionados*. What is undeniable, however, is that the 'disappearance act of the Canadian culture' that has been engineered by them has been swallowed whole by a significant portion of the English-speaking Canadian intelligentsia, and propagandized with gusto.

An excursus on this disappearance act

As I have shown in the last chapter, in denouncing the oikophobia (Scruton 2008) of John Ibbitson, and in defending the idea of a Canadian common public culture (Caldwell 2012; Paquet 2012) as an evolving set of reference points allowing convivial *vivre-ensemble*, a Canadian common public culture exists and some elements of this set are worth fighting for (Caldwell and Paquet 2016). But, by that time, the inexistence of Canadian culture had already become a 'convenient ideological device' in the discourse of Canadian federal politicians and technocrats.

Already in the 1980s, the *zeitgeist* of the country had developed a post-modern flavour: it was clearly stated in the literature circulated by the Secretary of State of the Canadian government to the prospective immigrants that they could bring their own culture in Canada 'because Canada had no culture of its own'. It had become part of the arsenal that the multicultural bureaucracy used to respond to those who were already expressing concern about the costs of the erosion of the social and cultural order as a result of a policy "inviting immigrants not to integrate into Canadian culture" (Paquet 1989). Indeed Sheila Finestone, the Secretary of State for Multiculturalism in the federal government, could proudly restate that startling view as 'common knowledge' in a TV interview in January 1995 (Gwyn 1995: 111). This convenient device was merrily absorbed into the cosmology of the Canadian intellectuals and media as a subterfuge to 'rationalize' as innocuous and inconsequential the effective *surrender* of the Canadian common public culture to the culture of others.[15]

This 'Canada has no culture of its own' argument is built on a very weak foundation:[16]

(1) some have underlined it as a moral disqualification based on the 'guilt ethic' preached by contemporary

[15] This surrender process from the 1980s on is clear. Beginning with the decision *not* to challenge (i.e., using the notwithstanding clause of the Canadian Constitution) the Supreme Court decision in the Singh case in the mid-1980s, supporting the claim of an illegal immigrant stating that since he had put his foot on Canadian tarmac he had all the rights of Canadian citizens except the right to vote. This was followed by the numerous restatements by political officials at the ministerial level about newcomers having the opportunity to bring their own culture with them since Canada has no culture of its own – from Minister Finestone in the 1990s to Justin Trudeau in the *New York Times* in the summer of 2016, repeating the same general message: Canada has no basis or inheritance nor a culture of its own, it is a new kind of country with a "pan-cultural" culture (Harris 2016). This propensity to accommodate has culminated with the recent concession of the federal government of Trudeau *le jeune* – allowing a newcomer to receive her Canadian citizenship at a public ceremony without having to show her face.

[16] This sort of argument reveals the profound schizophrenia of Canadian officials. It flies in the face of generations of intrusive policies by scores of Canadian federal officials (political and bureaucratic), propagandizing the existence of Canadian culture: restating *ad nauseam* how different we are from the Americans, defending an elaborate infrastructure to impose Canadian content on Canadian broadcasters, showering prizes on literature said to be Canadian, giving priority to Canadian topics in the financing of research, and deploying expensive activities to ensure the exposure of Canadian writers, artists and scientists to the international community, etc. Does this mean that all these activities to promote Canadian culture were a sham?

Christianity (Gottfried 2002: 68): separating the ROC (rest of Canada) from the three communities (Aboriginals, Quebec, immigrants) because these communities have been maligned (here or elsewhere) by the Western conquerors; and

(2) others have underlined this stance as a way to ensure that the vision of the multicultural paradise would never be indicted as a cause of any social and cultural disruption in the host community of fate because such a community had been spirited away.

For politicians and bureaucrats, culture-less Canada *à la* Taylor would appear to be strictly an *assumption of convenience* (in the sense one refers to a flag of convenience for a ship or citizenship of convenience) made to fence off the attack on mass immigration or the mounting criticisms of multiculturalism over time as potentially eroding the Canadian culture. For the intellectuals and media, it cannot be as easily explained; such probing as we have done does not allow one to escape the strong feeling of a form of intellectual dishonesty.

The escalation in the process of 'denial of Canadian culture' from Charles Taylor to Michael Ignatieff to John Ibbitson to Joseph Heath – without a scintilla of evidence to back it up, by the way, and purely as an intellectual *entourloupette* – has been repeated so often without being explicitly challenged that it has come to be regarded as conventional wisdom in a significant portion of Canadian public opinion.

In the case of Michael Ignatieff, the dismissal is characteristically mild and softly couched in terms of a warning about "exaggerating the importance of Canadian history for Canadians" (Ignatieff 1999). For him, Canada is neither about a history nor about a heritage, but only about a shared understanding about the plumbing of democracy (Gottfried 2002: 68): a gratuitous but oblique and softly elitist dismissal of common public culture that deserves no more attention.

In the case of John Ibbitson, discussed in the last chapter, his tack on the inexistence of Canada's common public culture is that it is an undesirable set of constraints on negative freedom (Bricker and Ibbitson 2013), that he wishes to occlude like the Underhill thin notion of nation (Underhill 1964).

In the case of Joseph Heath (2013, 2014), there would appear to be confusion between shared values and shared culture. While one may agree with Heath about the myth of shared values in Canada (Heath 2003), this has nothing to do with *manières de vivre* that have been agreed to as a way to facilitate *vivre ensemble*. Heath is more cynical. He sees no legitimacy in claiming a need to preserve the Canadian common culture. In his most cynical 2013 op-ed piece in the *Ottawa Citizen*, he clearly does not appear to defend multiculturalism as a genuine political philosophy based on the Berry hypothesis (Berry *et al.* 1977): the view that the more secure and comfortable the immigrants feel in the host country culture, the more likely they are to be tempted to integrate. For Heath, multiculturalism sounds more like a cynical decoy: "By generating the presumption of fair treatment in all public institutions (sometimes through exaggerated, bend-over-backwards gestures of accommodation), the multiculturalism policy encouraged immigrants to venture out of their communities, and join political parties, become police officers, and get jobs in places where everyone speaks the language of the majority" (Heath 2013: A13) – bend-over-backwards gestures of accommodation to give the newcomers a presumption of fair treatment and get them to integrate, even though multiculturalism policy states their right not to do so[17] – deception as national strategy.

The problem is that it does not work: recent Environics survey results for 2012 and CROP-Radio-Canada survey results in 2017 (Sondage Radio-Canada CROP, February 2017) suggest that despite over 30 years of bending-over-backwards, 70 percent of Canadians think that too many immigrants do not adopt Canadian mores – i.e., do not integrate – a marker that has increased over the last decade.

Canada's common public culture – a set of norms of *vivre-ensemble* that has evolved over time and that constitutes the foundation of our way or life – may not be a thick culture but

---

[17] But to integrate into what ... since for Heath there is no Canadian common public culture! I have ironized on Heath's position in a comment on his 2013 paper. My comment was not accepted for publication by Heath's co-author (Andrew Potter) who happened to be Editor in chief of the *Ottawa Citizen* at the time, but Heath's paper has now been withdrawn from circulation by the *Ottawa Citizen* and is therefore no longer retrievable.

whoever ordained that real cultures had to be thick? Newcomers have to accept this common public culture. It may evolve over time, but the laws of hospitality require that the newcomers accept them as a condition of entry. Equality of men and women, rule of law, etc. are not negotiable. Not stating it clearly as a condition of entry, and pretending to bend-over-backwards as a strategy of appeasement is a form of deceit. If later we wish to rescind our views on those exaggerated bend-over-backwards moves, can we be surprised if the newcomers accuse us of having acted in bad faith?

The common denominator in all those different ways to avoid having to face any trade-off between the old and the new culture is 'to spirit away the existence of the old culture'. This is nonsense but Canadians have tolerated this imposture for years.[18]

Imaginary exceptionalism and imaginary constitutional principle: Keith Banting and Roger Bernard as surfers on the Taylor wave

Taylor's message did not reach Canadian citizens in their homes, and each household has not been driven to speculate on the inexistence of a common public culture in the privacy of their living rooms. The demoralizing view that 'Canadians have no culture of their own' has been brought forth to the citizenry in oblique ways through the shaping of public opinion by the *pouvoir social*. All this has materialized over the last decades: a convergence of opinions – occurring via a process of inter-borrowing of various

---

[18] One should not underestimate the potency of *pouvoir social*: it often sways the most critical observers. For instance, even Andrew Coyne (2017) has been sideswiped into dealing in the same bilious way both with absorptive capacity in the economic, social and cultural sense of the term when it comes to immigration, and the silly anti-immigration vociferous statements of a funky candidate to the leadership of the Progressive Conservative party. This may explain why those who are less serene on these matters may get carried away into bizarre speculations in their desperate quest to avoid having to deal with the challenge to the common public culture by extraneous toxic forces. For instance Joseph Heath has proposed his own bizarre explanation of the aggressive Quebec *laïcité* policy: according to him, it could be explained by the fact that Quebeckers having failed to keep their own religion would have been led to ordain that others should not be allowed to keep theirs either (Heath 2013).

agents (political, technocratic, academic and media) emerging *not* from any basic inquiry or empirical evidence, but from convenient borrowing, by each group, without much critical thinking, mostly acting in order to bolster each groups' interests or cosmologies through opportunistic initiatives.

On the way to a vortex or an enclave

One of the most important dynamics in this bazaar of forces at work has been the electoral pressure on the Canadian federal government to respond to perceived pressure from the advocates of newcomers. With at present close to 25 percent of the population born outside of the country, and close to 50 percent in the case of a few large cities, mass immigration has become the elephant in the room: the undiscussed imperative for major federal political parties.

And the greater the response to that pressure, the laxer the immigration policy becomes, the stronger the contingent of Canadians born outside Canada, the more intense that pressure for even laxer immigration policy by lobbies (often trained by parliamentary studies centres) will be – whatever the unintended consequences on the integration of newcomers, and indirectly on the common public culture.

All federal political parties have had to develop an ever greater numbness when the economic, social and cultural costs and consequences of mass immigration and multiculturalism policy have been brought to their attention. They have also had to come forward with counter-arguments to defend their policies not as a crass political vote-getting ploy, but as a strategy designed in the best interest of the country as a whole. As a result, despite the consensus of experts about the limited economic or demographic benefits, at best, of indiscriminate mass immigration, all major federal political parties have generated deceitful information packages, claiming extraordinary economic and demographic benefits from mass immigration going much beyond Canada's absorptive capacity – i.e., Canada going beyond its capacity to integrate the newcomers.

In this bending-over-backwards to appease pro-immigration lobby groups, all political parties have also been led to embrace the gospel of diversity: to declare that optimal diversity is maximum diversity, and to chastise anything short of absolute and unconditional support for maximum diversity as reprehensible nativism. For over 40 years, multiculturalism has been marketed with gusto by the Canadian federal government as the 'Canada brand', and Canada's attractiveness for newcomers has been underlined not only as due to the fact that they do not have to worry about having to 'assimilate' when they come to Canada (for it would be abusive to ask them to shed their own foreign culture), but they do not even have to 'integrate' (for it would be disrespectful of their cultural rights to ask them to abandon their old way of life).

On both these fronts – economic-demographic and social-cultural – the technocracy, the intelligentsia, and the media have failed the politicians. As social science operatives to different degrees, they have provided technical, moral and communications support for the Canadian federal government views without as much as a scintilla of critical appraisal of the toxic nature of the policy mix, and no contribution (it would seem) to developing meaningful alternatives to what seemed to be dictated by electoral imperatives.

Over time, this set of Manichean ideas morphed into a 'new reference' that has not only gained general acceptance in political and bureaucratic circles, but has been promoted by the robust federal communication machine as the 'Canadian brand' (Kazemipur 2009: conclusion).

On the one hand, the no-culture view of Canada has been instrumental in exorcizing the critique of those who have complained about social and cultural costs of mass immigration and multiculturalism policy. This defensive move has entailed efforts to get rid of the thinnest and most liberal notion of nation à la Underhill (1964) – a group of people who have done great things in the past and want to do great things in the future – that permeates the Canadian ethos. The soul-less, pan-cultural Canada has become 'a representation of the mind' that has been proposed as part of the new reference. Such a creature borrowed whole from the Taylorian cosmology has the advantage of being fundamentally immune to any notion of erosion or corrosion because it does not exist: Canada being defined as an evolving mosaic of reference points in a multicultural soup that can only drift as 'an open-ended vortex'.

On the other hand, the groups described as the nuggets of recognized, legitimate and vibrant cultures *à la* Taylor (Aboriginals, Quebeckers and immigrants) are pronounced as having cultural rights, and are explicitly authorized and encouraged to maintain and enhance their cultures and nurture their positive freedoms. This has amounted to 'an invitation to enclaving', to developing strategies to re-enforce their innerness, and to making exorbitant requests for protection.

Canadian social science operatives have then been subsidized and deputized by the federal government:

- first, and primarily, to re-educate the primitive past-obsessed and culture-obsessed Canadians in the new sanitized ways of a Canadian world without cultural character: their role was to persuade Canadians that their only unity is through diversity, their fundamental quality is being without any over-riding qualities, and that this *citoyenneté sans qualités* is the way of the future – a future that Canada is pioneering; non-believers are branded nativists;
- second, and secondarily, to provide technical and moral support to those culture-rich groups (although it was a subsidiary task since, on the basis of the cultural rights granted, they had already organized to extract benefits from this status).

The rest of this chapter probes in a very general way the two sorts of surreal worldviews that have been nudged into existence in these two directions. In both cases, it is argued that the hyper-turbulent environment, having strained the limited adaptive capacity of groups and their contexts, collective action would appear to drive the systems either toward 'vortices' (in the first case) or toward 'enclaves' (in the second case) (McCann and Selsky 1984; McCann, Selsky and Lee 2009).

Toward the Banting vortex[19]

Keith Banting (2007) (but also others like Jeffrey Reitz (2011a, b) who hold similar views) are informed social scientists, conscious of the real dangers posed by the choice of the joint pursuit of mass indiscriminate immigration and multiculturalism. They know about the strained experiences in many Western European countries and the cautious warnings by many Canadian and US economists about the potentially deleterious effects of such choices (Paquet 2012; Borjas 2015, 2017). Yet, Banting (and acolytes) has been on a crusade for years to persuade the willing that one should not worry because Canada is 'an exception': it can be regarded as immune to all the problems to which other countries are exposed.

What is the magic potion that explains this immunity?

At the core of this issue is a 'puzzling paradox' connected with this 'counter-narrative' I underlined in *Moderato cantabile* (Paquet 2012: 25ff). It has to do with the fact that until the 1990s (when immigration levels were relatively low and within Canada's absorptive capacity), polls showed that some two-thirds of the Canadians polled held the view that there were too many immigrants; while for the first decade of the 21st century (when immigration levels were significantly higher in absolute terms and higher than absorptive capacity would suggest),

---

[19] The reason I have attached the name of Keith Banting to this 'narrative' or 'discourse' is that he has been the most persistent in this pursuit. He has also been most cautious in writing and has provided clear indications along the way that the empirical results on which that 'narrative' is built are fragile (Banting 2007). His associates and his financial backers are far less cautious, and, while it may be said to be outside his control, Banting has not always been very careful in correcting those politicians and bureaucrats who have purposefully bowdlerized his findings. Moreover, since he has left unexplored the search for the sort of mechanisms at work in 'explaining' how this alternative narrative has emerged and how it may not have been through an absolutely untainted process, such vacuum has probably allowed undue tainted interpretations to transmogrify his message. Finally, the fact that his work in this file has used some empirical work does not necessarily free him from the mortgage of the Taylorian cosmology. In any case, the fact that Banting presents his material as support for a 'counter-narrative' makes it legitimate to analyze it as such.

some two-thirds of the Canadians polled held the view that there were *not* too many immigrants.

How is it that Canadians' views have gone through such a puzzling, counter-intuitive trans-substantiation?

Taylor would argue that Canadians have become more 'tolerant'. Banting would argue that a 'new Canadian consensus' has emerged more or less by 'immaculate conception' from a new awareness that everything is all right, and there is nothing to worry about. Yet, both carefully refuse to notice the fact that two-thirds of the Canadians polled in the first decades of the 21st century complained about the newcomers 'failing to integrate' – and indeed they do not integrate as much or as easily as they had before and as they should – something hardly surprising, since they are invited by the Canadian policies not to (Sondage Radio-Canada CROP, February 2017).

How is one to interpret these paradoxical findings?

My own interpretation (Paquet 2012) has been that what might explain this counter-intuitive reaction of Canadians is the 'systematic disinformation campaign' of the federal government about the extraordinary benefits to be expected, economically and demographically, from mass immigration, in addition to the 'robust multiculturalism propaganda' bestowed by the Canadian federal government on the Canadian population to re-program the representations of Canadians.

This deceitful propaganda – compounded with the political correctness in a country where anyone insisting on taking seriously absorptive capacity and taking seriously newcomers' 'integration' must now expect to be openly accused of being a nativist, a racist and a bigot – as I have experience personally after publishing my 2008 and 2012 books – would suggest that polls are *not* representing what Canadians think but what Canadians have been 'led' to say to pollsters.

Therefore, the so-called 'new consensus' that Banting claims to have uncovered may be regarded as something more akin to a 'deceptive consensus' more than partly manufactured by the Canadian federal government marketing, with the complicity of a portion of the intelligentsia and the media.

On the matter of social and cultural costs of mass immigration (especially when compounded with a multiculturalism policy that states clearly that newcomers do not have to integrate into the culture of the host country), the discussion becomes murkier.

These dimensions have *not* been examined as thoroughly as they should be, measurements are not as reliable as one might like, and there is a strong ideological streak in those debates. Social costs incurred by the host society to underwrite the transition period (social housing, welfare support, language training, etc.) may be very substantial; excessive diversity may erode social capital and solidarity; and there may be a more fundamental erosion of the social and cultural order, e.g., the common public culture, the language base of the French Canadian minority, etc. Efforts to arrive at persuasive answers about the erosion of social capital by migration through these macro-correlations may not hold much explanatory power.[20]

What is clear is that the Canadian federal government has dutifully avoided any serious effort to gauge (1) if the host society can afford to shoulder these social costs without being unduly strained (financial affordability); (2) if the governance of the host society can be sustained without major administrative dysfunctions (administrative sustainability); and (3) if the common public culture of the host society might be eroded (cultural tolerability). This is probably due to the fact that the Canadian federal apparatus suspects that any serious cost-benefit study is most likely to show that the policy mix in good

---

[20] I am not persuaded by the Banting re-assuring macro-correlations between stable social policy expenditures and the portion of the Canadian population born out of the country. The data used are the resultant outcome of so many diverse factors and are unlikely to change instantaneously. Moreover, the analyses pertain to the period 1980-2000 – while the explosion of the immigration numbers is a phenomenon beginning with the late 1990s and after. I would conjecture that an analysis of data taking into account the full impact of the 20 years that follow the beginning of the tsunami will tell a different story. Consequently the basis for this act of faith and re-assurance is immensely fragile. (Breton *et al.* 2004). The more so because much of this kitchen-regressionism is measurement without theory: as long as one remains unclear about what mechanisms are at work to underpin the so-called exceptional character of the Canadian experience, this is nothing more than harvesting broad mushy data in search of re-assurance that nothing untoward has been noted as a way to support the belief in a mysterious phlogiston-like factor to explain Canada's so-called exceptional experience.

currency is very costly – financially for sure, administratively most certainly, and socially and culturally, probably.

Indeed, anyone examining the immigration issue through the lens of one of the best experts, George Borjas – who has recently urged the United States to limit immigration – will find it difficult to take seriously the view that any reasonable Canadian – economically, demographically, socially and culturally – should take seriously the rosy and magical Banting scenario (Borjas 2017). The case for an imposture is much more convincing.

A central piece in this imposture has been the ruse of the disappearance act of the Canadian culture.[21]

No other country (except in a moment of aberration) would have been able to draft the intelligentsia and the media into an uncritical and blind unconcern for the social and cultural malefits of the current policy mix. This sort of rationalization requires the surreal assumption that Canada is not a nation and has no culture of its own. It is only through that disappearing act that Canada can be presented as immune to the sort of malefits that ordinary nations with legitimate cultures might have to endure.

This epistemological coup has made any cost-benefit analysis superfluous.

Canada as an exception is a very elusive notion. And when it comes to explain what is making Canada exceptional, Banting is less than illuminating. His empirical work is certainly not enlightening on this point. The fact that one observes in the short run no drop in social expenditures with the arrival of newcomers is hardly evidence of anything … since they are a source of social expenditures.

---

[21] This disappearance act is an extraordinary event. Alain Finkielkraut has synthesized the Canadian twist as follows: *"Pour la première fois dans l'histoire de l'immigration, l'accueilli refuse à l'accueillant, quel qu'il soit, la faculté d'incarner le pays d'accueil"* (Finkielkraut 2013: 1113). One may add that this Canadian twist has already been borrowed by at least one other country. On January 5, 2010, Eric Besson, the French Minister of Immigration, stated that *"la France n'est ni un peuple, ni une langue, ni un territoire, ni une religion, c'est un conglomérat de peuples qui veulent vivre ensemble. Il n'y a pas de Français de souche, il n'y a qu'une France de métissage "* (Ibid.: 105). Allow me to add that Besson did not go as far as Canadian officials – he did not say France has no culture of its own!

If one cannot identify exactly why Canadians are concerned about the lack of integration of newcomers, but see no cost to the multiculturalist entitlement not to integrate, is there any other serious candidate for this sense of exceptionality of Canada except, by default, that so many Canadians have fallen prey to this fable that Canada has no culture of its own?

A significant portion of Canadian politicians, bureaucrats, intelligentsia and media would appear to have not only been sold the view that the mix of mass immigration and multiculturalism is not toxic but to suffer also from chronic learning disabilities when federal politicians entertain with glee the *scénario de la fuite en avant* – assorted speculations and fables about a Canada with a population of 100 million by 2100, based on the assumption of infinite absorptive capacity! The uncritical media, the progressive academics, the scared-fantasy-prone politicians, and the self-serving bureaucrats are already salivating. But is this not yet another hint that whether it is stated explicitly or not, all this would require one to assume that Canada has no culture of its own to be able to proceed fearlessly into such a future scenario.[22]

Canada is then drawn into a vortex: it is faced with a wicked situation for which no perceived realistic solutions exist in the short run; attempts at collaboration in integrative strategies are unlikely if not impossible, mental prisons are toxic, and the electoral dynamic somewhat inexorable. The intelligentsia and the media are in denial about the challenges ahead, and the *pouvoir social* blindly drives the vortex formation, learning disabilities, lack of collaboration, and the dissipation of adaptive capabilities (McCann and Selsky 1984).

---

[22] In the meantime, Ottawa wallows in 'big thinking' in this file: on March 21, 2017 at the Parliamentary restaurant in Ottawa, the Canadian Federation for the Humanities and the Social Sciences featured Keith Banting on "Immigration, Multiculturalism and Populist Backlash: Is Canada Exceptional?" Banting has now become condescending: the Opposition is contemptuously characterized as 'populist backlash' (the great unwashed), and the political-bureaucratic-intelligentsia elite has been invited to *une sorte de grand-messe* where the faith of the willing is going to be reconfirmed!

Toward the Bernard enclaves

One might use any of the privileged culture-rich groups in Canada to illustrate what that status has trigged in terms of strategy. In any of these cases, it would be easy to show that they have been very active in demanding less accountability and more beneficial largesse in the name of their recognized cultural rights.

Circumstances would have it that, at about the same time as the 'big thinking fiesta', on March 22, 2017, a few kilometers away from Parliament in Ottawa, there was another surreal event – the celebration of the victory, 'supposedly' clinched, some 20 years ago, through the effort of SOS Montfort – a populist movement – to prevent the local community hospital (Montfort) from closing or being assigned a more limited role.

The reality is less melodramatic (Paquet 2001).

An administrative commission on the rationalization and restructuration of the hospital system in Eastern Ontario was created in the mid-1990s. It produced a preliminary report in 1997 that appeared fundamentally flawed to most of the knowledgeable observers; a *front commun* was created to persuade the Government of Ontario not to accept the report because it was clearly inadequate.

Montfort, as one of the community hospitals of the region, chose not to join the *front commun*, and to carry its own fight under the banner of minority rights; SOS Montfort was a social movement, animated by Montfort, that presented an argument to the court synthesized in an affidavit prepared by Roger Bernard (2001). The argument presenting Montfort as embodying French presence in Ontario is summarized in a box (page 168); this argument was building on an imaginary unwritten principle supposedly contained in the Constitution, and an interpretation of the Charter of Rights that would amount to a commitment of government not to withdraw ever a service once granted to a minority group. The case was presented to the court and most surprisingly gained support, but the decision was appealed, and the court of appeal rejected the constitutional and Charter-based argument of SOS Montfort. As an aside, the Court of Appeal noted serendipitously that the commission had explicitly declared *not* to have taken into account Ontario's Law 15 on French Services, and therefore, on that basis alone, invalidated the sections of the report pertaining to Montfort.

The flawed commission report was a matter that could have been handled administratively and need not have used the constitutional and Charter routes. It was a significant administrative error committed by the commission that could have been corrected by bringing to the attention of the Government of Ontario that the commission had wrongly ignored Ontario Law 15 in its work. There were other errors in the preliminary report about the roles it suggested for the different hospitals that were indeed corrected through that process.

The rationale for Montfort to choose going its own way, and arguing minority rights may be regarded as the echo effect of the *zeitgeist* of the time that was importantly impacted by the Taylorian cosmology – separating those groups that are presumed *not* to have a culture from those who are presumed to have one.

Canada was declared by Taylor as a country with no culture of its own, with the consequences we examined in the last section. Those segments of the Canadian population that have been recognized as culture-endowed (Aboriginals, Quebeckers, newcomers) were declared holders of 'cultural rights', and encouraged by Article 27 of the Charter of Rights to pursue the affirmation and enrichment of their cultural rights.

In the case of Franco-Ontarians (akin to Quebeckers by osmosis), they would both appear to meet the Taylor criteria as a group (they can claim having been victimized and their culture could be regarded as Taylor-recognizable into existence) and to be legitimized in having rights to demand privileges as a result of being a recognized culture. This recognition was perceived as authorization for the aggrieved party to conjecture putative ills, to identify ominous catastrophic forces like 'subtractive bilingualism', and to invoke imaginary, unwritten, constitutional principles as a basis on which to build reparations.

The Montfort affair has displayed all these features, and illustrated the perils of being declared a culturally-legitimate group: there is no reason to believe that the legitimate excesses of the culture-haves cannot have the same potential toxicity as the illegitimate constraints imposed on culture-have-nots by the declaration of the inexistence of their culture. The collective action in the latter case fuelled a dynamic of vortex; in the former case, it has fuelled a full-throttle reinforcement of the enclave.

As in the case of the Banting 'narrative' examined in the last section, my interest here is to probe the SOS Montfort/Bernard 'narrative' as an predictable outcome of the logic of cultural rights for groups that have been recognized or quasi-recognized as culture-rich.

The Bernard Narrative*

The major proposition
The survival of a culture depends on the dynamism of its language

Minor propositions
a. the dynamism of the language is eroded by a bilingual context (i.e., not exclusively francophone) since it is improbable that Franco-Ontarians will require service in French.
   As a result bilingual institutions tend to generate 'subtractive bilingualism' (i.e., French taking second place).
   This is likely to generate de-culturation and assimilation, and to threaten the survival of the community.

b. Montfort embodies French presence in Ontario and is a symbol of the force and vitality of the Franco-Ontarian community.

Conclusion
Any diminution of the role of the Montfort or any concession to bilingualism is bound to accelerate the process of assimilation and lead to an irreversible loss, with important consequences for the survival of French Ontario.

Comments
Each of these propositions is highly questionable and can be challenged.
The causal link between language and culture does not hold.
The idea of subtractive bilingualism does not hold water either.
Making the local hospital, Montfort, into a pan-Ontarian symbol is frivolous.
Consequently the conclusion does not follow.

Adding to this weak argumentation the presumption that there is an unwritten principle in the Constitution of the country and in the Charter that would command that whenever a privilege is granted to a minority, it cannot be withdrawn, is pure fantasy (Paquet 2002). This has been confirmed by the Court of Appeal.

But the fact that the fable put forward by SOS Montfort has been supported by a lower court remains a cause for concern.

*(Bernard 2001; Paquet 2008: chapter 11)

While the groups defined as without recognized culture have been led to postures of hyper-toleration *vis-à-vis* groups with cultural rights, and have had a tendency to drift toward vortices, culturally-recognized groups have been driven to feel entitled to demand robust, if not unlimited accommodation, and therefore to be driven to the formation of protected enclaves.

The 'narrative' proposed by Roger Bernard is interesting because it provides the 'discourse' regarded as authorized by the Franco-Ontarian tribe. This is the one brought by SOS Montfort to the courts. Its contents are an echo of the sort of representation of reality in good currency in a portion of the community – and its excesses that have been granted credibility by hyper-tolerant believers in cultural rights are not that different from the excesses to which the family of fundamentalists, who have swallowed hole the myth of the inexistence of Canadian culture, have been driven.

What is particularly interesting about this situation is that those facts have had no effect on the way in which the very different fabled representation of the events has been transmitted and has endured. What was celebrated on March 22, 2017, with great pomp, had nothing to do with reality: it was the celebration by an enclave of believers, sharing a carefully distorted representation of reality in which the SOS Montfort movement was victorious and the reason why the mandate of the Montfort Hospital was not touched. This storytelling continues to be regarded as more real than reality. This is the stuff myths are made of.

One unfortunate aspect of this successful storytelling is that few of those who celebrated on March 22 realized how fortunate we were that the Montfort movement failed in its objectives, and that a form of resolution was arrived at on the basis of a technicality. For if the Montfort argument had prevailed, this would have meant that all minorities would have been worse off. For no responsible government would ever have been willing in the future to take action on behalf of any minority, if any such decision were to be regarded as made to remain in force in perpetuity.

A way out of the surreal

It is not the purpose of this paper to provide an alternative to the surreal processes described above that have driven our system toward a vortex in one case and toward an enclave in the other. What is clear, however, is that neither of these directions can be considered as holding interesting promise for the future. In the first case, the drift toward a vortex amounts to submitting to the pressures of faceless forces that only dedicated, post-modernists might find palatable; in the second case, the drift toward enclaving, *protection des acquis*, and retrospection holds little promise for the future development of the group.

In the case of the mass immigration-multiculturalism issue, the reprehensible trick has been the spiriting away of the existence of the Canadian common public culture in order to conveniently get rid of the very possibility of socio-cultural malefits from the deleterious policy mix. This is the key imposture to be denounced, and the response is to re-legitimize Canadian common public culture as the ground from which tolerable rates of immigration and diversity increases might be derived.

I have developed this argument in *Moderato cantabile* (Paquet 2012) together with the way in which one can derive from it a principled governance for immigration policy, and the recognition that the notion of absorptive capacity (economic, administrative, social and cultural) is a meaningful way to distill the sort of legitimate constraints one might impose on the flow of immigration, and the terms of integration to ensure that the common public culture is not unduly tainted by unreasonable flows and unreasonable terms of integration. This is bound to entail less toleration than what the current *laissez-faire* would suggest.

In the case of those groups who have been granted the privilege of having a culture of their own, and have fantasized somewhat in efforts to limit the freedom of others in the name of their so-called cultural rights, the way out is to recognize that enclaving is the source of fundamentalism and unreason. The answer is therefore to dis-enclave, and to reach out to the diaspora of other enclaves so as to provide a broader canvas on which to design less narcissistic arrangements.

I have sketched this idea further in *Tableau d'avancement IV* (Paquet 2017: conclusion). The only way to escape fundamentalism and narcissism is for tribes to ensure that they remain truly open (Goss 2014). Again this is bound to entail less toleration for unreasonableness, fundamentalism and the tyranny of minorities.

In both cases, toleration of unreason is a major source of learning disabilities.

Optimum toleration is not maximum toleration

The literature on toleration has been strongly biased toward its celebration as a virtue – be it an elusive, difficult one and impossible to define (Heyd 1996; Walzer 1997). Even if Walzer makes a passing remark about the fact that maximalism in matters of toleration could potentially lead to the dissolution of group life (Walzer 1997: 34), this is a very soft flat on a score that is *in toto* quite celebratory: tolerance is most naturally accepted as necessary for peaceful coexistence, while intolerance is associated with arrangements leading to civil war and persecution. Constrained toleration is nothing more than a *curiosum* added to the larger script – sprinkled carefully, especially in some footnotes, for use when impossible circumstances are in need of some exceptional conceptual perspective.

My view is that this attitude is a dangerous invitation to uncritical thinking, and has become toxic in a world under the spell of moral relativism and progressivist ideology, with its overwhelming load of sophistry, deception and imaginary entitlements. All this has generated a disposition and inclination to accommodate – and the more so as the preferences, entitlements and rights of others have become merrily confounded. Consequently, critical thinking has lost its lustre, and has become more or less associated with discourteous manners (Paquet 2014: chapter 1).

The social costs of toleration in discouraging critical thinking and blocking social learning have been immense as *consensus mous* and *molle pensée* have come to be in good currency, and *soumission* has ceased to be associated with the behaviour of slaves.

The purpose of this chapter has been to draw attention to both the tail ends of the distribution of toleration: 'unbearable intolerance' and 'hyper-toleration' as toxic attitudes, and to show how quiet submissions to the multiculturalism gospel or to the unreasonable request of a linguistic enclave, an Aboriginal group or an immigrant minority might not be wise.

I have shown that the lack of critical thinking by the intelligentsia and the media in Canada, in the face of the progressive tsunami and of the multicultural ideology, has allowed the most untoward drifts in the public discourse to take hold of public opinion and significant distortions to bend the representations of the social order in good currency. I have also drawn attention to the uncritical toleration of the bizarre ratiocinations of academics and journalists that has led to the obliteration of the notion of common public culture in Canada. This, in turn, has underpinned the puzzling support for mass immigration and multiculturalism policy by the ensuing occlusion of any discussion of their social and cultural costs.

I have also drawn attention to the excesses engendered by the hyper-toleration for the sacralization of some cultures (Aboriginals, French Canadians, and newcomers – as per Taylor, Walzer and others), the consequent veneration in certain circles of their folkways, and the hyper-toleration of artificial arguments put forward in order to give legal force to their preferences.[23]

Our intent has been to debunk both unbearable intolerance and hyper-toleration, and to reinstate the role of critical thinking in establishing the optimal level of toleration in each case.

In the cases we dealt with, first, I have been led to call for the resurrection of the notion of Canadian common public culture and most certainly for a vibrant challenge of the kafkaesque denial of a culture for the ROC – and, as a result, a call for debunking the fable that Canada has no culture of its own which has emerged from flurries of groundless denials invented by many culprits (politicians, bureaucrats

---

[23] One might have chosen other examples of untoward drifts into pneumopathology like the unreasonable relaxation of accountability rules for Aboriginals in their responsibility to account for financial transfers from the federal government (i.e., from public funds); or the near acceptance of sharia law in Ontario under the sponsorship of Marion Boyd, former Attorney General of Ontario in the Rae government – a disaster stopped *in extremis* by Dalton McGuinty; or the creation of a public school for Blacks only in Toronto – which went unchallenged; etc.

and intelligentsia) and inexplicably tolerated by the citizenry; second, to call for some reason back into the discussions built on the so-called cultural rights of Aboriginals, Quebeckers, and newcomers – i.e., to bring reasonableness back, and to constrain emotions in dealing with groups on whom cultural rights have been bestowed.

If some balance is *not* brought back into the toleration debate, given the asymmetry that would appear to have become conventional wisdom in Canada – veneration for the culture of newcomers and denial of a culture for the host country – we may slide into a *soumission tranquille* ... and the pneumo-pathological haranguers – those who claim Canada is an exception – may perpetrate irreversible damage to our country. Their regrets later when they will have to come to see the wrongs of their ways will hardly compensate for the damage created along the way (Houellebecq 2015; Gingras 2015). For hyper-toleration for their twaddle will have been responsible for the toxicity of the vortexes and enclaves they have made possible.

References

Banting, Keith G. 2007. "Canada as Counter-Narrative: multiculturalism, recognition and redistribution," *www.optimumonline.ca*, 37(3): 2-15.

Bernard, Roger. 2001. *À la défense de Montfort*. Ottawa, ON: Le Nordir.

Berry, John W. *et al.* 1977. *Multiculturalism and Ethnic Attitudes in Canada*. Ottawa, ON: Supply & Services Canada.

Borjas, George J. 2015. "Immigration and Globalization: A Review Essay," *Journal of Economic Literature*, 53(4): 961-974.

Borjas, George J. 2017. "The Immigration Debate," *The New York Times*, February 27.

Breton, Raymond *et al.* 2004. *A Fragile Fabric?* Montreal, QC and Kingston, ON: McGill-Queen's University Press.

Boudon, Raymond. 2005. *Tocqueville aujourd'hui*. Paris, FR: Odile Jacob.

Bricker, Darrel and John Ibbitson. 2013. *The Big Shift – The seismic change in Canadian politics, business and culture, and what it means for our future.* Toronto, ON: HarperCollins.

Caldwell, Gary. 2012. *Canadian Public Culture.* Ste Edwidge de Clifton, QC: The Fermentation Press.

Caldwell, Gary and Gilles Paquet. 2016. "Disinformative, ideological, and oikophobic : on a piece of storytelling by Quixotic John Ibbitson," *www.optimumonline.ca*, 46(3): 57-66.

Coyne, Andrew. 2017. "Immigration rage puts rights at risk," *Ottawa Citizen*, March 9, NP4.

Duchesne, Ricardo. 2016. "Charles Taylor's Philosophy of Minority Ethnic Identity and the Suppression of Eurocanadian Identity," *The Occidental Quarterly*, 16(2): 3-19.

Finkielkraut, Alain. 2013. *L'identité malheureuse.* Paris, FR: Stock.

Gingras, Yves. 2015. "Les soumissions tranquilles ou Houellebecq en Ontario," *Le Devoir*, October 14.

Gingras, Yves. 2017. "McGill et Potter et le symptôme du déclin des universités," *Le Devoir*, March 28.

Goss, Sue. 2014. *Open Tribe.* London, UK: Lawrence & Wishart.

Gottfried, Paul Edward. 2002. *Multiculturalism and the Politics of Guilt.* Columbia, MO: University of Missouri Press.

Gwyn, Richard. 1995. *Nationalism without Walls.* Toronto, ON: McClelland & Stewart.

Hanes, Allison. 2017. "Charles Taylor sees the light on religious garb restrictions," *Montreal Gazette,* February 14.

Harris, Ashley. 2016. "Justin Trudeau thinks Canada is a country without a culture of its own or personality," *Debate Post*, September 16.

Heath, Joseph. 2003. *The Myth of Shared Values in Canada.* Ottawa, ON: Canadian Centre for Management Development.

Heath, Joseph. 2013. "How to avoid the next turban controversy?" *Ottawa Citizen*, June 18, A13

Heath, Joseph. 2014. "Misunderstanding Canadian Multiculturalism," *The Global Brief*, March 24.

Heyd, David. 1996. *Toleration – An Elusive Virtue*. Princeton, NJ: Princeton University Press.

Houellebecq, Michel. 2015. *Soumission*. Paris, FR: Flammarion.

Ignatieff, Michael. 1999. "Do we need Canadian history?" *National Post*, September 4, B5.

Kazemipur, A. 2009. *Social Capital and Diversity – Some Lessons from Canada*. New York, NY: Peter Lang.

McCann, Joseph E. and John Slesky. 1984. "Hyperturbulence and the Emergence of Type 5 Environments," *The Academy of Management Review*, 9(3): 460-470.

McCann, Joseph E., John Slesky and James Lee. 2009. "Building, agility, resilience, and performance in turbulent environments," *People & Strategy*, 32(3): 44-51.

Onfray, Michel. 2014. *Le réel n'a pas eu lieu – Le principe de Don Quichotte*. Paris, FR: Autrement.

Paquet, Gilles. 1989. "Multiculturalism as National Policy," *Journal of Cultural Economics*, 13(1): 17-34 (reprinted in Gilles Paquet. 2008. *Deep Cultural Diversity*, chapter 4).

Paquet, Gilles. 2001. *Si Montfort m'était conté… Essais de pathologie administrative et de rétroprospective*. Ottawa, ON: Centre d'études en gouvernance.

Paquet, Gilles. 2002. "Montfort et les nouveaux Éléates," *Fancophonies d'Amérique*, No. 13: 139-155.

Paquet, Gilles. 2008. *Deep Cultural Diversity – A Governance Challenge*. Ottawa, ON: The University of Ottawa Press.

Paquet, Gilles. 2012. *Moderato cantabile – Toward principled governance for Canada's immigration policy*. Ottawa, ON: Invenire.

Paquet, Gilles. 2013a. *Tackling Wicked Policy Problems: Equality, Diversity and Sustainability*. Ottawa, ON: Invenire.

Paquet, Gilles. 2013b. "Joseph Heath's Golden Rule" in G. Paquet, *Tackling...*, p. 149-152.

Paquet, Gilles. 2014. *Unusual Suspects – Essays on Social Learning Disabilities*. Ottawa, ON: Invenire.

Paquet, Gilles. 2017. *Tableau d'avancement IV: un Canada français à ré-inventer.* Ottawa, ON: Invenire.

Paquet, Gilles and Christopher Wilson. 2016. *Intelligent Governance – A Prototype For Social Coordination.* Ottawa, ON: Invenire.

Reitz, Jeffrey G. 2011a. "Immigration: The United States and Canada," *The Economist,* May 20.

Reitz, Jeffrey G. 2011b. *Pro-Immigration Canada: Social and Economic Roots of Popular Views.* Montreal, QC: Institute for Research on Public Policy.

Scruton, Roger. 2008. *England and the Need for Nations.* London, UK: Civitas.

Scruton, Roger. 2014. *How to be a Conservative.* London, UK: Bloomsbury

Sibley, Robert. 2013. "Young men can be turned to good or evil," *Ottawa Citizen,* April 29.

Sondage Radio-Canada CROP, February 2017.

Stein, Janice G. 2001. *The Cult of Efficiency.* Toronto, ON: Anansi.

Taylor, Charles. 1989. "The Rushdie Controversy," *Public Culture,* 2(1): 118-122.

Taylor, Charles. 1992. *Multiculturalism and the Politics of Recognition.* Princeton, NJ: Princeton University Press.

Taylor, Charles. 1994. "The Politics of Recognition" in A. Gutman (ed.). *Multiculturalism: Examining the Politics of Recognition.* Princeton, NJ: Princeton University Press, p. 25-73.

Taylor, Charles. 2013. "L'interdiction des symboles religieux serait une erreur," *Le Devoir,* August 23.

Taylor, Charles. 2017a. "Le temps de la réconciliation," *La Presse,* February 14.

Taylor, Charles. 2017b. "Charles Taylor réfléchit sur la tolérance des Québécois," *Radio-Canada,* February 9.

Underhill, Frank H. 1964. *The Image of Confederation.* Toronto, ON: Canadian Broadcasting Corporation.

Walzer, Michael. 1997. *On Toleration.* New Haven, CN: Yale University Press.

CHAPTER 13

The Perils of the Politics of Guilt

"Quousque tandem abutere, Catilina, patientia nostra."

– Cicero

P aul Edward Gottfried suggests that there are three ways in which political regimes 'manage' consensus: by using the intelligentsia and the media to falsely propagandize that there is an agreement when there is none; by appealing to the guilty conscience of the listeners as a leaven; or by treating dissent as a sort of illness (Gottfried 2002: 72ff). Trudeau II's regime has made use of those three methods with gusto, but it has out-performed most preceding governments in using the 'politics of guilt': choosing to exploit shamelessly one of the most sensitive fibres of Canadian souls – the sense of fairness (Fulford 2017).

This device has been used to excess in the hope of surreptitiously sneaking through all sorts of unpalatable concessions to interest groups that would never have been found acceptable by the citizenry had they been presented without that unholy garb of correcting unfairness or penance for past sins. Unfortunately, given the erosion of critical thinking in Canada (Paquet 2014: chapter 1), little has been said to expose these impostures.

In this enterprise, the Prime Minister has explicitly built on the bizarre bloating of the notion of 'victimhood' that has come to be in good currency in Canada in the frenzy of the post-Charter era. This mindquake has been scrutinized by Richard Gwyn.

Gwyn showed that, through a series of decisions by the courts, the notion of disadvantaged person or group has considerably broadened in Canada: it is now a stigma claimed to be brought forth even by the presence of a 'chilly climate' or a 'seemingly hostile environment' (whatever these notions may connote) (Gwyn 1995).

Together with the politicization of the notion of diversity as an over-riding good – with the notion of 'cultural defense' being legitimized by the courts, and used to exempt certain citizens from other cultures from certain everyday obligations of ordinary Canadian citizens[24] – the displacement of the concept of 'victimhood' has generated the stunning result that, today, most of the segments of the Canadian population are on the way to having the possibility of claiming some disadvantage and, therefore, of regarding themselves as potential candidates for victimhood, with all the symbolic and material benefits and bounties attached to this status in our new surreal world.

La faute plutôt que le scandale

The general cosmology thereby accredited is now serving as a broad conduit for many groups seeking the support of the courts for all sorts of claims of victimhood, and pressing for the cowardly accommodation of governments to their claims.[25] The

---

[24] Richard Gwyn (1995: 197ff) has mentioned the case of a reduced sentence for a man who had assaulted his 11-year old stepdaughter over a two-year period because he had only sodomized her, thereby (in the words of the judge) "preserving her virginity which seems to be a very important value in the (Islamic) religion."

[25] The idea of a 'cowardly reaction' of governments to claims of victimhood does not quite do justice to the real endeavours of some governments: elected officials are not only cowardly and passively reacting to claims by interest groups, they have become so politically sensitive to the possibility of a scandal erupting, and to their being indicted as guilty of having failed victims (real or imaginary) in any way, that they have developed the pre-emptive strategy of actively searching for potential victims, smoking them out, persuading them that the government regards them as victims so as to be able to apologize to them for the 'mistreatment' (real or imaginary) they have suffered at the hands of Canadians ... before their fate might emerge on the public forum and become the source of a scandal. Already in 1992, Premier Bob Rae of Ontario, in the face of certain social tensions, chose to appoint Stephen Lewis as a special advisor on race relations, and asked him (and a small team) to report on the state of

new national game seems to be finding a way to tickle the 'guilt bone' of the Prime Minister or of the courts. This has been at the source of a string of apologies (with or without direct financial compensation) for victimization (real or imaginary) built on some sibylline scribbling of progressive courts in their interpretation of the Charter. Progressive, in this context, connotes persons, organizations or institutions consubstantially driven by blind, myopic and impulsive compassion or so-called 'generous' ideologies, instead of reasonableness in their activities.

The result has been a systematic distortion of the rules of the game in our democracy, through maneuvers that have allowed disingenuous interest groups to take advantage of the legal flourishes of the Charter, and of the zealotry of the courts, to extract, from crafty governments, strategic apologies, and other unwarranted advantages. Over time, this abuse of the Canadians' sense of fairness has led to the emergence of a 'sense of unfairness' in the citizenry, and to a fragilization and delegitimization of democratic institutions associated with these shenanigans.

Some questionably rich 'settlements' for victimhood have generated outrage in the general public, and led citizens to worry about what might be in store for Canadians in the future: ever more frivolous claims of victimhood, ever more

---

systemic racism in Ontario. In a matter of weeks, Lewis confirmed that the systemic racism existed in Ontario. This led to the creation of an Anti-Racism Secretariat. The Couillard government in Quebec has announced in March 2017 the creation of a *comité-conseil* to consult Quebeckers on systemic racism. This led to vigorous debates in the Quebec National Assembly and in the media: it was perceived as a device to generate a guilt complex for Quebeckers opposing multiculturalism, mass immigration, and the like (which have nothing to do with systemic racism), or indeed for suffering from *"une inquiétude pourtant dominante dans notre époque: celle de devenir étranger chez soi"* (Bock-Côté 2017). So the politics of guilt is well anchored in Canada, and goes much beyond the world of Justin Trudeau. It is made possible by the Canadian ethos that would seem inclined to treat more kindly an admission of sin (real or imaginary) than the scandal of being accused of the sin of insensitivity to the fate of victims (real or imaginary). This has led elected officials to develop a proclivity to make untoward use of the sense of fairness of Canadians by playing on their sense of guilt (organic or fabricated). This is obviously unfortunate, but the fact that these shenanigans have so often used Anglo-French Canadian self-hate as a political lever is even more troublesome (Black 2017a).

unreasonable settlements demanded as compensation, ever more normalization of reprehensible practices by groups seeing the possibility of taking guilt-prone politicians to the cleaners with the helping hand of progressive courts, sanctimonious ambulance-chasing lawyers, and the ever compassionate intelligentsia and media?

Some overly kind souls have ascribed the collusion of Trudeau II with such impostures to his naïvety. Cynics have ascribed it to his propensity for endless searching for feel-good ways to bribe all the malcontents. Somewhat more observant fellows have suggested that this is the *modus operandi* of the 'therapeutic state', bent on replacing effective but politically unpopular arrangements by symbolic gestures that make officials feel good and warm, even if such alternative arrangements are counter-productive.

Whatever consolation might be provided to anxious observers by such forays in psycho-pathology to explain the emergence of this new cosmology, the behaviour that has ensued from this propensity to use guilt as a lever has generated economic, political and societal costs, and foisted pathologies onto Canadian society in the form of:

- acquiescence to the worst wishes of the feel-good progressives, and to an ever growing level of irresponsibility on the part of so-called deserving groups because they have supposedly been 'maligned' in the past;
- legitimacy being bestowed on imaginary cases of victimhood in the past as substitutes for taking real action to repair *real* flawed governance arrangements in need of repairs now;
- emergence of ever new waves of unwarranted entitlements and criminal irresponsibility as the *new* normal in Canadian society;
- the ever greater dominance of a petulant therapeutic state driving out responsible stewardship by sprinkling feel-good accommodations for anyone claiming victimhood (real or imaginary); and
- the general weakening of real accountability across the board from those failing to honour the basic obligations

of citizenship, while legitimacy and authority are being loosely granted to untoward behaviour on the basis of the edicts of adjudicatory agencies (including the Supreme Court): the judgments of such agencies being falsely regarded as infallible and unquestionable, and their sibylline musings about complex issues (issues that they often would appear not to fully understand) being falsely interpreted as executive orders (Paquet 2006). Both these types of distortions have served as alibis for unwise and irresponsible governments to err sheepishly (or strategically) on the progressive side (i.e., on the side of compassion rather than on the side of responsibility and reasonableness).

Indeed, this new covenant has become the new moral philosophy of the progressives who regard their distorted view of reality as more real than the reality these views are trying to capture (Onfray 2014).

A few examples

Scaling down accountability for so-called maligned interest groups

From the beginning of his first mandate, Trudeau II has signaled the prominence of his politics of guilt. His first move was an exoneration of the financial accountability requirements of Aboriginals under the *First Nations Financial Transparency Act* – an act legislated by the Harper government in order to ensure minimal accountability requirements on Aboriginal groups receiving generous bounties from the public purse. Whether it was intended or not, the Trudeau government thereby became complicit in the misuse of public funds by the many Aboriginal groups that had been clearly exposed by the auditors. By the end of 2015, only 38 of the 531 bands had not complied with the provisions of the Harper government legislation, and those were most likely the very bands where something most reprehensible had to be smoked out – like leaders of impoverished communities paying themselves outrageous salaries while the community was denied even basic amenities (Freeman 2015).

Deliberately cancelling this Harper government initiative explicitly designed to increase accountability was criminally irresponsible – not only rewarding the worst culprits, and re-instituting a veil of secrecy on scandalous use of public funds by some groups, but also formally sacralizing the Aboriginal pseudo-entitlements to non-accountability for their use of public funds – all this in the name of some imagined guilt that Canadians should carry *vis-à-vis* First Nations.

In June 2017, the Trudeau government further abolished two other Harper laws designed to eliminate untoward practices of labour unions: the laws requiring labour unions to hold secret accreditation votes (to put an end to a long tradition of intimidation in union meetings), and the law requiring financial information about union expenses above $5,000, to avoid unauthorized use of funds collected on the authority of labour laws. Radio-Canada (June 19, 2017) sheepishly referred to these abolished laws as 'anti-union' – but casuistically put the expression between inverted commas – probably, to demonstrate the exemplary neutrality of the public broadcaster in such matters! Abolishing these laws was clearly a shameful concession to interest groups that have been known to indulge in malfeasant practices and financial shenanigans.

In a somewhat cruder parlance than the one in good currency among the progressives, these groups were granted back the veil of secrecy behind which they could continue their malpractices. These Trudeau-inspired so-called 'correctives' were presented to the citizenry as ways to right the wrong that Aboriginals and labour unions had supposedly suffered at the hands of the Harper government – a mistreatment Canadians were told by the Trudeau II government they should have felt guilty about.

Such cartooning of the Harper government as anti-Aboriginal and anti-union by the Trudeau government, and the ridiculous claim that a prejudice had been inflicted on these groups by demanding that they be as accountable as all other groups receiving public funds, or collecting funds through legal statutes in Canada – were most disingenuous claims. Yet, since both Aboriginals and labour unions were presented as disadvantaged groups, the loud dissent one might have reasonably anticipated in a normal country did not materialize.

Indeed, such actions, however offensive they may appear to reasonable citizens, are hardly noticed any longer, and almost never chastised.

Dealing symbolically with past 'sins' in order not to have to correct real current structural flaws

It is obviously easier to make apologies for past sins than to actively work at redesigning flawed organizations and institutions that make current governance dysfunctional. The successful bids by Aboriginal groups and labour unions to gain exemption from standard accountability rules have been perceived as a game-changing move in Canada: the new game is based on producing certifiable victims to whom the country should be offering official apologies and cushy exemptions.

The extensibility of the guilt list that Trudeau and his epigons have come up with is impressive ... at times seeming to include the whole middle.

Are there limits to the generalizability of this panacea? It would appear that there are not.

The recent case of a young man who went to the Middle East with his family to join a terrorist group is exemplary of things to come if Trudeau II cosmology prevails: he was caught in the act, and incarcerated; later he confessed to the crime, and offered moving apologies and regrets to the wife of the person he was accused of killing.

Now, years after, we are told that this US tribunal was as illegitimate as those of Pol Pot, that he confessed under duress, and that his apologies to the assassinated person's wife were disingenuous. Moreover, we are informed that he supposedly did not receive quite the support he felt entitled to as a Canadian citizen when he was in prison, and that some Canadian diplomat visitors in his prison shared some immensely unclear information with the American authorities detaining him. According to the woolly prose of the infallible Supreme Court, Canada was at fault in all this.[26]

How far should Canadians be carried away on a national guilt trip as a result of a questionable edict of the Supreme Court that is regarded by those closely involved as unwarranted? What is the proportionality between the 'guilt' that Canadians might feel in this whole affair, *and* the canonical *and supposedly fair view* of the Trudeau government that this jihadist should be offered not only apologies, but also $10.5 million in compensation? Can one not reasonably conjecture that an unhealthy combination of a Supreme Court not necessarily capable of appreciating the complexities of the case and wrongly prone to be oversensitive to the lofty prose of sections of the Charter, along with a government somewhat overly prone to guilt trips, might have triggered a toxic mixture likely to generate, now and in the future, unreasonable *débordements*?

---

[26] Persons, like Daniel Livermore, who were "among a small group in Foreign Affairs Canada who dealt with the Khadr case" have disagreed with the Supreme Court conclusions when it arrived at judgments in 2008 and 2010. They suggest that Foreign Affairs Canada "was inadequately represented in presenting its case to the courts. The shallowness of the government presentations contributed to the Supreme Court's misunderstanding of some of the case's finer details" (Livermore 2017). Livermore regards all this as "a trifling matter today" and is willing to stand by the judgments of the Supreme Court – right or wrong – when it indicted Canada for "state conduct that violates the principles of fundamental justice." This is a most generous, if difficult to understand, attitude. Whatever has been discovered by inquiries into kindred matters such as the Maher Arar affair – the court case that may be regarded as having set the bar for the Khadr case – would appear to be even less conclusive about the responsibility of the Canadian government in such matters (Livermore 2010). Most certainly, it is not a matter of black and white. Given the doubts about the Supreme Court decisions, the decision of the Trudeau government to settle most generously out of court in the civil case presented by Khadr's lawyers on his behalf – complete with admission of guilt for Canadians – may have been politically convenient to flush out an inconvenient issue, but it remains questionable, especially for those who do not regard Supreme Court statements as infallible or, in this case, as calling for any such settlement.

Indeed, if allowed to proceed unchecked by some critical thinking, might these not be the ingredients of more and more 'perfect storms'.[27]

Some mechanisms at work

The last half century has been dominated by the progressive mindset in Canada. This has translated into both a mental prison and a crippling epistemology generating a worldview akin to what Eric Voegelin would probably call *pneumopathological* – a worldview that characterizes persons "'living' in a fantasy world of self-righteousness" (Sibley 2013). This is not the place for a disquisition about the progressives and their gospel, but it may be useful to underline that, for the progressives, maximum

---

[27] Only the most hyper-tolerant Canadian souls and the most uncritical Canadian minds can swallow the sophistry used by the PM to cover his tracks in the Omar Khadr case, and persuade Canadians that they are guilty and have to pay for their Khadr sins. Canadians were subjected to a surreal three-act play. First, the Prime Minister argued that the Supreme Court brandishing the Charter had *forced* him to offer apologies and financial compensation – a matter quite open to question since the Supreme Court had never mentioned any remedy in its opinion. In the second act, the Prime Minister argued that paying a $10.5 bounty was a *prudent* move since the civil court proceedings launched by Khadr and his lawyers might have ended up with the court granting the detainee much more money. This second line of defense underlined two important points: (1) apologies and financial compensation are *not* really a matter of Charter and Supreme Court, and (2) the Trudeau government was not so much principled on those matters as moved by fear of an even more insane decision by the courts. In any case, the citizenry did not buy either of the first two arguments of the Prime Minister. More recently, in the third act, Prime Minister Trudeau found his groove on this matter by reverting to his basic collective guilt problematique: "when a Canadian's right are violated, everyone pays" (Platt 2017). Given the immense degree of subjectivity of the definition of citizen Khadr's rights (in this case), brandishing an idolatry of rights amounts to imposing a politico-moral mold that completely eschews the complexities of interpretation of the case that is required: this is "abstraction in the service of convenience" (Minogue 2010: 244). In parallel, as a sideshow, senior Liberals (ministers and staff) are now stridently attacking those who dare to criticize the Trudeau government's handling of the case by charging that their dissent, widely propagated in the United States, is threatening to affect negatively the NAFTA renegotiation talks – intimating that additional collective guilt should be bestowed on the dissenters for the putative economic costs of their dissent (Stone 2017).

diversity and outcome egalitarianism are fundamental norms. Any limit to diversity or to egalitarianism is perceived as violating the canons of a progressive society. While these ideas, in general, may appear innocuous, when diversity and egalitarianism become *dogmatic absolutes*, they become toxic.

Culture of the host society as an inextinguishable source of guilt

Radical progressives claim, for instance, that any reference to some fear of erosion of the 'common public culture' of the host society is out of bounds when discussing the absorptive capacity of immigration by the host society. This is the case even when the norms invoked have been developed over centuries to help bring forth decent societies (i.e., societies that do not humiliate people) (Margalit 1996): they are regarded as offensive and not constituting a legitimate basis for screening entry into the host society.

In this extreme form, progressiveness generates *oikophobia* – a propensity to denigrate the foundations of one's culture – since defending one's own culture and rules of *vivre-ensemble* is regarded as delegitimizing the norms of others (Caldwell and Paquet 2016; Scruton 2008: chapter 8).

Indeed, the progressives' declaring all points of views and cultures equally legitimate, and one as worthy as the other – another part of the dogmas of radical progressives – culminates in delegitimizing the defence of any particular culture, like the culture of the host society, however precious it may be in itself, and however fundamental it may be to one's society.

In my paper on "The obscenity of hyper-toleration," I bemoaned the demise of critical thinking that brought forth this philosophy of 'anything goes' (Paquet 2017). I was not the only one taking a dim view of this progressive outlook. Already in 1996, William Gairdner made a succinct and eloquent case for Canadian culture (Gairdner 1996: 45ff). His perspective may have been persuasive to some, but it did not displace the progressive view in good currency.

In the same paper, I have also denounced the madness of the notion that all cultures are equal – a view that broadly underpins a certain form of multiculturalism, and denies that indiscriminate mass immigration could cause damage to the culture of the host society (Paquet 2017). The Canadian progressive response to those who have called for prudence, and claimed that the 'common public culture' of the host country might be eroded unduly by mass indiscriminate immigration – has been intriguing and quite a *révélateur*. A posse of intellectuals has designed what they regard as the perfect defence against those calls for prudence: the Canadian culture cannot be eroded by indiscriminate mass immigration, they say, because Canada – at least for Canada outside of Quebec, and separate from Aboriginal communities, and newcomers coming from other cultures – has no culture of its own.

This is a view that has been propounded by a wide array of opinion-molders from Charles Taylor on to Justin Trudeau (Duchesne 2016; Harris 2016). Justin Trudeau has publicized this view in multiple interviews to media across the continent – the view that immigrants can bring the culture of the old country with them when they migrate to Canada because Canada has no culture of its own – a view that has been in good currency in Ottawa in progressive circles since the late 1980s.

This 'cultural nihilism', *vis-à-vis* the Canadian common public culture and the host country in general, has been denounced in the last chapter. According to Gottfried, this cultural nihilism view of the Western world as guilty of having imposed duress on the rest of the world in the past underpins the view that it should accept to unconditionally share its own resources and even its homeland as an element of compensation for earlier malignment (Gottfried 2002). The self-flagellating notion that the West (and therefore Canada) has victimized the rest of the world has led to a bizarre intriguing corollary that non-victims in this egalitarianism world of ours are "implicit categorical victimizers" (*Ibid.*: 15). And, those assigned this collective guilt – the "implicit categorical victimizers" – would appear to have masochistically accepted that role.

To explain this phenomenon, Gottfried puts a lot of emphasis on what he calls "a Protestant deformation": a deformed Protestant cultural mold built around a faith that emphasizes human depravity, individual salvation, and the need for divine grace to lead to salvation. Such a cultural mold tends to make a society guilt-prone, and has left Canadians (it is inferred) ill-equipped to fight this sort of status category (implicit categorical victimizers) some may wish to assign to them. Indeed, according to Gottfried, some have so fully internalized their 'fate' as victimizers that they have been led as "the repentant Protestant" and as a "humbled and self-debasing sinner" to go forth and bring enlightenment to others, as a crusader on a never ending global mission (*Ibid.*: 16)

There may be other forces underpinning this 'culture of guilt', but it remains clear that the English Canadian intelligentsia and media has been surprisingly and incomprehensively willing to accept the idea of treating citizens as "objects of socialization" (*Ibid.*: 15) of which some "feel good about whoever they are" and others disavow their inherited identities. A significant number of the members of the English Canadian intelligentsia would appear to have joined the latter group.

In such a cultural context, it is easy to fathom how much damage an imprudent guilt-prone magician's apprentice like Trudeau II (and his epigons and imitators) can inflict on a country in which a significant portion of the population would appear ready to accept any sort of "guilt" its PM might wish to dish out to them.

This toxic tendency has shown how dangerously ill Canadian democracy is: it would appear that Canadians seem to have forgotten the "core conundrum of modernity" according to William Gairdner:

> ... *namely that there can be no moral framework, and therefore no true community without a **judicious public intolerance** [my emphasis]. In other words, there can be no public sense of virtue without a public sense of vice. In the end, what marks any civilization is a conscious and clear set of widely accepted "shalls" and "shall not" that constitutes an ideal way of life. A folk vision of the good. Without this, a civilization soon deforms and despiritualizes; it ceases being a home and becomes a motel to the extent that the people check out of any deep concern for the whole. I think we have at least one foot out the door* (Gairdner 2001: 4).

In the search for those who might be regarded as responsible for the fact that so many Canadians have lost sight of this "judicious public intolerance", it might it be reasonable to turn to the two important clutches of opinion-molders – the progressive intellectuals and media, and the would-be postmodern politicians.

Progressivism and the toxic intermediation of the intellectuals and the media

This paper is not the place for a full study of the many ways in which the corrosive power of guilt is co-related to the Protestant culture in the Anglo-Saxon world, or of the extent to which the peculiar intermediation of the progressive intelligentsia and media may be responsible for channelling its impact in destructive ways. Caldwell and Paquet (2016) have hinted at the importance of the intelligentsia and the media as prime movers of the *pouvoir social à la* Tocqueville (Boudon 2005), and a most powerful mechanism of distortion of communication in a democracy like Canada.

a) The progressive ideological grip distorts the production and dissemination of knowledge. The Jordan Petersen affair – where a scholar unwilling to subject himself to the sophomoric diktats of ideologically-inspired students about grammar has been subject to harassment by the coward authorities of the University of Toronto (one of the best Canadian universities) to appease the zealots – has revealed the weakness of our intellectual defense against progressivism in Canada.

The fact that one year after those dishonourable events, it is sufficient that a clutch of ignorant students brandish the word 'fascism' for another university in Toronto (Ryerson) to cancel an event about freedom of speech involving Professor Petersen, shows that freedom of speech is now routinely denied by Canadian universities: in a most servile way, they bow to the intimidation of minorities of progressive goons, with the media approving this sort of censorship as warranted as long as it does not interfere with the licence for the extreme left progressives to spread their gospel.[28]

But there are other ways – less blatant but equally toxic – in which the progressives corrupt the public discourse by disseminating distorted information and interpretation of current events.

Two very recent examples, picked at random, underline the toxic capacity of the intelligentsia and the media to actively disinform and to fabricate a distorted view of what is said and done.

The first one is the occasion of a recent speech of Donald Trump in Poland.

In a paper published on July 12, 2017 in the *National Post* (de Souza 2017), Raymond de Souza reported on that speech: "Trump delivered a powerful argument that Western civilization – rooted in certain ideas about God, the human person, and liberty – depends upon more than force of arms or a surfeit of material goods to survive." He quoted Trump arguing that it takes "a commitment of the will" and asking the question "Do we have the desire and the courage to preserve our civilization in the face of those who would subvert and destroy it? … if we do not have strong families and strong values, then we will be weak and we will not survive."

The reaction of the North American progressive intelligentsia startled de Souza:

- *The Washington Post*: "Trump's White Nationalist Dog Whistles in Warsaw"
- *The Atlantic*: "The Racial and Religious Paranoia of Trump's Warsaw Speech"

---

[28] Minister Ralph Goodale, as interpreted by *The Globe & Mail*'s front page (Leblanc and Stone 2017), may pretend to be worried about extremism but he merrily and most irresponsibly mixes fascists, neo-nazis, racists, on the one hand, and those worried about immigration beyond absorptive capacity, on the other. He would appear to convey the message that there is extremism only on the right – indeed he seems to regard the right as identical to far-right extremism. His fight against extremism would then appear to be less on extremism than on the right. Nowhere is there a hint that there might be far-left extremism, for the left is by definition associated exclusively to peace and love movements – obviously! – as starkly demonstrated by the violence in Quebec City on August 20, 2017.

- Doug Saunders of *The Globe & Mail* (de Souza dixit) "took leave entirely of the actual speech conjuring up the darkest of his anxieties: "Trump shocked European observers by using the language of extreme-right and white-supremacist movements to make the case for ethnic exclusion and isolationism"

De Souza was somewhat shaken at what the European observers generated in Doug Sanders' comments: supposedly "horrified by someone who thinks that there is a distinctive culture of liberty that is worthy of defence." This led de Souza to remind his readers that Justin Trudeau obviously does not seem to share Trump's concerns about our civilization since he has declared to *The New York Times* that newcomers migrating to Canada can bring their own culture since Canada has no culture of its own. While this sort of press reporting may be music to the ears of the progressives, de Souza was not impressed, and concluded that "Trump came to Poland to sing a different, more venerable, hymn" (*Ibid.*)

The second instance was on the occasion of the war of words between Donald Trump and Kim Jong Un, and of the recent events in Charlottesville.

As Conrad Black remarks, a review of the press coverage of this so-called North Korean crisis, in Canada and in some other Western countries, would have the readers believe that the main culprit, and the one who is threatening nuclear war in this war of words, is Donald Trump, and not the lunatic North Korean leader (Black 2017b). Western commentators have become so blindly anti-Trump that they have become amnesiacs: their taste for appeasement would appear to know no bounds, and one could legitimately believe that they would wish to have us condone the ways of President Clinton who naïvely paid a $4 billion bribe to North Korea to stop its nuclear military program – which North Korea did not do – or the suave but empty language of the lines in the sand *à la* Obama which Obama would bombastically issue (that he would intervene if the Syrian government ever indulged in chemical warfare) – but when it did, Obama merrily ignored his commitment – thereby losing all credibility. One of the few commentators that did not join the progressive choir on this occasion was former Canadian Charles Krauthammer – hardly a Trump supporter – who declared the 'fire and fury' statement "worthy of President Truman".

As to the civic dispute about the removal of the statue of Confederate General Lee in Virginia, there was escalation by both sides in the face of local law enforcement making no serious effort to constrain violence. It ended up in a tragedy that provided an opportunity for the media to falsely impute to Donald Trump all the odium of the situation because he was not willing to ascribe all the blame exclusively to one side – how could the progressives ever be responsible of any violence? Indeed, the political correctness and the black-and-white Manichean imperative of the progressives ordain that all the blame be assigned to one side (the right one). Even some saner members of the Canadian media like Andrew Coyne mindlessly joined in the outrage directed to President Trump.

One has a sense that it is almost by a miracle that the citizenry can be reasonably informed: for the intelligentsia and the media would appear to have a fundamental propensity to dis-inform *pour la cause*. Indeed, this is a credo of the progressive press. Nothing summarizes this progressive frame of mind more effectively than a poster with a picture of Salvador Allende still in circulation with a quote from him declaring: *"Pour un journaliste de gauche, le devoir suprême est de servir non pas la vérité, mais la révolution"*.

b) As for the reasons why the progressive intelligentsia and media would play such a role in a liberal democracy, there may be many. But I would like to draw attention to an explanation proposed by Ryszard Legutko. The Legutko thesis is that their travails in progressive liberal democracies have developed "affinities" with some of the totalitarian traits of Soviet-type regimes (Legutko 2016).

In theory, a liberal democracy is supposed to be a neutral arrangement of rule by consent with some guarantees for minorities. It is meant to be agnostic and neutral about ideals, pluralistic in its sympathies, and tolerant of dissent. But *since the liberals rebranded themselves progressives* – most vibrantly in the last decades – and announced with a new boldness that they had developed some sense of 'historical necessity' and a new 'impatience with foot-draggers', things have changed (Crawford 2017).

In such a context, Legutko suggests, progressive intellectuals have begun to pontificate in the name of 'what will be' – even though a large part of humanity, less perceptive and less intelligent than them fails to see it. For those imbued with such a mission of building a 'true liberal-democratic society', this implies "the withdrawal of the guarantee of freedom for those whose actions and interests are said to be hostile to what the [true] liberal democrats conceive as the cause of freedom" (Legutko 2016: 20) – a sermon that has a totalitarian flavour.

Crawford's book review synthesizes Legutko's argument: *"progressive* purity, based on abstraction from social reality, sometimes has to be guarded by policing the speech of real individuals who are putatively the objects of the progressive's enthusiasm or the speech of those who are in more intimate contact with these individuals, and threaten to complicate the picture" (Crawford 2017). This leads Crawford to the following *envoi*: "Legutko's book will appeal to people who can point to no overt political oppression, but who feel that the standards of acceptable discourse increasingly require them to lie, and to accept the humiliation of doing so" (*Ibid.*).

This whiff of totalitarianism has become the handmaiden to progressivism's propensity to invent victimhood and to ordain guilt and reparations not only for having allowed prejudice to exist in the past, but also discipline and punishment for not having lived by the new 'right' thinking or for having offended the extreme sensitivity of those who wish to extract as much as they can from their recently discovered victimhood.

The erasure of the name of the Langevin Building in Ottawa; the disappearance of a plaque mentioning that Jefferson Davis, the President of the Confederate states, had lived there, removed by the Hudson's Bay in Montreal; the mauling of a member of the Senate of Canada for insisting that there were not only malefits caused by residential schools for Aboriginal children; the project of erasing the name of John A. Macdonald from every school in Ontario for his malignment of First Nations; and the taking out of circulation a guide prepared by alderwoman Apollon of Gatineau (with the cooperation of the provincial authorities) to help newcomers adjust more easily to local mores on the basis of a single complaint by a newcomer who said that he felt insulted by this guide – all this is 'revisionism' on steroids – as a former politician labelled it – an echo of the erasure of the comrades fallen in disfavour from official politburo portraits in Stalin's time. All this cultural cleansing may not be as brutal as the Puritans' witch hunts in the 16th and 17th centuries in Europe and in the United States, but they emerge from the same spirit: different clergies but the same *basses oeuvres* (Schiff 2015).[29]

Politicians and adjudicators would appear to be incapable of judicious public intolerance

It would be unfair to unload all the responsibility on the intelligentsia and the media. They have fanned the fire and fuelled the hunts most irresponsibly, but they have built on the cowardice of politicians and courts. The Justin Trudeau post-modern cultural nihilism brings front and centre the responsibility of Canadian politicians and adjudicators in failing to generate or nudge forward the sort of "judicious public intolerance" necessary to defend our culture and civilization.

The rhetoric of victimhood is in the process of forging a new bargain between the governors and the citizenry: the acceptance by the citizenry of a 'servile' status against the promise of future security. At the core of this process is bribability and bribery, and the final product is 'dependence of mind', i.e., allowing the beliefs and passions of *others* to determine one's own beliefs and passions (Minogue 2010: 5).

Our concept of society: "is no longer an association of independent self-moving individuals, but rather an association of vulnerable people whose needs and sufferings must be remedied by the power of the state. The idea of 'vulnerability' has become such a cannibal that it now covers not only the victims of the misfortune or delinquency but even the delinquents themselves. It is not only the victims of the knife crime, for example, who have turned out to be 'vulnerable' but also those who do the killing" (*Ibid.*: 9).

---

[29] It is fascinating to see how easily this far-left totalitarianism is routinely occluded by the intelligentsia. Only a minority of observers have denounced clearly like Joseph Facal (2017) that over the last decades it has become clear that *"pour certains, la violence de gauche a toujours été moins moralement condamnable que la violence de droite."*

In a world where *la peur du scandale* drives politicians, and where the fundamentalists and puritans reign by intimidation, the implication, Minogue adds, is an implicit recognition that society has failed in its duty to equip its members with decency and integrity; this in turn raises questions about moral agency:

> ... *governments take over the tasks that individuals used to do for themselves... it thus becomes our habit and our interest – and our habit because it is our interest – to do what the government requires. After all, who are we to stand out against democracy? The state can supply these benefits only, of course, by taking more and more of our money in taxation... whatever may be left of (his or her money) the individual can devote to 'the satisfaction of impulses rather than to the management of autonomy... to the point of falling in with the correct opinions'* (Ibid.: 9-10).

> *We still admire freedom and the virtues associated with it – courage, pride, self-reliance, and such like, even though other admirations may be invoked to cover this or that betrayal of our independence* (Ibid.: 10).

This is what Minogue refers to as "sliding into ... 'the servile mind'" (Ibid.: 11).

In this world,

> ... *convenience trumps responsibility ... We have moved from a morality of respectability to one of benevolence ... the steady drift in which controlled and homogenized individuals are given advantages on condition that they fit the place authority suggests for them ... (a world in which safety for the servile spirit) lies in surrendering one's interest to the basic idea of appeasement, and it raises difficult questions of judgment because compromise is sometimes the rational and proper thing to do. To the servile mind, however, it is always the right thing to do"* (Ibid.: 339-340).

In the dialectics of government and citizenry, both parties evolve as the game and the circumstances change, but if, in the original situation, deceit and manipulation prevail, and critical thinking is absent, a servile spirit emerges and fills the conversation.

In this context, the *problematique* of guilt thrives. It generates a system imbued by sentimental moralism and, in the long run, has the capacity not only to allow the servile spirit to take hold, but also for the common public culture to be destroyed. Nothing in this evolving process in Canada is determinate, but no one should imprudently presume that things will necessarily turn out to be all right in the end.

Indeed, such assurance that one should not worry too much, that it will turn out to be all right in the end, if and when it ever gets installed in the mind, may be the sure sign that catastrophe is near. In Ionesco's play *Rhinoceros* – a play in which a series of persons are transformed into rhinoceroses – a sure sign that a particular character is going to be the next to be transformed into a rhinoceros is that he petulantly declares himself to be immune to such a fate.

Conclusion

In the evolution of democratic societies, upheavals of populism are often ugly and unpleasant ways by which the democratic process attempts to recalibrate itself, and rectify its imbalances. So one must "hope" that such upheavals will "furnish periodic therapy" for the system, but one cannot expect those events to always be "decorous or seemly or rational" (C. Vann Woodward quoted by McClay 2017a: 126). This is the case whether turbulence emerges organically or whether it is nudged into existence by commissars from the intelligentsia and the media or whether it comes from both sides.

It may be said that, with the Trump administration, the United States is going through one such moment of shock therapy in the process of disturbing the seats of power and privilege. And, a good majority of Canadians sanctimoniously look down on this episode in horror – declaring the event, in chorus with the US progressive intelligentsia, somewhat "deplorable" (*pace* Hillary Clinton) and endangering democracy.

Canadians should be careful before adopting such a contemptuous stance.

For it is not clear what will turn out to be more toxic for democracy in the long run – the boisterous buffoonery of Donald Trump, or the underhanded clownesque act of deceit of Trudeau II and his aficionados fiddling with the guilt wand, and sanctimoniously ensuring that the religion of progressivism, with its whiff of totalitarianism and blast of exemptions of responsibility for certain supposedly victimized groups, is crystallizing in Canada.

For the time being, the 'overground' Trump shake-down would appear to be generating chaos, and the progressive voices which, in a most disingenuous way, are also actively trying to sabotage any reform plan Trump may have, sound re-assuring when they claim the shock therapy will not work.

The 'underground' Trudeau deceitful initiatives to selectively undermine accountability and responsibility in Canada, and his myopic politics of guilt (with its gospel of selective empathy for designated classes of victims) would appear to be met favourably by the blindsided progressives.

In the final analysis, however, when the dust has settled, Trumpian buffoonery will shake the American democratic system, and, through the catharsis it generates, might well make it stronger. In any case, it may turn out to be less corrosive than the Trudeauesque insidious destruction of civic responsibility by inventing victimhood everywhere and, in the name of historical justice (whatever that means), feeding the "mounting tide of unassuaged guilt, ever in search of novel and ineffective, and ultimately bizarre, ways of discharging itself" (McClay 2017b: 53).

The US Trump storm may leave no permanent scar on US democracy; the politics of guilt of our *"compassionné"* Justin Trudeau most certainly will on Canada. By the way, this bizarre word *"compassionné"*, which would be considered a *barbarism* in normal French, is not mine, but a self-defining label of Trudeau II's own making.

References

Black, Conrad. 2017a. "Aboriginals deserve a fair deal, but enough with us hating ourselves," *The National Post*, August 4.

Black, Conrad, 2017b. "The media misconstrues the situation in North Korea, Charlottesville," *The National Post*, August 18.

Bock-Côté, Mathieu. 2017. "Vous avez dit racisme?" *Le Journal de Montréal*, July 30.

Boudon, Raymond. 2005. *Tocqueville aujourd'hui*. Paris, FR: Odile Jacob.

Caldwell, Gary and Gilles Paquet. 2016. "Disinformative, ideological and oikophobic: about a piece of storytelling by Quixotic John Ibbitson," *www.optimumonline.ca*, 46(3): 57-66.

Crawford, Matthew B. 2017. "You can't say that! Has liberalism taken a Soviet turn?" *The Weekly Standard*, August 21.

De Souza, Raymond J. 2017. "If Europe's elite think that Trump's defence of Western liberty is 'racist', they'd have hated Churchill," *National Post*, July 12.

Duchesne, Ricardo. 2016. "Charles Taylor's Philosophy of Minority Ethnic Identity and the Suppression of Eurocanadian Identity," *The Occidental Quarterly*, 16(2): 3-19.

Facal, Joseph. 2017. "*Si on parlait aussi du fascisme de gauche?*" *Journal de Montréal*, August 24.

Freeman, Alan. 2015. "The Transparency Act is one Harper law that should have been left alone," *ipolitics*, December 24.

Fulford, Robert. 2017. "Welcome to Canada, a country obsessed with always being fair," *National Post*, July 7.

Gairdner, William D. 1996. *On Higher Ground – Reclaiming a Civil Society*. Toronto, ON: Stoddart.

Gairdner, William D. 2001. *The Trouble with Democracy*. Toronto, ON: Stoddart.

Gottfried, Paul E. 2002. *Multiculturalism and the Politics of Guilt*. Columbia, MO: University of Missouri Press.

Gwyn, Richard. 1995. *Nationalism without Walls: The Unbearable Lightness of Being Canadian*. Toronto, ON: McClelland & Stewart.

Harris, Ashley. 2016. "Justin Trudeau thinks Canada is a country without a culture of its own or personality," *Debate Post*, September 16.

Leblanc, Daniel and Laura Stone. 2017. "Canada puts pressure on allies to monitor far-right extremism," *The Globe & Mail*, August 23.

Legutko, Ryszard. 2016. *The Demon in Democracy – Totalitarian temptations in free societies*. New York, NY: Encounter Books.

Livermore, Daniel. 2010. "The Inquiry Model: Lessons from the O'Connor and Iacobucci commissions," *www.optimumonline.ca,* 40(4): 1-15.

Livermore, Daniel. 2017. "The case of Omar Khadr," CIPSBLOG, July 13, 4p.

Margalit, Avishai, 1996. *The Decent Society.* Cambridge, MA: Harvard University Press.

McClay, Wilfred M. 2017a "Populism," *The Hedgehog Review,* 19(2): 125-127.

McClay, Wilfred M. 2017b. "The Strange Persistence of Guilt," *The Hedgehog Review,* 19(1): 40-54.

Minogue, Kenneth. 2010. *The Servile Mind – How democracy erodes the moral life*. London, UK: Encounter Books.

Onfray, Michel. 2014. *Le réel n'a pas eu lieu – Le principe de Dion Quichotte*. Paris, FR: Autrement.

Paquet, G. 2006. "Une déprimante culture de l'adjudication," *Options Politiques,* 27(5): 40-45.

Paquet, Gilles. 2014. *Unusual Suspects – Essays on Social Learning Disabilities*. Ottawa, ON: Invenire.

Paquet, Gilles. 2017. "The obscenity of hyper-toleration," *www. optimumonline.ca*, 47(2): 13-32.

Platt, Brian. 2017. "'Extensive' vetting process found no reason Payette shouldn't be GG, Trudeau says," *National Post*, July 20.

Schiff, Stacy. 2015. "The witches of Salem," *The New Yorker,* September 7.

Scruton, Roger. 2008. *England and the Need for Nations*. London, UK: Civitas.

Sibley, Robert. 2013. "Young men can be turned to good or evil," *Ottawa Citizen*, April 29.

Stone, Laura. 2017. "Liberals say Khadr campaign could affect NAFTA talks," *The Globe & Mail*, July 20, A7.

PART IV

Design Challenges:
A Small Sample

CHAPTER 14

Getting the Governance of Canada's Federal Capital Right

"capital, the window through which the world peers
into one's country..."

– Beth Moore Milroy

Introduction

Canada has one of the most difficult federal capitals to govern, because, as Donald Rowat noted, "Canada's constitution grants the power over local government to the provinces ... and the control over Ottawa's metropolitan area is split between two provinces (with different majority languages and legal systems). ... Legally, the federal government has no control over its own capital area" (Rowat 1993).

This has not prevented the federal government from the late 1960s on from formally regarding the cities on both sides of the Ottawa River and their surrounding areas as 'the National Capital Region' (NCR). It has invested massively in the construction of federal buildings on the Quebec side of the river, and has planned to direct 25 percent of its new office space there.

What has not been established is a governance structure of this *de facto* federal capital region that would ensure the required degree of coordination among the urban/rural agglomerations on each side of the river and the various federal authorities.

Federal and provincial governments have refused to give serious consideration to the idea of a federal district, and the population, when consulted, has been divided on this question. As a result, a baroque polycentric governance structure has emerged, composed of a crown corporation (the National Capital Commission), diverse federal departments, the administrations of the two cities and of surrounding areas, along with the provincial governments of Quebec and Ontario.

A mandate review of the National Capital Commission (NCC) in 2006 proposed an enhanced status for the NCC (to become an agent of Parliament), a sharper focus on planning, a refurbished toolbox (so as to make the NCC into the Grand Coordinator of the federal presence in the area), and new rules calling for greater openness, greater involvement of the partners, a reformed board of directors, and the development of a culture of consensus (Paquet *et al.* 2006).

Some changes along these lines have taken place, but unfortunately the governance problem is still not resolved. The federal government still has no direct control over its own capital, and the extreme timidity of the NCC in exercising its mandate is largely the result of the open hostility of certain "partners" to any form of collaboration.

In this chapter, I set out an approach to the problem of coordination, suggest a structure and some mechanisms for making it operational, and some safe-fail mechanisms to ensure that the voices of all the important stakeholders are heard.

Local, federal and mixed goods and services

The main challenge facing the federal capital region is that it serves many quite different constituencies: various local populations, as well as the Canadian citizenry as a whole. In an ideal world, one would be able to separate cleanly the local goods and services provided for the benefit of these local populations from the federal goods and services provided for the benefit of all Canadians at home and abroad. However, in the real world, trying to do so is fraught with disputes.

A useful approach is to identify, at least notionally, three categories of public goods and services: those goods and services that (A) are routinely provided by localities to their inhabitants (for example water, sewers, refuse collection, snow removal, and social services); (B) are provided exclusively for the benefit of Canadians at large (either domestically or in dealing with the external world in the form of national security, bureaucratic services to Canadians abroad, diplomatic services, etc.); and (C) serve both purposes to some degree, (for example, national ceremonies that aim at forging national symbols and boosting national pride but that entail local benefits, from tourism and the like, or costs in the form of impediments to local activities and services).

Such a partitioning would have to be negotiated by the NCC and its local partners, and would require some accommodation. It should, however, be possible to arrive at a workable arrangement that is technically feasible, socially acceptable, and not too politically destabilizing if the NCC were mandated to shoulder these responsibilities and thus to take on seriously this overall negotiating task. Concretely, this would entail that (A) goods and services be entirely left to the responsibility of local governments, (B) goods and services be funded by the federal government, with (C) goods and services the subject of specific financial arrangements (conditional grants from the federal government, cost-sharing based on the degree of the 'national interest', or adjustments to be taken into account in establishing payments to the municipalities from the federal government in lieu of property tax).

Multi-level governance: fixing the NCC's mandate

Governance is defined as effective coordination when power, resources and information are in many hands. In the National Capital Region, there are many different groups of stakeholders at the federal, provincial and local levels, each one with a portion of the relevant information, power and resources. So, a simple two-tiered (federal and local) arrangement can only poorly accommodate the multiple relationships of these stakeholders with each other and with the other affected entities (the other parts of the federal government, Eastern Ontario, Western Quebec, Ottawa-Gatineau, etc.).

The Report of the Panel reviewing the NCC Mandate in 2006 (after a six-month study period and extensive consultations with a wide variety of stakeholders) made a number of recommendations to renew NCR governance. These included:

I.   an enhanced NCC role to oversee the federal government's policy of assuring a 75/25 Ontario/ Quebec ratio of federal employment and investment in the NCR, and to coordinate inter-provincial and federal government transportation initiatives on both sides of the Ottawa River;

II.   that the plan for Canada's capital be tabled with the Standing Joint Committee of the House of Commons and Senate on the Library of Parliament, and approved by Parliament, in order to enhance the legitimacy of the NCC and its interventions along with its partners in the federal capital region, and thus the credibility of its definition of national interests in the accommodations required from the various partners;

III.   that a Federal Council for the federal capital region (or some such instrument) be created to ensure the inter-departmental coordination absent in the activities, operations and responsibilities of federal agencies in the federal capital region. Such a federal council (to be added to the 13 such councils for each of the different regions in Canada) should be composed of the senior officials of the federal departments and agencies in the NCR so as to allow the Treasury Board Secretariat that coordinates the work of the other 13 to better grasp the specific problems of the federal capital region;

IV.   that a Troika composed of the mayors of the Ottawa and Gatineau and the Chair of the NCC (with additional stakeholders invited as required) meet quarterly to coordinate activities and priorities, and nurture the commitment needed for collaboration, as recommended by the Ottawa 20/20 Summit (Chaiton and Paquet 2002);

V.   that a municipal consultative committee of senior officials from the NCC, the City of Ottawa, the City of Gatineau, and the MRC des Collines-de-l'Outaouais be established to meet quarterly to act as a problem-solving working group open to the full participation of the other local partners on any relevant issue; and

VI. that a quinquennial roundtable of all the relevant stakeholders (similar to the current practice at Parks Canada) be convened to ensure that the evolving plans and activities in the NCR are discussed and critically appraised by all those in a position to do so. The results of the deliberations of the advisory committees of the NCC (Planning, Design and Architecture; Environmental and Assets Management; Parliamentary Precinct, Official Residences and Heritage Buildings; and Celebration, Commemoration and Promotion) could thus be usefully communicated to this broader community and nationwide feedback sought.

The missing link: federal-provincial partnership

However elaborate the structures suggested above might appear, they will not in themselves suffice to ensure effective collaborative governance for they do not give a sufficient place to a few other stakeholders that need to be brought to the table – in particular, the governments of Ontario and Quebec that have constitutional authority on portions of the territory of the federal capital region. Their interests – financial, jurisdictional, ideological, etc. – in the federal capital region are quite important and diverse.

There are many issues that could not readily be resolved by the existing structures (such as inter-provincial bridges, transport infrastructures, rules and regulations to simplify life in the NCR trans-border community) without a tripartite negotiating committee with representation from the governments of Canada, Ontario and Quebec, set up to meet annually to find ways to eliminate blockages and irritants stemming from the federal-provincial interface.

Resolving such matters will take time (as it did in the case of mutual arrangements for the inter-provincial circulation of construction workers within the federal capital region), but the process should generate over time a set of precedents that would make these issues easier to resolve in the long term. Such a forum might lead to the development of social innovations sensitive to provincial principles like *l'intégrité du territoire* for Quebec. An example can be found in the experience of La Société du Havre de Montréal – a non-profit corporation created jointly by the federal government, the Quebec government, and the City of Montreal "to propose the major elements in a concerted plan for the development of the harbour front and the urban areas around it, as well as an implementation structure and financial strategy" (Gordon and Juneau 2011: 96).

Special purpose inter-jurisdictional authorities for river stewardship or infrastructures of all sorts have been experimented with in Canada and the United States to allow federal, provincial/ state, and local voices to participate effectively in the governance of what could only be joint initiatives because of the need to take into account potentially divergent interests and invite the contribution of many parties.

Such a tripartite committee would be essential to develop fail-safe mechanisms that would come into play in the case of differences of opinion that could lead to destructive stalemates. These would take the form of arbitration processes (as is done internationally), or imaginative arrangements (such as three-way financing of special purpose, non-profit corporations in which any one of the (federal, provincial or local) partners might take the lead depending on which one is best suited to do so most effectively).

By adding to the institutional landscape, these structures will make decision making for the federal capital region more complex. But this is inevitable: the problems posed by the federal capital region are complex, and the arrangements likely to be up to the task need to be complex too.

While the production of local public goods and services can be assigned to the municipalities, the production of the variety of federal and mixed public goods and services (material, symbolic, etc.) requires the collaboration of many partners in a federal capital like ours. Such collaboration is contingent on structures and forums, providing opportunities for the requisite sharing of information and negotiating arrangements, including suitable platforms for experimentation.

The federal capital region as a smart mega-community

It would be unwise to presume that the only key actors in the federal capital region game are state actors. A thriving and inspiring federal capital region has to be a smart community, i.e., one that learns fast and well, a fuzzy geopolitical entity that has assets, skills and capabilities, but also a soul, a collective intelligence, and a capacity to transform (i.e., to learn) that reflects the contributions of all sectors – private, public and civic. Social learning is the means by which we make the best use of all the community's intelligence and resources (intellectual, social, physical, financial, personal, etc.) (Paquet 2005: chapter 7).

To create a smart community, based on collective intelligence and social learning, we need to uncover ways to organize the various elements of the NCR as a mega-community (i.e., "a public sphere in which organizations and people deliberately join together around a compelling issue of mutual importance following a set of practices and principles that will make it easier to achieve results" (Gerencser 2008: 53). 'Civic architects' are required to work at improving the learning relationships, networks and regimes, and to transform them as required. There is also a need for a range of interventions by 'civic engineers' to invent mechanisms to reconcile the different logics and belief systems, and to invent mechanisms and monitoring instruments likely to stimulate and support collaboration by helping them to gain access to this super-vision. Moreover, smart communities need 'civic entrepreneurs' who can play a significant role as 'interpreters' and 'promoters', helping to define the style of the community.

It is unfortunate that the contribution of the NCC towards the emergence of a smart mega-community has been anaemic, except when Douglas Fullerton (1969-73) and Jean Pigott (1985-92) were at the helm of the NCC.

Conclusion

For much of its history, the NCC has not been the catalyst required to give impetus to the emergence of an ardent civic architecture, engineering and entrepreneurship for the NCR. My diagnosis is a lack of *affectio societatis*: the engagement to commit with creativity, imagination and gumption to the partnerships required for the progress of the region. Instead, the NCC has shown a certain aloofness in the interpretation of its mandate and – except episodically – has eschewed a pro-active duty to intervene to undergird the development of the civic architecture, engineering and entrepreneurship in the NCR.

There are other sources for the lack of *affectio societatis* in the NCR, but, through its failure to nurture the required vibrancy, the NCC has contributed to the grievous lack of interest for the NCR, both in the Ottawa/Gatineau area and in the rest of the country. The result has been a fractiousness that continues to keep the NCR as a geographical rather than a living entity. It is not sufficient to add federal buildings and jobs on the Quebec side of the Ottawa River to transform the NCR into a living entity.

For the NCC to foster the work of civic architects, civic engineers and civic entrepreneurs will depend on its developing a kind of 'super-vision' that can help overcome the crippling fractiousness. The NCC has been unwilling up to now to engage in this sort of reframing of perspectives directly, for fear of exacerbating certain tensions (cultural, linguistic, geographic, etc.) and, perhaps, antagonizing the Quebec government that has been somewhat hostile to the silent integration of the NCR. Such timidity will have to be overcome if a super-vision and the requisite *affectio societatis* are to materialize, and the mega-community is to progress.

NCC stewardship will entail taking on the role of educator and animator to reframe the views of the public realm and to initiate the learning process necessary to bring to the surface whatever latent consensus exists among the parties that need to collaborate (Paquet 1999: 194ff). This sort of role has not been regarded as a central function of the NCC in the past – except, perhaps, during the Pigott era.

The indictment of the Canadian capital by Andrew Cohen in his 2007 book *The Unfinished Canadian* is more than a *cahiers de doléances*; it is a call to action to change a whole culture. And it is unlikely to materialize without the combination of three unpopular virtues – responsibility, compromise and patience – and the mobilization of the collective intelligence and capacity for social learning of our mega-community. There are no short-cuts, no magical solutions. Such a transformation will need more than new information or new analyses; it will depend on something much more profound: a change in the "code of honour" (Appiah 2010) – from one based on entitlements (claiming humiliation when preferences are frustrated) and on envy (resentment of the success of others) to one based on reciprocity and mutual responsibility

Already there are signs that our code of honour is evolving (albeit very slowly) as we move from a language of rights and entitlements (a world of either/or) to a language of reasonable accommodation (a world of more-or-less) to deal with contentious issues: what is honourable is less and less the fundamentalist *pur et dur* stand than the creative and fruitful compromise. We are seemingly rediscovering the crucial importance of the principle of fair-play as an over-riding Canadian principle: it is already guiding important national conversations and defining limits to the Canadian disposition to excessive tolerance. This may help in making the federal capital conversation less confrontational and more forward-looking.

So even if I am not hopeful, I have hope.

References

Appiah, K. Anthony. 2010. *The Honor Code – How Moral Revolutions Happen*. New York, NY: Norton 2010.

Chaiton, Alf and Gilles Paquet (eds.). 2002. *The Ottawa 20/20 Smart Growth Summit – A Synthesis*. Ottawa, ON: Centre on Governance.

Cohen, Andrew. 2007. *The Unfinished Canadian*. Toronto, ON: McClelland & Stewart.

Gerencser, Mark *et al*. 2008. *Megacommunities*. New York, NY: Palgrave Macmillan.

Gordon, David L.A. and André Juneau. 2011. "Bridge Mechanisms for the Federal Capital Region" in R. Chattopadhyay and G. Paquet (eds.). *The Unimagined Canadian Capital – Challenges for the federal capital region*. Ottawa, ON: Invenire Books, p. 87-104.

Paquet, Gilles. 1999. *Governance through Social Learning*. Ottawa, ON: The University of Ottawa Press.

Paquet, Gilles. 2005. "Smart Communities and the Geo-Governance of Social Learning" in Gilles Paquet. *The New Geo-Governance – A Baroque Approach*. Ottawa, ON: The University of Ottawa Press.

Paquet, Gilles. *et al.* 2006. *Charting a New Course.* Report of the Panel on the NCC Mandate Review. Ottawa, ON.

Paquet, Gilles. 2010."Immigration and the Solidarity-Diversity-Security Nexus," *www.optimumonline.ca,* 40(4): 73-93.

Pquet, Gilles. 2011. "Le nationalisme québécois dans une ère de surfusion," *www.optimumonline.ca,* 41(1) : 50-68.

Rowat, Donald C. 1993. "Ways of Governing Federal Capitals" in John Taylor *et al.* (eds.). *Capital Cities – International Perspectives.* Ottawa, ON: Carleton University Press, p. 159-160.

CHAPTER 15

Ontario Higher Education as Governance Failures

"You see how circumstances are to blame."

– Lydia Davis

Introduction

When one examines any complex social system showing signs of stress, it is rare that one can identify a single source for the difficulties. Usually, the poor situation is ascribed to circumstances and to an array of faceless forces that have shaped it in a dysfunctional way. Recognizing this reality is a form of wisdom for those who want to focus on problems to be addressed rather than on culprits to be punished. This has many advantages over the propensity to look for a scapegoat: it forces attention on the issue and plausible remedies rather than on crime and punishment. Yet, this is rarely done by commissions of inquiry (usually chaired by former judges); they almost naturally succumb to the temptation of ignorantly pointing the finger toward supposedly guilty parties, while doing very little to help those in charge in redesigning the flawed system.

The Clark *et. al.* study of the higher education system in Ontario, entitled *Academic Transformation*, has been exemplary on this front. In its study of the poor state of affairs of the Ontario higher education system and of its necessary academic transformation, it has avoided like the plague naming names. Rather, it has very carefully deconstructed the process that has led to the present situation, and has shown convincingly that it is not sustainable (Clark *et al.* 2009).

In its careful efforts to avoid indicting anyone, however, it has not been as explicit as some would have liked about exposing the foundations of the overall governance failures that have resulted in the present situation. As a result, given the vagueness of some of the maybe too delicately worded recommendations, it may allow the major stakeholders – those channelling an immense amount of public monies into that system, those purporting to properly manage this mess, those agents complacently benefitting from the gratifications of the system, and those poor students being badly treated by such a system – to all look at each other in disbelief, without understanding how they should get involved in the repair process, or even to accept the very idea that they will all have to get involved as partners in the required renovation.

The inquiry and the argument

For this study, funded by the Higher Education Quality Council of Ontario, the Council has mobilized four experts, each with a sound knowledge of the system, but with quite varied experiences, and significant acumen about the fundamental dynamic conservatism of organizations. This has helped in guarding the inquiry from being hijacked by any of the various interest groups dedicated to the preservation of the *status quo*.

The thesis of the book is that "the present approach to the provision of baccalaureate education in Ontario is not sustainable" (Clark *et al.*: 1). The emergence of the present approach is traceable to a number of past decisions that might be summarized as follows:

- the decision that colleges would have no role in producing baccalaureates;
- the decision that publicly-funded universities would have complete autonomy in defining their mission, purpose and objectives;
- the drift from the universities being focused on teaching to institutions focused on research, regarding themselves as needing to be research universities, and very strong external and internal pressures and incentives to proceed in this direction;

- the concurrent pressure by political authorities to expand accessibility: not only to further increase the university participation rate, but also to ensure a higher participation of disadvantaged groups (requiring more attention than the traditional clientele); and
- the pressure on universities to accommodate the trend away from liberal arts and sciences toward career-focused programs.

This has led to research-focused universities, entirely driven by their own sense of purpose, and funded in such a way that only 40 percent of their faculty members' time is purportedly dedicated to classroom activity, where they are being asked to cope with a greatly expanded clientele and mission. This model has proved:

- extremely expensive;
- unable to provide the requisite variety for a clientele with a great diversity of backgrounds, aspirations and learning styles; and
- not necessarily able to provide the quality of education one might expect from universities, as they have come to rely more and more on part-time personnel to provide teaching services.

In 2000, colleges and private post-secondary education institutions saw a policy change: they were allowed to award baccalaureates. But this has not modified the situation appreciably: a very small number of such programs have been approved, and a very small number of students have been enrolled in them over the last decade.

If it is to be able to meet the objectives pursued, with the minimal quality required in the face of the significant increase in enrolment that is foreseen, the only option facing the Government of Ontario, we are told, is either a massive increase in the level of public funding, or a radically transformed higher education system.

The report

The Clark report addresses these issues in three steps. First, it describes the changes in the environment of higher education that have generated the two important pressures on the Ontario higher education system: (1) toward accommodating a greater participation rate and the demand for greater accessibility, and (2) toward a greater focus on knowledge production by universities by demanding that they give more relative importance to research (*Ibid.*: chapters 1,2,3). Second, it examines the forces that have constrained the college and university responses to these pressures: one-size-fits-all funding, the limited accountability and quality insurance in place, and the particular design of Ontario's post-secondary system. Third, it puts forward some broad recommendations for the modification of the existing institutions and the creation of new ones.

A book that puts forward such a stark argument must be prepared to face the wrath of a higher education system that has successfully resisted externally driven change over the last 50 years every time proposals for transformation have been put forward. Consequently, much of the book's *force de frappe* is built on the evidentiary base it has mustered, and on the sharpness and persuasiveness of the recommendations.

Stylized facts

One of the great strengths of the Clark report is the solidity of the evidentiary base, the clarity of the unveiling of the causation mechanisms generated by decisions arrived at (wittingly or not) over time, and the starkness of the historical review that shows clearly how many reasonable forewarnings and suggestions have been effectively scotched by the effective lobby of higher education institutions, with the result that the situation has been allowed to deteriorate unhampered.

The Ontario higher education system (when it pertains to baccalaureates) has been until very recently *de facto* a monopoly of publicly-funded universities subject to tuition-control. It is not surprising that it has not displayed the sort of capacity and willingness to differentiate and innovate that has been experienced in other jurisdictions where more competition prevailed. Traditional universities have lobbied effectively to prevent colleges from granting baccalaureates, arguing that as a condition of quality of education, teachers had to be researchers (a mythical argument clearly demolished by empirical evidence), while cynically subjecting a substantial portion of their undergraduates to baccalaureate teaching by part-time faculty with little or no research activity (*Ibid.*: 12).

This crass defence by universities of their funding base (getting government to enforce barriers to entry in the baccalaureate market) might not have been so disastrous had it not been that universities (encouraged by many sirens) have concurrently shifted their focus of interest and attention away from teaching toward research. This shift toward a research-focus paradigm was defended in the name of national competiveness and productivity. This entailed a dramatic relative reduction of the resources allotted to teaching – the very task they wanted to monopolize. The chasm between responsibilities and resources was made all the more dramatic by the one-size-fits-all philosophy adopted by the Government of Ontario that refused to discriminate and deal differently with the University of Toronto and Nipissing University – both supposedly being research universities!

The Clark report shows how the challenge of a politically mandated increase in accessibility, combined with an expectation to contribute to national productivity and competitiveness, could not be met – given the limits on fiscal resources, the monopoly granted to universities, the undiscriminating government funding formula, and the unfounded myth of the teacher-scholar as a non-negotiable *sine qua non*. Something had to give.

The thing that was sacrificed was the quality of education. Some universities contracted out more than half of their undergraduate classes to low-paid, part-time, freelance instructors (some of them harried graduate students), having to handle ever-larger classes while allowing their regular professors to retreat to other activities.

This system is unsustainable: the lack of external competition and the effective rejection of any effective coordination mechanism among universities have generated a system that does not have the requisite variety; the existing undergraduate education system serves the students badly; and because it is cost ineffective, it represents a wasteful use of public monies by the government. The only group that would seem to benefit is the elite group of regular full-time faculty members unburdened by teaching – but even this group is now under stress, since it is slowly becoming a vanishing breed which the system cannot afford any longer (Stainburn 2010).

The problem has been long in the making and, at different times over the last 50 years or so, different committees have been set up to examine ways in which the system might be refurbished. While the Clark report does not dwell at great length on these efforts, it says enough for the reader to understand that such recommendations as came out of these committees have been effectively scuttled by the dynamic conservatism of the university lobbies.

Dealing with the governance failures

Although the language of the Clark report is particularly careful, and the use of adverbs is at times aesthetically impressive, the subliminal message is stark: it is the diagnosis of a series of governance failures. Governance might best be defined as effective coordination when power, resources and information are widely distributed into many hands. Efficiency, effectiveness, continuous improvement and social learning, and innovation depend on effective coordination and collaboration.

The whole analytical part of the report richly documents a variety of disconnections and blockages, the effective cartellization process, the resistance to change, the remarkable cognitive dissonance and myopia of key actors, etc. – all forms of governance failures. Consequently, the simple tweaking of some mechanisms here or there could not suffice. The report had to propose a set of reforms that would transform the governance of higher education in Ontario (i.e., reshuffle the deck of rights and responsibilities, and modify the way in which the higher education system in Ontario is steered).

The blueprint for transformation starts with a friendly reminder of two sets of imperatives.

The first imperatives are the features of a higher education system that would best meet the expectations of the stakeholders in general: accessibility, diversity, specialization, efficiency, effectiveness, economy, flexibility, quality, giving due attention to teaching, appropriate attention to high-quality research, etc. It is meant to remind the reader of the multi-dimensional character of the system, and of Ashby's law of requisite variety that states that one cannot regulate a system of complexity X with an apparatus of regulation of complexity less than X.

The second set of imperatives are the principles that can legitimately be defended as foundational for the higher education system if it is to make the highest and best use of its diverse loci of power, of the resources available and of the information in the minds of all the stakeholders (autonomy of the institutions, stewardship of the government, freedom of choice of students, etc.). It also is insistent that none of these principles – *and this is a very crucial point* – should be allowed to trump all the others, if one has any hope of meeting the legitimate expectations of the stakeholders, including clients obviously.

While these basic statements appear to be uncontroversial, they set the stage for a major overhaul of the system. In order to get a higher education system that meets the standards aimed at, it is clear that the autonomy of the institutions is going to be eroded (or at least restricted), if only by new competitive and regulatory arrangements that need to be put in place, and that are bound to have some impact on the margin of manoeuvre of the individual institutions.

The Clark report shows its respect for the awesome power and immense dynamic conservatism of the universities' lobby in refusing to confront the universities head-on with an obligation to change. Indeed, it is only in its last recommendation (Clark *et al.* 2009: 201-2) that the report lobs the real grenade: the need for a system redesign that cannot and will not emerge from individual institutional adjustment or voluntary agreements, but through government action to ensure appropriate capacity, structures and processes.

In a way, this last recommendation is a requiem for the leadership and direction of existing institutions that have failed so miserably. While the government redesign imperative takes the form of a veiled threat in the report, it is clear that this last recommendation represents the starkest and most important challenge to the Government of Ontario – the need to follow the lead of Alberta and BC and accept responsibility for redesigning the system and for providing direction in the light of needs and circumstances.

Despite the superbly diplomatic way in which this last recommendation is couched, the Clark report is throwing down the gauntlet: it remains to be seen if the government of Ontario will have the courage to take it up.

The other proposed transformations presented in the earlier portion of the last chapter might be summarized under three headings: new institutions, new products, new processes. But it should be clear that all such major or minor tweaking will not amount to much if the redesign work called for in the last recommendation is not firmly in place.

1) On the new institutions side, the report is bold.

Given, on the one hand, the dynamic conservatism of the universities and the unlikelihood that they will willingly transform themselves, and, on the other hand, the probability that if and when colleges embark on baccalaureates they will immediately want to become research universities also, the Clark report has a sense that the conversion of existing institutions into what is now needed would be immensely difficult. Between the lines, one may read a strong impression of both an anticipation of massive resistance by existing institutions to pressure for change, and a whiff of the probable lack of courage of the Government of Ontario in confronting them.

So, in what might at first appear to be a *solution de facilité*, the report suggests the creation of a new institution – the teaching-focused university. It might be costly, but since there will soon be a need for a massive extension of baccalaureate-producing facilities, especially in the GTA but also elsewhere, it may be a very astute way to create instantly a new sector ("designed and staffed to fulfill a new type of mission, unencumbered by their history, institutional culture, and contractual relationships" (*Ibid.*: 183)). It might be easier than trying to convert existing institutions, and might allow the design of new funding arrangements that might entice universities and colleges to adjust later.

2) On the new products side, the report is skilful and subversive.

First, it resuscitates the idea of the three-year degree (but it does not dare to suggest a natural extension of the idea: the acquisition of a three-year degree through various certificates). This is seen as both a cost-reduction initiative, but also implicitly as a way to indicate that there is much more one can cover now with the help of new technologies in three years than what used to be possible in yesteryear. In an effort to mollify the academic snobs, the report makes soothing remarks about its not becoming the old pass-BA, but the logic for this is elusive.

Second, it suggests a new array of products offered through an "Ontario Open University." This is a concept that has been extraordinarily successful in the United Kingdom, and has been embraced in other regions of the country. The dual possibility of open admissions and much flexibility through technology to outreach to individuals who do not have access to universities and colleges would be valuable, and would provide alternative ways of accessing post-secondary education.

Third, it proposes a rethinking of the notion of quality of post-secondary education products. This is subversive because it openly challenges the old view of "quality" defended by traditional research universities. While the report does not take a stand on the issue, it calls for a debate that is bound to reframe completely the notion of quality of higher education. Such a debate will undoubtedly force all stakeholders off their traditional defence mechanisms, and may even trigger a refoundation of the whole notion of what we mean by quality education.

3) On the new processes side ...

The report focuses on obvious blockages that have prevented the higher education system from making the highest and best uses of existing resources. Some of these exhortations to efficiency and effectiveness, balance and differentiation within college and university sectors, and ease of college-university transfers are likely to fall on deaf ears: this has been the case for the last 50 years.

The ace in the hole here is the invitation to the Government of Ontario to revisit, in a comprehensive way, its approach to funding. The call for detailed public reporting and the invitation to a "more differentiated system of funding that would allow for a balance between reasonable constraints in the public interest and the preservation of institutional autonomy" (Ibid.: 190) is presenting the Government of Ontario with the major tools it will need to be able to redesign the system: (1) the transparency that will tend to eliminate abuses and feather-bedding; and (2) the incentive-reward systems that need to recognize that the difference between the University of Toronto and Nipissing University is not one of degree but one of kind, calling for unashamedly differential treatment.

Envoi

This project has been an initiative of the Higher Education Quality Council of Ontario, which deserves much praise. The role of such a group is to provide fruitful new perspectives on pressing issues and advice as to how one might respond to them.

The Clark report was released in November 2009. The seriousness of the governance failures of the higher education system in Ontario can no longer be denied. It can only be hoped that the Council will advise the Government of Ontario accordingly, and in the strongest of terms.

Whether the Government of Ontario will heed such advice (and challenge the corporatist interests in the pursuit of the public interest) is another matter altogether.

Post-scriptum in the summer of 2017

As is obvious to anyone who is not comatose, little has been done of consequence since 2009. The university lobbies have managed to scuttle this ambitious project.

Or is it that the elected officials have criminally failed the citizenry, and have been allowed to do so unscathed by a citizenry that has lost any capacity to live up to its burden of office and any interest in forcing elected officials to manage the public household reasonably? And where are the media and the intelligentsia in times when their wake-up calls should have been heard and are sorely missed? And where is the university professoriate at a time when some evidence of critical thinking about their own fouled nest should have been heard?

As the old Somali maxim would have it, it is very difficult to wake up someone who only pretends to sleep!

References

Clark, Ian D., Greg Moran, Michael L. Skolnik and David Trick. 2009. *Academic Transformation – The Forces Reshaping Higher Education in Ontario.* Montreal, QC/Kingston, ON: McGill-Queen's University Press.

Stainburn, S. 2010. "The Case of the Vanishing Full-Time Professor," *The New York Times,* January 3.

CHAPTER 16

The Challenges of 2020 for the Canadian Armed Forces: A Citizen's Perspective[30]

Introduction

The Canadian Armed Forces (CAF) are in the throes of a major transformation. While in the past their main role was to maintain combat readiness, they are now confronted with additional roles such as peace keeper and orchestrator of emergency missions in collaboration with the United Nations (UN) or North Atlantic Treaty Organization (NATO). This is posing important new challenges.

Not only is the specific role of the CAF being modified, the institution is also forced to adapt to important changes in its environment that have little to do with its original vocation. In a pluralistic, heterogeneous, fractured and turbulent social context, the need for legitimacy by the CAF requires that it become more adaptive to change, more representative of this social reality and capable of maintaining more rigorous ethical standards than the general citizenry.

The CAF have a reservoir of excellence (history, institutions and competencies) that has been quite effective in helping Canada face important crises in the past. But it may be that these very competences and capabilities are not quite what is required for the new emerging roles of the CAF. Moreover, there is a need

---

[30] This paper was co-authored with Robin Higham.

for the CAF to redefine their relationship with the citizenry, to transform their set of competencies, and to recognize that they may have to face permanent change as their new state of affairs.

This is because emerging forces in the environment are calling for nothing less than the abandonment of the traditional relationships between CAF personnel and the citizenry: while in the past armed forces personnel and civilians may have been able to maintain somewhat separate facilities, and the CAF were allowed to live more or less according to their own rules, a new set of accountabilities has materialized that are forcing the CAF to negotiate a new moral and social contract with the citizenry.

It is our view that these new emerging relationships between the CAF and the citizens (but also with international agencies, provincial governments, etc.), as they partake in international peace-keeping missions or act as domestic crisis relief forces, are forcing the CAF to transform its core competencies to do these new jobs well. Indeed, the CAF has to become a true learning organization, capable of adapting continually to changing circumstances, and to modify its core competencies accordingly: change has become a permanent reality.

In the face of these transformations, the CAF has to engineer workable ways to respond.

This paper has been prepared to help promote a discussion within the CAF. It should be clear that it is not proposing answers, but putting forward a number of stylized trends that we consider rather important, and a certain number of propositions about the likely impacts of these trends. It is for the CAF to decide whether these trends and the implications we have drawn from them are plausible, and to determine what must be done to prepare the officers of 2020 to deal with them effectively.

Trends

The pace of change is accelerating. Indeed, this is the most important characteristic of the new turbulent environment. This turbulent environment is constantly transforming the role of institutions and this process has not spared the CAF.

While there have been many exercises by the CAF to scan the environment to detect what might be the most meaningful trends (international, technological, resource management) and even an effort to probe the national/societal trends, there may have been too little done on this latter front.

In our view the national/societal trends are of the greatest importance; they may even overshadow all the others.

The CAF, like other agencies of governance in Canada which seek to reflect the full spectrum of Canadian values and priorities, must be sensitive to: what our national norms are (as contradictory and complex as they may be); how those values are evolving; and how the organization fits with those current values and their anticipated directions of change.

The federal Policy Research Secretariat recently addressed the issue of what trends matter to Canadian governance in a general way. It identified eight broad areas where current socio-economic trends are particularly relevant for the general governance of Canada: environmental pressures, globalization, value change, population aging, technological change, Canada-US relations, social differentiation, and multiple centres of power. These are not equally important for the CAF, but we have drawn from these general discussions a few trends that should be regarded as the most relevant:

Globalization: the increasing capacity of events and actions which take place outside the national jurisdiction, to affect conditions in the country (climate, air and water quality, biodiversity, human security, human rights, public health management, international crime control ...), particularly in ways which offend national norms or frustrate pursuit of national priorities.

Differentiation: the trend toward greater ethnic, regional, linguistic, religious, gender, etc. identity, seeking specificity through behaviour thereby eroding social cohesion, national identity, etc.

Horizontalization: the weakening of traditional social hierarchies, the flattening of political authority.

Fragmentation of federal government responsibility by its transfer: outward to multilateral authority, downward to provincial and regional authority, or laterally to private and civic partners.

Public cynicism: a decline in public trust, in confidence in representative democratic institutions in general, and the concurrent insistence on more citizen engagement.

Our own trends research has allowed us to identify two major interfaces that may deserve particular attention in the CAF 2020 project: the new importance of **diversity** and of the **trust/ ethics** nexus.

The diversity factor

One aspect of these trends is the extraordinary transformation of the fabric of Canadian society. We have become much more diverse and pluralistic over the last 30 years. As a consequence, many Canadian institutions have faced a growing chasm between their own texture and the new fabric of Canadian society at large. This has led to a growing disconnect between the institutions and the population.

Moreover, when the Canadian institutions have grappled with diversity, it has been largely by treating it as a constraint that must be merely accommodated. This containment response may prove to be insufficient.

The CAF must accept the challenge of "serving" a larger number of constituencies that are very diverse in terms of their cultures and expectations by accepting to reflect this new reality in order to maintain their legitimacy. This means not only a change in the recruitment of personnel but the development of new capabilities to make this diverse group work effectively and creatively together at all the tasks with which the CAF are now charged.

Officers and leaders of these new CAF units will have to be gifted *animateurs* who will have to be immensely sensitive to the multicultural nature of their 'followership' and to the challenges it creates. In the new Canadian environment, maintaining relevance means that public and private institutions must make space for legitimate and positive diversity.

The ethics/trust nexus

If the new pluralism creates new challenges, the new accountabilities that have evolved in parallel with it have also transformed the stage fundamentally. The citizenry is no longer accepting any use of the *raison d'état* with equanimity. The challenge of governance for the armed forces is to find ways to transform its highly hierarchical and bureaucratic operations into a more nimble and agile governance system.

It may well be that democratic regimes require pockets of autocracy to survive (be it the Supreme Court, the Bank of Canada, the military, etc.), but *the burden of the proof falls fully on the shoulders of those performing these higher-order tasks to demonstrate that they have designed governance systems that have wisely economized on the degree of autocracy, and remained as fully accountable, open and transparent to all stakeholders as possible.*

Accountability refers to the requirement to 'answer for the discharge of a duty or for conduct' in connection with the despatch of an obligation. This presupposes an agreement on (1) what constitutes acceptable performance and (2) what constitutes acceptable language of justification for the actors in defending their conduct. But since in the complex world in which we now live, officials are confronted with (a) many interfaces with different stakeholders with different claims to authority (hierarchical superior, professional colleagues, clients, etc.); (b) many types of accounts demanded (political, managerial, legal, professional, etc.); and (c) considerable complexity, heterogeneity and uncertainty in the circumstances surrounding the activities for which one is accountable – the very complexity of the burden of office results in a great deal of fuzziness in the definition of accountability.

Stewardship in such de-bureaucratized and less hierarchical governance systems cannot be engineered in a top-down manner. Stewardship is not a task or a position, but a process. It is a misconception to look at stewardship as manipulating an object outside of and independent of the steward: managers who labour under this misconception unconsciously undermine the reorganization or cultural change they initiate.

Stewardship is about constant cultural change within the organization. To modify a corporate culture, three ingredients are necessary: 1. a capability for meaning-making, 2. a capacity for community-building, and 3. an ability to inspire trust and confidence.

Meaning-making: The new governance requires continually *making sense of people's experience* by putting it into a larger context: providing a sense of purpose, a story of why people do what they do, and shaping the organization by building a shared vision with its stakeholders, appropriate to the demands of the new situations.

Community building is about developing and nourishing relationships within and between organizations. It is all about skillfully recognizing and resolving dilemmas, inconsistencies, contradictions and paradoxes. This requires the mastery of dialogue, the capacity to suspend judgment, and to question one's assumptions.

Trust and confidence: *Stewardship* cannot emerge unless one can promote adaptive capacities rather than inappropriate expectations of authority: for stewardship is influencing the community to face its problems. This cannot be accomplished without trust. In short, the heart of the matter is not goalseeking and control, but intelligence and innovation: the definition of standards and norms, and the negotiation of a moral, intellectual, and emotional normholding pact, that is built on a multilevel dialogue in which (1) stewards and community are in some measure the shaper and the shaped, and (2) the whole institutional process becomes itself the learning process, and the source of the redefinition of norms and standards as a result of that experience.

To bring about this kind of *stewardship*, a thorough renewal of our ways of selecting, evaluating and coaching stewards is required. Leadership in the military has often been somewhat mistakenly regarded as a forceful top-down thrust by those in authority. This view of leadership was derived from a notion of governance characterized by hierarchy and vertical lines of command. In fact, effective stewards lead change from the bottom up by reflecting the values of their followers, after having done considerable listening, since effective stewards are not only principled but pragmatic. They tend to bring their followers beyond their limits, but not too fast or too far. The steward must earn the trust of his followers by persuading them that he has their needs and aspirations at heart. This bottom-up stewardship cannot evolve unless steward and followers develop a capacity to appreciate the limits imposed by mutual obligations.

This new moral contract within the military must also reflect the foundations of the moral contract between the military and the citizenry. This latter contract demands from the military a much higher standard of ethics than from the citizenry as a *quid* corresponding the *quo* that grants to the military the legitimate use of coercion. If this higher standard of ethics were not reflected in the workings of the military enterprise and given requisite importance in the selection and promotion of stewards, the citizenry could be legitimately concerned.

Implications

These transformations are bound to have an impact on the governance, accountabilities and stewardship requirements of the CAF. This, in turn, will modify considerably the sort of requirements that are likely to be of import in the work of officers.

1) On the governance front, the compounded constraints imposed by the new trends would translate into a number of important modifications in the governance regime:
   - the military's governance would have to become more open, transparent, participative, and deliberately non-hierarchical to take advantage of distributed intelligence, and it would have to systematically devolve decision making to the lowest possible level;
   - the military's governance would be bound to develop ever greater capabilities in non-violent, dispute-settlement matters as part of the new role of the profession;
   - the military's governance would become a multi-stakeholder governance, giving a great deal of attention to balancing the importance of local, national and international forces in its deployment and activities;
   - the military's governance would tend to become more in-line with the rest of the public service and its compensation packages (with due attention to danger pay and related matters).

2) On the accountabilities front, it would also translate into important changes:
- the military would have to become open to 360-degree accountability and break with a long tradition of self-reference;
- the military would have to accept the dominium of some powerful agencies to monitor these moral contracts (the equivalent of the Office of the Auditor General and of the Public Service Commission in the civilian world);
- the military would have to accept the challenge of resolving by negotiation many of the paradoxes and dilemmas it now resolves by fiat;
- the military would have to redefine completely the benchmarks by which it measures the performance of its officials, and the nature of the arguments it is in the business of using, but it must also find ways to give full marks for creative accountability.
3) On the stewardship front, a major redefinition would ensue:
- the military would build more and more on collaboration and *esprit de corps* and on true bottom-up stewadship;
- the military would develop a new culture of motivation based less on obedience than on achievement in one's own learning, and as part of a learning team;
- the military would develop a new pattern of recruitment, training and promotion based on the new values;
- the military would develop greater capabilities to partner with civilian organizations in a manner that allows it to concentrate on its core competencies.

Responses from the CAF

It is not for civilians to define the necessary adjustment in the preparation of officers in the light of the trends mentioned above. However it may be useful to draw attention to a number of plausible targets that might be envisaged for 2020: change of the military culture, change in the nature of the training of officers, change in the relation between the military, the citizenry and the like.

It is our view that this cannot proceed but in three overlapping phases corresponding to a triple process of transformation: a mind-quake, a long period of conversation, and a demographic transition.

1) The mind-quake will occur with a declaration that might be regarded as some sort of Magna Carta, redefining the role of the military in Canada. This would be a joint declaration of the Prime Minister of Canada and of the Chief of Defence Staff, following a period of consultation with the other stakeholders in order to achieve, at the very least, a modest consensus on the new directions in which the new vision of the military and its role in society would be developed.

2) This would have to be followed by a period of one year during which the integrative moral contract would be debated by the stakeholders in a multiplicity of forums, with a view to preparing a more elaborate but short statements, spelling out some of the details of the covenant at a well-defined date. This would be the occasion to look back at Canada's history and at its contribution on the world scene, at its contribution to inventive dispute settlement, but also an opportunity to reflect on the role a small to medium-sized country like Canada could play on the world scene, as well as the sort of role the 'new military' might play in managing internal crises.

3) This would be followed by a long period during which the recruitment, training and promotion process would be amended to ensure the creation of the sort of military organization we wish to create. The example of the US Army might be of the utmost importance for Canada since it has gone through this sort of revitalization. However much might be learned and borrowed from the American experience – what will be required is a *Canadian version* of this process of refurbishment, taking into account both Canadian values and Canadian circumstances.

Conclusion

In all modern organizations from all sectors, governance has considerably evolved over the last few decades. While it had a fiefdom-quality in other times, the governance of large organizations developed more elaborate and bureaucratic structures to orchestrate collective action in more recent times. As long as the environment remained relatively stable, bureaucracies thrived as their rules remained valid and effective.

But, as the pace of change accelerated, problems facing modern organizations became less structured and ever changing, and the bureaucratic system, with its slow capacity to transform its rules, began to show signs of dysfunction. This led to efforts to partition private and public bureaucracies into smaller self-contained and more flexible units. Private companies created a multiplicity of more or less independent profit centres; public organizations like the government of Canada have gone the same route with the creation of special operating agencies. But these efforts to make use of more customer/client/citizen-sensitive mechanisms have often proved insensitive to third-party effects and external economies, and poorly equipped to appreciate and foster synergies.

As a result, an effort was made to re-introduce the requisite amount of cooperation in the governance of organizations through the development of a variety of informal links, *liens moraux,* based on shared values and new corporate cultures.

Such clan-type governance systems are fundamentally built on intelligence and innovation: a capacity to tap the knowledge and information held by active citizens, public servants and stakeholders at all levels, and to get them to invent ways out of their predicaments. The governance system must ensure that institutions promote and ensure the highest level of social/ organizational learning and the appropriate degree of risk-sharing. This, in turn, requires the engagement of all stakeholders in governance.

The CAF has to face the same challenges, and it can best be done by the stewards of the CAF deciding the nature of the transition and the strategy most likely to generate the desired results.

CHAPTER 17

A Culturally-challenged RCMP[31]

"Is it possible to impose a modern governance structure
on a police force?"

– David A. Brown

Introduction

The Brown Report into matters relating to RCMP pension and insurance plans, tabled in June 2007, identified improprieties having compromised the confidence and trust that Canadians place in the RCMP. The Task Force is therefore faced with the challenge of proposing ways in which order, but also trust, may be restored.

In the mandate of the Task Force, the challenge has been partitioned in two main strands: matters pertaining to governance and culture (mandate items, ABC); and matters dealing with the development of a more ethical, fair and equitable workplace (DEFGH).

The core issue behind all these concerns is the culture of the RCMP.

Summarizing the results of his inquiry, David A. Brown refers to (1) the culture of the RCMP as characterized by "mistrust and cynicism," (2) to senior management not having responded to issues "in a manner that was transparent, timely, effective or thorough," but having projected "an attitude of disinterest and

---

[31] This document was originally produced for the Task Force on Governance and Cultural Change in the RCMP.

callousness," and (3) to the Force's values – honesty, integrity, commitment, respect, accountability and professionalism – having been "routinely disregarded by management". He also pointed to "the governance structure and the culture at the RCMP" as the root cause of the difficulties and to one of the key problems being that a single individual had "unchallenged authority" (Brown Report 2007: 3-4).

In chapter 7, of his report, David A. Brown underlined the autocratic approach to leadership, the apparent lack of respect and civility, and the lack of consultation with the Senior Executive Committee, and denounced the 'tone' at the higher echelons of the RCMP ascribable to the autocratic style of the commissioner, the absence of oversight, and the culture of intimidation and unquestioned obedience to lawful orders.

Consequently, without a sound understanding of the forces at work in the culture of the organization that have led to the aforementioned improprieties, one is unlikely to get at the source of the problems.

One may be tempted to slap on the organization a series of additional oversight and controls that may appear to solve the problems, but this may, in fact, accentuate them in the longer haul. A set of new controls instituting a number of additional mechanisms based on systematic distrust would only re-enforce a certain perverse aspect of *esprit de corps* (bent on protecting one's own at all costs), and tend to feed a subterranean culture of deception as excessive controls come to prevent proud professionals and highly-skilled experts from performing their jobs well.

This is the reason why this paper takes a moment (before proceeding explicitly with the different items in the first portion of the mandate) to set the stage in a sufficiently broad way to ensure that the search (1) for new governance and management mechanisms and (2) for a transformation of the organizational culture – is anchored in as full an appreciation of the context as possible.

Preliminary considerations

First, members of a legitimate and credible police force are 'professionals' whose work entails (like other professionals –

medical doctors, lawyers, etc.), the delivery of services to citizens most often in situations of crisis. Such work calls for action in real time to be carried out according to some accepted rules, but also for the exercise of judgment and initiative in the light of circumstances that differ from place to place and from time to time.

Second, and consequently, the burden of office of such professionals can only be defined in broad and somewhat fuzzy terms. Basic principles have to be seen as prevailing at all times, but there is a need for much interpretation. This, in turn, means that there must be much 'empowerment' of the professional on the front line. As a result of the essential fuzziness of the notion of burden of office, the notions of accountability (what account has to be rendered) and ethics (what is acceptable performance) are of necessity also fuzzy.

Third, one should avoid falling into the 'illusion of totality'. Not everything that the RCMP does is tantamount to professional acts. There is also, apart from these professional acts, but intermingled with them, much work that is ordinary functional management (HR, finance) that simply and solely must meet the standards of good management. There is also much scientific work that must meet the requirements of good science. Moreover, at the different layers in the organization, members have immensely different responsibilities. As a matter of consequence, it would be unreasonable to conceive that any *effective governance apparatus would not have the requisite degree of variety*. A single regime will not fit all circumstances.

Fourth, a governance regime is always evolving as a result of challenges revealed by past experience and of correctives regarded as necessary as a result of past failures. This is the basis of social learning. In that sense, the basic test of the new regime called for by the recent crisis at the RCMP is its capacity to avoid the sort of improprieties that have been observed in the past. Learning from this legacy is a tricky exercise: one must not redesign the organization to help it fight only this particular last war. One must keep in mind the broader flaws revealed with a view that, at a minimum, the new regime should make past improprieties immensely less probable, but that it should also make the organization more capable of learning.

Fifth, no regime, however cleverly designed, can promise zero error. The design must therefore be geared to quick learning and minimization of repeat mistakes. Too tight a structure may buy error minimization at the price of zero creativity and initiative. In an organization dealing in real time with critical issues, this would be catastrophic. Consequently, the temptation to impose command and control arrangements (however strong such a temptation might be in the post-Gomery world) should be countered very strongly, and maximal effort should be put on designing a *distributed regime* that has much nimbleness, much learning capacity, and not only resilience (i.e., the capacity to spring back undamaged even when put under stress by unusual events), but also antifragility (i.e., the capacity to spring back stronger and improved from such experiences).

In the design of a governance apparatus likely to minimize the probability of re-occurrence of the noted improprieties, but also to perform as well as possible as a modern national police force, a number of considerations have to be kept in mind.

1) There is a mix of reliability and innovation needed to qualify as a first-rate modern police force. This requires a new focus on *capacity to transform* in the face of new challenges (terrorism, globalization of criminal activities, and the like), while maintaining a close link with the various communities and stakeholders the force serves, keeping alive a vibrant *esprit de corps* that will facilitate effective collaboration, and developing an altogether new level of sophistication in skills and capabilities to be able to meet these multiplex challenges.

2) This new degree of sophistication required of science-based modern policing calls for a much more complex organization of the work. Front line officers, highly skilled scientists, sophisticated intelligence and communication specialists, expert financial and logistics experts, competent human resource managers, perceptive and thoughtful continuous trainers and coaches, etc. are all necessary for the police force to perform in its whole portfolio of different tasks. Each of these groups has a piece of the information, of the power, and of the resources required for success. Governing entails recognizing the different families of

functions (routine functions, management coordination, strategic planning needs and the like), but also ensuring that they all mesh together, and acknowledging that, as the organization becomes more complex, the heightened level of coordination required at all levels is bound to be ever more challenging.

3) At the bottom of the governance pyramid, where the routine functions lie, most of the information necessary to do a good job used to be available within the organization. Conversely, at the top of the pyramid, where strategic planning dominates, much of the information necessary to do a good job used *not* to be available within the organization, but had to be gathered, analyzed and assessed on the basis of external sources of information.

In the recent past, at all levels of the pyramid (routine, management, governance/leadership), an ever larger number of activities have come to depend much more than heretofore on external sources of information, on constant communication and collaboration among the different layers and segments of the organization, on a continuous need to update and refurbish professional skills, capabilities and sensitivities (as all professionals have to do), and therefore on better intelligence and communication.

Failures of police forces in dealing with terrorism and other new threats have been generally ascribed to poor intelligence and communication, and to a lack of appropriate upgrading of skills, capabilities and sensitivities.

This change in the context and in the nature of the challenges has entailed a reframing of the mindset of police forces that is daunting especially for organizations with a strong and vibrant culture based on a long tradition. In the same way that honourable and famed universities find it more difficult than newly minted ones to change their ways, honourable and famed police forces are bound to have more difficulties changing their ways than those that have more shallow roots.

4) Any profound transformation in an organization under stress, after a messy moment or a crisis (or when the very mandate of the organization has been felt to be in need of review) cannot be easily performed instantaneously. It is

difficult both (i) to get rid of bad habits that have been the source of *distrust*, and (ii), at the same time, to establish new arrangements based on *trust*.

Yet one cannot inflict on the organization a process of permanent restructuring without destabilizing the organization and destroying its soul. So the challenge is to find ways to launch a process of change that would be allowed to be modulated along the way. This means that the change must be seen as simple, instantaneous, draconian and definitive, but must also be planned and seen as stepwise, continuing and unfolding.

A standard nugget of governance wisdom is that one cannot usually pursue X objectives with less than X instruments. If one wishes (i) to get rid of improprieties at the highest level, (ii) while encouraging a cultural change throughout the organization that enables it to develop a mix of new skills, capabilities and sensitivities, (iii) together with the new variety of disciplines the new work entails, and (iv) maintaining the best element of *esprit de corps* that has been one of the major strengths of the Force over time, (v) while getting rid of the creeping tendency to defend the not-defendable to save the organization from ever being embarrassed and colleagues from ever being found at fault – many instruments will have to be used, and positive results on all these fronts may require a particular sequencing of interventions.

5) There are many families of levers available to help trigger the required transformation: transparency, suasion, incentives and coercion. Different mixes of these instruments are embedded in any change in the structure, accountability and oversight apparatus, but also in the culture of the organization. There may be a tendency in the post-Gomery world to play up coercion, hard accountability and ferocious oversight across the board. This may be a toxic mixture. A more useful strategy to intervene in any complex organization is to regard it as a portfolio of activities and functions, each requiring often a slightly different mix of uses of these levers.

6) Playing down the ferocious oversight and hard accountability may appear to be a weak response to a scandal that has rocked the trust the population had in the RCMP, and may be received badly by a citizenry often

poorly informed and intent on heads rolling when there are improprieties. But it may be even more dangerous to appear to mindlessly admit that a whole organization is rotten because some improprieties have been discovered at the top.

What is most useful is not a shotgun approach but (i) a rifle approach aiming at correcting what has to be corrected and transformed, structurally, (ii) while explicitly recognizing that much of the corpus of activities and many functions that have remained untainted need not be tampered with structurally, but (iii) with a full appreciation that, in the case of the culture of an organization like the RCMP, the mindset cannot be transformed or repaired (and trust regained) without all the members being involved.

7) In intervening in any large organization, as in intervening in the human body, it is quite risky to try to resolve all perceived mishaps and failures only at the very locus where the impropriety has been spotted. Often, headaches have their source in other parts of the body. For instance, as chapter 7 of the Brown report suggests, much that has gone wrong in the financial management or the human resource management or in other areas of the RCMP has had to do with culture: some of the preconditions that have made these improprieties possible had to do with a certain mindset that is more diffuse and cannot be excised with a scalpel, but only by cultural change.

8) As the Force becomes ever more professionalized (even if it means differentially professionalized), better designed governance structures, refurbished professionalism, and a head-on approach to cultural change (however difficult it may be and however long it might take) may be the most promising instruments.

A tentative diagnosis

The improprieties mentioned by the Brown Report have revealed a profound *malaise* within the RCMP:

- deception has occurred,
- denial of accountability at the top also,
- failure of internal control was obvious,

- an imperial authoritarian management style prevailed,
- intimidation was rampant,
- complete lack of oversight was flagrant, and
- a chasm between formal structure and real operations was observed.

What was revealed is an ethos that permitted the authoritarianism and intimidation by a few to override the principles of the many, and a 'culture of fear' to prevent any effective challenge by subordinates of abusive behaviour by superiors. This translated into *a perverted esprit de corps* at the top (loyalty to the organization right or wrong), and into a law of silence in the middle ranks for those who had any aspiration to promotions. It also led *to non-mounties taking a three-monkey type attitude:* I did not hear anything, I did not see anything, I did not say anything ... it was none of my business. Cynicism at the bottom could not but blossom and become contagious.

These interrelated perversions could not but cascade down into a variety of cover ups at the lower levels that may be difficult to identify and prove, but for which there is much anecdotal evidence: officers being relocated after some offense very much in the manner that bishops of the Roman Catholic Church relocated offending priests – in good conscience, they said, to 'protect' the reputation of the organization, and to live up to what is 'owed' to colleagues that are members of the club.

Such deep-rooted unprincipledness cannot be eliminated by simple carpentering of the structure, accountability arrangements or oversight institutions. Such carpentering would help, but will not suffice. It must be complemented by initiatives striking at the very culture of the organization. A *révolution dans les esprits* is required.

The dilemma such a situation poses is akin to the ones faced by medical doctors when they have, as a last resort, to use draconian shock/radio/chemo therapies aimed at eliminating the source of a life-threatening disease. The side effects of such therapies are always devastating, but they often save the patient. However, they may also kill the patient.

Such intrusive and draconian initiatives in the case at hand cannot avoid having to do more than dealing with material and legal realities. They must attack frontally the symbolic texture of the organization, and aim at nothing less than changing the self-image, the myths, the narratives that have carried the organization through much of its glorious past, the very mindset of the organization. The therapy must amount to nothing less than a change of identity.

If one is to deal with a mindset, surgery or organ replacement will not suffice.

A framework

One must recognize that organizations are social systems that contain *structure, technology and theory*. The structure is the set of roles and relations among members; the theory pertains to the views held (inside and outside the organization) about its purposes, operations and environment; both structure and theory reflect, but, in turn, influence the prevailing technology of the system; and these dimensions hang together so tightly that changes in one produces change in the others (Schön 1971: 33). Any successful transformation will have to take this dynamic into account.

It follows from the tentative diagnosis of the last section that a fixation on modifying only the structure does not sound promising. Any meaningful attempt must work at the three levels. The easiest lever to use is obviously *technology* (physical and social): modifying the tools usually generates less of a mobilization of the forces of dynamic conservatism, and it may have much reverberation on structure and theory. When Bratton inflicted a Blackberry on his police officers, he changed their self-image, their mindset, and the very nature of the way the police force defined its business in Los Angeles.

The most difficult element to change is the mindset and the sense by members of an organization of the sort of business they are in. Many organizations have died rather than modify their sense of the business they are in.

In the case of the RCMP, the right mix of interventions must be designed with the full recognition that even though technology and structure may have to be seen as tinkered with more explicitly because it is easier, what is really at stake is modifying the 'theory' the RCMP has of itself.

New structures, plastered on the organization as it is, might have little impact. The same forces at work that allowed the improprieties of the past to occur would still be at work and would regenerate the virus that has stunted the organization in the recent past.

One cannot expect a *bouleversement* of the organization of the sort that would appear to be required without structure, technology and theory all being on the table and put into question. Pretending that structural change will suffice, and reacting later with surprise, astonishment and improvisation to predictable consequences when this approach proves flawed, may not be the way. One might want to work explicitly on ways to deal with the whole nexus of issues right from the start.

The instrumentation used in modern science-based policing – in the whole range of its activities from CSI to CIA – is extraordinarily complex. It is bound to shape the day-to-day activity of RCMP over time, the recruitment necessary for this new breed of officers, the continuous education and training required, etc. It is also bound to demand a governance structure immensely more complex than what was involved at the time of the cavalry.

The structural changes suggested by the analysis of the Brown Report are obviously important. Strengthening accountability and building some oversight are essential. But one has to avoid instituting distrust by imposing rigid structures that will ossify the organization. A potential result might be the replacement of some rigid structure by another, with little gained in the process when so much could be accomplished by tackling both structure and culture as the Brown Report strongly argued.

Dealing with the mindset will be infinitely more difficult and painful. Any psychoanalysis leaves an individual transformed, with a different sense of self. An organization subjected to socio-analysis and socio-therapy will be forced through the same fundamental transformation of mindset and self-image.

Can a fundamental refurbishment of the organization to ensure it is superbly fit to do its job of modern policing allow the quaint image of the RCMP officer on his horse to stay in place? Should it?

Responses at three levels but also at a fourth one

It would be simplistic to pretend to allocate the vast array of activity areas, and of lines of business the RCMP has responsibility for, according to only one principle. It must be the result of a fairly detailed analysis of those activities and lines of business. But one cannot proceed further without at least trying to identify the different portfolios that might be considered separately when redesigning the governance apparatus.

Modern governance suggests that decision making should be distributed to the point closest to where the action is, to where effective decision making is possible. This entails that 'subsidiarity' has to be accepted as a basic principle: as much decentralization as possible, but as much centralization as necessary for best performance.

This is based on the recognition that there are inevitable organizational failures in large organizations as a result of cognition, motivation and design failures. More decentralized organizations have the merit of being made of smaller units, and therefore the consequences of failures are likely to be less important.

Moreover, smaller sub-organizations are likely to ensure better overall results both because of the reduced size of the targets they are confronted with, and of the consequent 'multistability' of an overall organization that can delegate sub-tasks to segments of the organization best able to deal with them, and protect the rest of the overall organization from the impact of local failures in this specific area.

Yet, on the other hand, certain basic functions pertaining to the very mission of the RCMP and its broad strategic directions must rest at the centre.

For instance, one of the main weaknesses revealed by the Brown Report has been the lack of a governing board providing both the stewardship and the general oversight of the organization. As a result, the equivalent of the CEO could indulge in what could be regarded as whimsical reallocation of resources or take important decisions for the Force without having to render account to anyone. Such an arrangement is unacceptable.

So some refurbishment is necessary at the very top to begin with.

At the macro level

A. A *governing board* on the model of the Canada Revenue Agency and the Bank of Canada might be envisaged. Such a board would be required to perform two basic jobs: (1) to create an effective oversight mechanism for the CEO and an apparatus where he/she must render account *ex post*; and (2) to be the locus where the broad mission of the organization will be defined (and constantly redefined) *ex ante* and where social learning and the stewardship of the organization will be shaped. Without this layer of central guidance for the organization, there is no real control on the management of the Force.

The degree of hands-on control by the governing board will vary considerably for the different portions of the portfolios.

There are tasks that the governing board cannot delegate. They have to deal with the definition of what businesses the RCMP is in, of the broad principles that should guide its management, and of the monitoring and discipline that must be enforced to make sure that the management stays on course.

Such a governing board would also clearly and symbolically establish that, in a democracy, civilian oversight is required to impose civilian order on police organizations. This would eliminate the view that the RCMP operates outside the normal order of government.

What has been claimed *de facto* by those trying to impose authoritarianism in the management of the Force is that the police forces are outside the law if not above it. They have claimed, at least implicitly, *exceptional status* for the organization. From this claim follows naturally the right to operate in exceptional ways. This perception has to be questioned explicitly and corrected.

There may be times for *l'état d'exception* when, for instance, the government invokes the *War Measures Act*, but, in normal times, the police force must be operating normally under civilian rules. The improprieties confirmed in the Brown Report, and more importantly the attitudes documented there, were possible because the organization saw itself as not really bound by normal rules. Unless this *état d'esprit* is eradicated, no change in the book of rules will have any impact.

In the same spirit, such a governing board would have to also quash the idea that a police force is a para-military agency. Again, this is most important both in symbolic and in real terms. So even though the creation of the governing board is seemingly a move at the structural level, it would also have much of an impact at the symbolic/theory level, and one should ensure that such a move is so explained very well to all inside and outside the Force.

The composition of the governing board should not be allowed to be polluted by the sort of patronage appointments that are so usual in such circumstances. Indeed, it should be explicitly stated that, since Canada's security depends on the quality of this board, a mechanism (like Cabinet approval) might have to be put in place to minimize the risk of such appointments not being of the highest quality.

The board should be composed of expert Canadians of outstanding reputation, and chaired by an eminent Canadian who has the necessary expertise.

It might also have a number of *ex officio* members drawn from the judiciary or from other expert bodies to ensure that it has a strong component of expertise about the new challenges that the RCMP is facing.

B. At the same time, in order to make sure that the governing board is seen as dealing proactively and robustly with deception and misinformation, another mechanism might be put in place: the creation of *an ombudsperson* – a person to whom issues of deception and misinformation may be reported – who will have extraordinary powers (as an agent of Parliament or something of the sort) because of the extraordinary importance of trust in the RCMP.

The central concern here is the existence of a mechanism (whether it is a person or a process) to insure that any issue raised inside or outside the organization would be investigated and suggestions for action and repairs put forward. The report of the ombudsperson (or of whatever other mechanism that might be said to exercise the same type of function) would be filed with the CEO and the board, and action would be expected at the next board meeting: the CEO would be expected to announce in what ways he/she has handled the matter, and if the board were not to be satisfied with the way it has been handled, it could mandate action.

The ombudsperson or such a process should perform *both a redress and a learning function*. There is a need for deception and misinformation to be punished, but it is equally important that it be understood that a *learning culture* needs to be instituted: mistakes are a source of learning: cover ups being punished extremely harshly, but open discussion of screw ups becoming not only possible but welcome as a way to improve social learning. In this context, a look at the After Action Program in the US Armed Forces might be useful.

C. A third action might be the *clarification of the mandate of the committees* of the governing board charged with oversight of the *vertical* functions, regional portfolios or other *transversal* activities.

These different portfolios would normally be assigned to an Assistant Commissioner. But it should be clear that the governing board is unlikely to have a full grasp of the working of the organization unless its committee structure is such that functional, regional, transversal and other portfolios have a clear and unambiguous connection to one of the committees of the board.

At the meso level

As for the broad directions for the redesign of external oversight and internal accountability activities, the general philosophy should be that these two functions are complementary.

In the ideal world (where trust prevails), soft accountability and oversight suffice. However, after a crisis of confidence, it might be necessary to impose a transition phase: harsh accountability and oversight until trust is earned.

Indeed, what is aimed at over the medium term is the development of *earned trust*, and this should be stated clearly in the mandated redesign.

Moreover, the design of the mixes of accountability and oversight for different portions of the organization should be allowed to differ.

For instance, in a world where empowerment of persons on the front line is to be encouraged, harsh oversight and soft accountability for field operations may be required: much latitude to improvise, but after action evaluation that is quite rigorous.

On the other hand, soft oversight and harsh accountability might be much better for back office activities where management standards are known and easily enforceable.

The need to balance oversight and accountability entails designing a higher or lower degree of decentralization depending on the nature of the activities. For each portfolio of activities, the governing board should clearly establish the requisite pattern of accountability/oversight.

The oversight/accountability world

		Accountability	
		soft	harsh
Oversight	harsh	x	w
	soft	y	z

D. A most important appointment might be that of a Deputy Commissioner, charged with the relationships with the stakeholders and responsible for continuing education in the Force. It is quite clear that, in a vast organization with such complex and numerous portfolios of activities where coordination and communication problems have been important, a Deputy Commissioner might be charged with constant communication with the wide variety of stakeholders, with a view to ensuring that retroaction is most effective at the top, and that any blockage encountered in the lines of business, that might prevent maximal and most effective collaboration, will be quickly eliminated.

This is all the more important if the governance is going to be distributed and the likelihood of communication failures rather high.

It would also help significantly in underlining the importance of understanding the horizontal and transversal links in light of what the variety of stakeholders expect. Such a function would be an *insurance policy* against silos at the senior executive level and in the boardroom.

However, such a function would risk being strictly ornamental if it did not connect with the whole process of continuing education that is necessary in any corps of professionals. What is the point of noting particular flaws in the dispatching of duties ascribable to lack of skills, capabilities or sensitivities if there is not instantly some corrective introduced at the very locus where the training and continuing education is shaped.

Such lack of follow-through is plaguing continuing education in the public service and proves very costly, but one cannot afford to put up with it when public security is involved.

Indeed, especially at the cultural level, there is no way to ensure that the needed repairs will be made without making use of continuing education. Only a Deputy Commissioner, whose function is transversal, might have the authority to ensure that the requisite transformational work pertaining to the whole Force and its mindset will be carried out.

Some additional comments are made on this matter under heading H below.

    E. Senior management and the governing board have to ensure that, at each meeting, some attention is given to routine monitoring of both (1) the *variance* noted among services within the organization at any level, and (2) the degree of *fluid communication* between headquarters and the different portfolios.

The amount of police contracting of the RCMP in all sorts of contexts is quite significant. This form of work can best be monitored locally or regionally, and it can best be done by those to whom such services are rendered. This might entail a dramatic decentralization of such activities, and the design of administrative, staffing and financial management capabilities that go with it.

The governing board and senior management may wisely approve and encourage some tailor-made arrangements to adjust to local circumstances, but some oversight function has to be developed to ensure that the interpretation of rules stays *within a certain corridor of acceptable variance*, that local and regional practices and mores are not at too much variance. This can be arranged by using a matrix form of arrangement where these activities are mainly monitored at the local levels, while a subsidiary audit responsibility kicks in at the functional level from the centre through periodic audits, if it proves necessary – which it may not.

Conversely, matters of national security, integrated market enforcement teams, and a variety of issues where international collaboration, secret service type work, and FBI type activities are required, would need to remain highly centralized, but not necessarily concentrated.

Networks are the fabric of intelligence work, and there needs to be some way for these centralized activities to benefit from the large number of ears and eyes that may be mobilized by the Force throughout the country.

The burden of the proof in partitioning the activities into distributed and non-distributed ones should be on the shoulders of those who want to centralize: unless the case can be made that these activities cannot be conducted efficiently in a decentralized manner, they should be decentralized, and the bulk of the innovative work should focus on inventing ways to maintain workable coordination when much decentralization prevails.

Indeed, this is the main challenge of distributed governance – governing in a decentralized organization – to invent soft and non-intrusive ways to maintain oversight from afar and to keep the communication channels open between the centre and the periphery, while building strong accountability links between the peripheral groups and the clients they serve, who are best able to demand hard accountability for performance.

In the case where strong accountability at the centre dominates the scene, the oversight function is much more to ensure that communication channels are open that allow information from afar to be tapped and analyzed.

In both cases, some hybrid form of organization is likely to provide the best performance.

F. It is also the role of senior management and of the governing board to ensure that *safe spaces are provided throughout the organization for appraisive retroaction on a continuous basis* after the completion of field operations. What is of interest here is the input of junior or non-executive or non-Mounties staff who have been involved in the operations, and should have an opportunity to be heard at debriefing time.

The After Action Program in the US Army has shown that even in military organizations, it is possible to gain extraordinary insights into what has gone well or not (with a temporary suspension of the notion of ranks). Pascale *et al.* have explained how this most powerful mechanism of social learning has been used profitably, both in the US Army and in the private sector (Pascale *et al.* 1997).

But such mechanisms and safe spaces have to be seen to exist as an explicit and forcefully stated wish of the very top of the organization, and with the strong explicit support of the board and senior management; it also has to be experienced by all participants as an effective learning tool, with explicit feedback to participants about what has been learned and what changes it has triggered. Otherwise the process will quickly atrophy. Senior management and the board should be known to insist that the existence of such safe spaces is necessary to ensure a sound process of social learning in the organization, and their contribution to such events should testify to their keen interest in it.

The results of such ongoing experiments would be expected to be part of the routine monitoring activity of senior management and the board under E., but there might be a special effort to ensure that the requisite mechanisms are in place for such after-action-learning to occur. This is absolutely fundamental, but especially difficult in an organization that has suffered from a culture of intimidation.

At first, it is likely that there will be much cynicism when such practices are introduced. This is also where the generational chasm will most probably show its ugly face: too many older members of the Force might have been schooled and have lived in the culture of unquestioned obedience for too long to have any appreciation of the importance of critical thinking throughout the Force. The younger generation may have been less deeply acculturated into this sort of mindset despite their 'basic' training.

At the micro level

At the micro level, the most important and the most difficult task is to maintain the *focus of attention of the individual members* simultaneously on both (1) the task at hand and (2) the broad mission of the Force.

In an organization that has been traumatized and that one wants to transform from a culture of entitlement at the top and blind obedience at the bottom to a culture of pride, collaboration and learning, this requires a restoration of the fundamentals.

G. The first big lever is professionalism. Professionalism provides the experiential and existential notion of *relational accountability*. Officers who are fully aware of their burden of office navigate these waters easily. But it requires that a notion of the burden of office be fully internalized. And this is where the culture of the organization plays its full role. Invisible institutions and unstated informal conventions have an immense impact on the day-to-day activities. They act as a coordinating instrument, but also as constraint, blockage, agent of cognitive dissonance.

Culture is not only or even mainly shaped by accountability or oversight (i.e., top down), but by experience and interaction at the local level. It is distilled by a large number of actions reinforcing one another: habitualized choices tending to become the norm by imitation, contagion, and as a result of mutual expectations.

Organizational culture is the sum of these habits, norms, expectations that have developed over time as a result of the process of acculturation generated by training, collegiality and governance stories and myths shared by the members of the club. And these habits and norms are nurtured, maintained, and enhanced by their constant invisible presence in day-to-day activities.

At the micro level, culture, pride, and the like are most powerful agents of effective coordination, accountability and ethics. The need to have challenge and oversight functions within the organization becomes a moot point when the organizational culture is sound. Such add-ons might be seen as efforts to institutionalize distrust.

There is a multitude of ways in which this professionalism has been used in the past. The point here is to understand that these ways may need to be *refocused*: from a sense of blind defense of the club to a redefinition based on a burden of office being defined as more demanding than in any other occupations, and as calling for a higher degree of integrity and ethics than in non-professional work. This might call for an oath of office like the Hippocratic Oath for medical doctors.

    H. This centrality of the burden of office might require a massive investment of resources to transform the mindset of the members of the Force. It will require that the Force be subjected to a socio-analysis and a socio-therapy, not unlike what troubled individuals, who have to go through in psycho-analysis and psycho-therapy.

What is involved is nothing less than a redefinition of the rapports of the members of the Force at all levels with *les autres* – persons that are regarded as aliens as distinct from them, as another species, as animals – into *autrui* – persons with whom they see some commonality, for whom they may have some empathy.

Such transformations have been successfully effected on a smaller scale when some mental health institutions or homes for seniors discovered that patients were abused by the staff. What had to be done was to modify the "relationship" with the patient by redefining the patient as *autrui* not *autres*, a person like me and not one of another species.

When one has a capacity to regard persons and groups with whom one has professional relationships like persons of one's own species, one can hope to fathom their needs, and one might be able to change one's own way of acting. Without such extraordinary internal transformation in the mindset, any change in structure is bound to fail.

The culture will not be changed unless interpersonal relationships are transformed. And this transformation is profound and difficult in individuals. In fact, the defense mechanisms are so strong that most members are likely to be in strong denial and to object vehemently to any such process of transformation when it is suggested to them.

Indeed, one must anticipate the same antagonism from members of the Force that one faces when one suggests to an individual that he/she may be in need of psychological help. There is a negative aura attached to psychological disorder and mental illness that leads it to be occluded and denied, with disastrous consequences. The same may be said of disorders at the organizational culture level: they are summarily dismissed as unreal, unimportant, and irrelevant in day-to-day operations, and therefore as calling for no therapy at all. Good stewardship will be required to persuade the members of the Force to accept to take part in this transformational process.

This is where the role of the Deputy Commissioner might be crucial. He/she will have to explain that this is part of the development of critical thinking, of the process of becoming aware of assumptions one is not aware one is making, of better self-knowledge as a way to become a more effective professional. Psychologists have to go through this process in order to help persons with psychological disorders. Members of a police force need the same transformation to be able to do their jobs well.

How can this mammoth task be accomplished?

Subtly … and often in an oblique way.

Most often through occasions developed when getting the members involved in training (for they regard it as legitimate and do not feel threatened). On such occasions, transformation can often be successful through *organizational bricolage* or modification of technology, for again this is not threatening.

The use of *vous* instead of *tu* in schoolyards has done well to reduce schoolyard violence. The insistence by the New York chief of police that members of the force use the subway to and from work so as to expose them more fully to the citizenry they interact with has transformed their view of the citizenry they work for.

But in the case of the RCMP, such baby steps may not suffice. A vast process of learning and development-centred cultural transformation may be necessary.

Indeed, other very large organizations have launched successfully such a process. G. O'Donovan has shown how the Hong Kong and Shanghai Corporation, the second largest financial institution in the world, now headquartered in London, has engineered such a successful transformation through a five-year strategy (O'Donovan 2006). This is not the only way to proceed, but it should indicate that this sort of initiative has proven feasible and successful in an organization of more than 15,000 employees throughout the world.

Such cultural change has to be associated with continuous education and must translate into specific changes in day-to-day practice. Tact and civility are minor virtues that were not present in the RCMP at certain levels. This may be a powerful starting point. But what has to be transformed is the whole set of relationships with partners and stakeholders, the lenses through which they are perceived and defined, the way in which one defines oneself *vis-à-vis* them.

Generative governance

There may be a need to frame the discussion of these structural and cultural changes in such a way that they will not be rejected as abhorrent from the start. This may require that they be explicitly interpreted and understood as ways and means to move to *a new form of governance and stewardship,* for these latter goals are regarded as legitimate and imperative after a crisis.

One way to present this ensemble of responses, and to get all to engage willingly and creatively in the process, is to present it as a way to move from a focus on Type I (fiduciary governance) and Type II (strategic governance) toward Type III (generative governance) using the language of R.P. Chait *et al.*'s *Governance as Leadership* (Chait *et al.* 2005). Type I governance focuses on the stewardship of tangible assets; Type II on partnerships; Type III on stewardship. Good governance entails a mix of the three components.

The Brown Report has revealed Type I governance failures, and it calls for some fiduciary repairs. Trustworthiness must be ensured through better financial controls and routine oversight, but it may not suffice. The Report also reveals Type II governance failures: these flaws pertain to the definition of what business one is in, what are the core competencies to be nurtured, what is the business model, what is the architecture of the organization that best fits the mission, what are the priorities, what are the benchmarks to use? The structural repairs suggested would remedy some lack of oversight at the macro level, but the governing board and its committees (in consultation with the CEO) may have to set in place a management structure that will ensure that these matters are better handled.

Most importantly, however, the Brown Report reveals Type III governance failures: a lack of capacity for generative governance – a capacity to discern problems, to make sense of them, to frame the problems differently, and to look at the business in a different way – because of the stultifying culture of the organization. This, in turn, calls for a different way of thinking, a different mindset.

Such a new mindset cannot be produced only at the top: then it would entail a perpetuation of the hierarchical governance of the past and of the culture of intimidation and unquestioned obedience … with a few flats and sharps. What needs to be transformed in the way to do business, the framework within which issues are viewed entails a change in the mindset.

This is the sort of thinking that led to community policing: broken windows not seen as simple trade marks of crime-ridden neighborhoods, but preventing broken windows as part of a larger effort to create order and safety.

The overall strategy might usefully be labeled: *toward generative governance.*

Guideposts

A more elaborate study would require a fuller appreciation of the complexity of the context, of the constellation of different interests in play, of the foundation of the power base of the different groups, and of the range of levers available to intervene in subtle ways in processes one can only control partially and imperfectly.

But this may be regarded as a start.

Some general principles are likely to lead to better governance:
- the principle of maximum participation to ensure that as much knowledge as possible is made available, and that any commitment made in inclusive meetings will tend to be honoured;
- the principle of subsidiarity that posits that the best decisions are taken by those who are directly concerned, and that a decision should be taken at a more remote level only if it cannot be done well at the local level;

- the principle of multistability simply suggests that the best way to get a stable system is to partition it in sub-systems. This prevents the whole system from having to adjust completely to each perturbation and shock: each sub-system that is most apt to take care of a particular adjustment may then be asked to take care of it.

These principles are not necessarily equally important in each particular case, but they combine to suggest ways in which one may want to design organizations likely to generate the highest level of social learning.

From these principles (and there may be others inspired by the particular circumstances of the RCMP), one may suggest a number of mechanisms that would appear to best serve these principles.

Some mechanisms of a generic sort might prove useful:

- the creation of forums or safe spaces for information exchange, interaction and negotiation;
- the change in the nature of 'relationships' and the development of moral contracts and seemingly innocuous arrangements that often are the root of trust, and making inter-personal relations easier;
- the provision of settings leading to the confrontation of frames of references, to social learning, and to the generation of a basis for reframing that may lead to getting out of what first appeared as an impasse;
- mechanisms of intervention to counter some dysfunctional cleavages between beliefs and reality: cognitive dissonance, and the like;
- the design of fail-safe mechanisms to prevent the multilogue to degenerate in meaningless consensus and to prevent sabotage.

But these general mechanisms have to translate into stratagems to ensure that they are not allowed to remain ineffective. As we mentioned earlier, these stratagems simply impact on the organization through simple avenues: transparency, suasion, incentives and coercion

The case of the RCMP is interesting because of the generational cleavage that is likely to stand in the way of an abrupt transition from the old order to the new one. The paramilitary and hierarchical nature of the old order is bound to continue to have an impact on the 'acceptable' strategies in the short run. If what is proposed tends to be perceived as laxity and lack of effectiveness, or 'soft', it will fail.

On the other hand, if it maintains assumptions about the optimal regime having to remain authoritarian, there will be no buy-in from the younger generation.

The new culture has to build on what both generations have in common: pride and *esprit de corps*.

It also has to start with a reframing of the vision and mission in a manner that puts much emphasis on power *with* and not power *over*, learning, on a police corps that is intent on remaining at the frontier of new scientific, physical and social technologies in its efforts to meet effectively the challenges of modern policing, and on a police force that is ready to experiment to get there ... even with reframing completely the notion of policing – from coordination by the use of force to coordination with the use of as much force as necessary but as little force as possible.

Preliminaries for a strategy: a summary view

As mentioned earlier, after a crisis of the sort the RCMP went through, nothing less than a transformation of the whole governance process is required. Generative governance is the objective sought.

This transition might require a two-tracked effort.

First, *a modification of the structure of governing*: a strong civilian governing board, connected fully to the operations of the organization through many channels – the reports of the CEO, the intelligence of an ombudsman process reporting to both the CEO and the Board, and the various committees charged with managing, but also monitoring, the terrain in all sorts of ways.

Second, *a transformation of the mindset*: through an ambitious and systematic process that will swamp the whole organization and transform the culture through a massive exercise in continuing education.

Track (1a) Implementing immediately transparency and openness

The central rule might be that each official should be kept fully informed, and that disloyalty will be interpreted as not having fully informed one's superior of anything untoward. Thus the sins are deception and misinformation.

But it is unreasonable to presume that modern governance can be built exclusively on the principles of transparency (panopticon) and accountability (generalized distrust).

Track (1b) Putting in place the structural repairs suggested above

Concomitant with the new philosophy of transparency and openness, one would put in place a new governing board, and an ombudsperson process, with the clear mandate of reviewing the management, accountability and oversight structure within one year.

Track (2) This second track might aim at implementing generative governance at the RCMP

This would mean evolving from the traditional notion of accountability (TA) to a more relational notion of accountability (RA).

TA is a mechanical top-down *ex post facto* rendering of account mainly as a tool of control and with a view to punishing mistakes. RA is a more encompassing, continuing disclosure of what one is doing or intends to do as a tool of learning and with a view to negotiating the best possible approaches.

But this will not occur unless there is a transformation of the culture.

The only way for this to work might be to get from the Commissioner and from the Chair of the Board a clear message that nothing less than this will do, for nothing less than such a cultural change will allow the RCMP to regain the trust it formally had.

Such trust might be regained by two important bottom-up changes:

- the refurbishment of the burden of office as professionals so as to ensure that excellence in performance will ensure respect will be regained; but also
- the refurbishment of all relationships so as to build on power with, empathy, and the rule of civility first – as much force as necessary, but as much civility as possible in dealing with all ... as a part of the refurbished notion of professional members of the Force.

This would constitute a major challenge for the Deputy Commissioner or whoever shoulders such functions to operationalize such a cultural transformation strategy, based on the continuous education component that would be presented as absolutely fundamental in the ongoing conceptual refurbishment required from any professional.

Conclusion

Mapping the terrain is what we have tried to do.

A few key points deserve particular attention:

- the importance of dealing with the symbolic/theory dimension frontally and to avoid counting exclusively on structural change;
- the importance of being diffident about challenge functions, whistle-blowing and other such instruments that are likely to institute distrust;
- the importance of moving to distributed governance as much as possible;
- the need to redefine *esprit de corps* explicitly and frontally for this will be the rampart behind which much deception will be engineered; it has been done well in the case of drunk drivers – a real friend takes away his keys;
- the importance to think about the Deputy Commissioner (or a process akin to it) as a positive complement to the negative role of the Ombudsman (or a process akin to it): the latter is there to detect and correct mishaps, the former works actively at experimenting with new ways like the VP-R&D in an industrial firm;
- the importance of fleshing out the notion of relational accountability;
- the importance of spelling out fail-safe mechanisms;
- the importance of finding a way to make massive socio-therapy palatable, and to make it fit naturally into the process of continuing professional education that is in good currency in all serious professions, and a strategy of generative governance.

References

Chait, R.P. *et al*. 2005. *Governance as Leadership*. Hoboken, NJ: Wiley.

O'Donovan, G. 2006. *The Corporate Culture Handbook*. Dublin, IE: The Liffey Press.

Pascale, Richard T. *et al*. 1997. "Changing the Way we Change," *Harvard Business Review*, 75(6): 127-139.

Schön, D.A. 1971. *Beyond the State State*. New York, NY: Norton.

CHAPTER 18

About the Office of the Auditor General[32]

"From the dew of the few flakes that melt on our faces
we cannot reconstruct the snowstorm"

– John Updike

Introduction

These notes are not meant to be a comprehensive summary of the discussions in the two workshops Lorna Marsden and I chaired on April 29, 1993. The conversations were too rich and the exchanges too stimulating for our short document to be able to do justice to them. At best, we feel that it is possible to present some highlights of the discussions to ensure that the most important points made in one or the other of the workshops are recorded and may help the Auditor General, within the context of his existing roles and responsibilities, in his Office's deliberations about the "deficits and debt" issues.

We have prepared these notes without attribution in order to avoid maligning or misrepresenting the views of individuals. Our summary may also have simplified unduly or sanitized somewhat the variegated messages we heard over the day. Moreover, what follows does not correspond to the recollections of any one person

---

[32] Revised version of the closing remarks of the two *animateurs* (Lorna Marsden and Gilles Paquet) at the Colloquium on Deficits and Debts, organized by the Office of the Auditor General of Canada, April 28-29, 1993.

attending the seminar, since our single document has blended the messages heard from the members of the two workshops, which were held simultaneously.

While the two workshops followed parallel lines on most issues, in some areas their work was clearly complementary. Participants should not be held responsible for what may have been our lack of perceptiveness or sensitivity on a number of those complex issues.

Perceptions and indicators

A portion of the day was spent matching a number of perceptions of the central issues behind this "deficits and debt" syndrome and the sort of relevant indicators that might convey well to Parliament and to the general public the depth of concern harboured by a good many specialists. The mandate of the Office of the Auditor General was seen first and foremost to be a servant of Parliament and only secondarily to be a servant of the citizenry and the media that shape public opinion.

First, the problem of "deficits and debt" was cast in *national* terms (i.e., as the general state of affairs encompassing "deficits and debt" at all levels of government). This is a relatively new phenomenon that has arisen mainly as a result of the growing awareness that the different levels of government are in the nature of communicating vessels: What is at stake? Is the accumulation of deficits at each level amounting to a growing national debt level?

Second, the issues identified under the label "deficits and debt" were largely regarded as symptoms of a more fundamental *malaise* pertaining to a range of problems – from productivity to governance, to fiscal management, to a misunderstanding of the real fundamental weaknesses of the Canadian economy. For some it was a symptom, misread and misunderstood, that revealed a critical situation. As a result, the warning signals of financial deficits were interpreted quite differently as either a reflection of a concern about policy inaction or as an indicator of a poor understanding of the nature and role of the deficit financing and debt.

Third, and as a natural consequence of the earlier point, there was no agreement on the extent of the concern that should be generated by the "deficits and debt" signals: while some expressed views about brinkmanship, others insisted that fixation on the "deficits and debt" problems would appear to obscure rather than enlighten public debates, mainly as a result of the masking of the accomplishments "deficits and debt" have enabled us to finance. As a result, there was much disagreement about the immediacy or urgency of the crisis even though a majority of the participants viewed the situation as an emergency.

Finally, there was concern expressed about the lack of information about the *causes*, not only the *sources*, of the deficits/debt issue, and about the diversity of diagnoses that underpinned this problem set. For some, it was a sign that we should rethink the role of government altogether; for others, this was a problem of vulnerability as a result of extensive external debt; for still others, the matter was simply a problem of the psychological reduction of the existing margin or manoeuvrability that government perceives it has. Put simply, there were obvious differences of opinion about the nature of the problem, the seriousness of the problem, and the capacity of the socio-economy to overcome these strains.

Unsurprisingly, no single indicator describing the condition of deficits or debt appeared sufficient to gauge the situation, but there was concern that too wide a range of indicators would produce yet more confusion. A battery of indicators was proposed by participants in keeping with both their diagnosis of the nature of the *malaise* and their sense of what might most appropriately convey the message to parliamentarians and citizens: public debt-to-GDP ratio, debt per capita, debt charges as percentage of government revenue (interest bite), program spending to government revenue (program bite), total public debt to government revenue, percent of public debt held by foreigners, bond rating, yield differential between government long-term bonds in this country as compared to those in the US, etc.

Most of the indicators mentioned either were already available or could be made available easily. It was generally felt that a battery of three to six indicators (clear, precise, reported at regular intervals on a consistent basis, incorporating historical trends and comparative data for other countries, but also data on the federal and provincial deficits/debt situation) would be most useful. A majority of the participants argued for the indicators to be provided on a quarterly basis at least and for a concerted effort to ensure the dissemination and the analysis of the information in the media.

Over and beyond the provision of simple deficits/debt indicators, some improvements in the overall presentation of public finances were suggested. First, a case for more detailed information was made. It was noted that the last budget, for instance, provided much less information than usual. Second, there was a strong case made for the preparation of separate operating and capital budgets, for the preparation of 'national' financial information, consolidating federal and provincial affairs, and for a closer scrutiny of the shuffling of cash balances to the next fiscal year.

The general sentiment was that much of the work to generate a better understanding of the deficits/debt issues and to improve the sophistication of the analyses would be difficult to translate into information benchmarks that would be meaningful for every parliamentarian and citizen. It was felt that the present data set was simply too complex and too macro-economic in flavour to be meaningful for most parliamentarians and citizens.

Finally, there was a strong sentiment that one cannot expect, in the present context, any existing market or agency (provincial, national or international) to issue clear and reliable early warning signals about danger points. Financial markets may register the *crisis* but may not foresee it; agencies like the IMF, the OECD, etc., while well informed, are in many ways forced to be prudent and to attenuate nasty signals both to avoid triggering a crisis and to avoid embarrassing the national governments on which they depend. Bond-rating agencies may be a more sensitive recorder of market moods, but there is often confusion when the different agencies issue different signals.

All this pointed to the need for a source of reliable, authoritative information, compiled critically, that would complement the existing data sources. There is also a clear need for more effectiveness in communicating ongoing information about the deficits/debt situation to Parliament.

What can the Office of the Auditor General do?

The colloquium addressed the issue of What the Office of the Auditor General (OAG) can do in a variety of ways and with some ambivalence. Central to the debate was the high degree of credibility and legitimacy of the OAG. It was felt that this was such a valuable asset that any action by the OAG that might compromise its credibility should be avoided or at least discussed thoroughly. This trade-off (effectiveness/legitimacy) was not universally celebrated as a key constraint. Some suggested that the credibility of the OAG might be enhanced by its becoming the source of reliable information on the deficits/debt issue.

One may summarize the debates under a variety of headings. While these do not exhaust the full range of discussions, it provides a sense of the differences of opinions as to how far the OAG should go.

OAG as modem auditor

It became clear during the debates that the role of the OAG – as with private sector auditors – is evolving. While the auditors of yesteryear were satisfied with expressing an opinion on the fairness of presentation of financial statements of companies, more recently they are being encouraged to encompass some responsibility in drawing the attention of shareholders to the structural and fundamental weaknesses of the entity. Recent court decisions are pushing auditors of private firms to pay more attention to these concerns.

The OAG must face the same pressures, as the standards of what is expected from an auditor are evolving. If the concern "Canada Inc." proved to have been in danger (as some claim) and were to run into a serious financial crisis, both internal and external creditors might legitimately ask why the Auditor General had not found it in his mandate to issue some warnings. A clear majority felt strongly that this was the Auditor General's responsibility, yet, no one felt that they could unequivocally advise the Auditor General as to how far he should go.

OAG as generator of numbers

As for the sort of information the OAG might disseminate, there was a precise notion of warranted limits. It was felt that the OAG should stay clear of making forecasts of any sort and be satisfied with a critical appraisal of the costs of poor marksmanship by the Department of Finance. The general idea was that the OAG should restrict itself to the job of clarifying and certifying the accuracy of the most relevant indicators and of complementing the list of these relevant indicators, if essential.

The OAG could provide or urge government to provide a fair estimate of the real costs of services. Such cost figures could act as a shadow price system to heighten sensitivity to the need for prudence in the consumption of public goods and for cost containment in the management of the public household.

OAG as definer of standards

While not becoming the major provider of new numbers, the OAG would play a crucial role in contributing to the definition and establishment of a set of standards of reporting not only for the federal government, but for all portions of the public household. It might, for instance, foster the practice of having separate operating and capital budgets. This would enlighten the public considerably, since the OAG might also suggest important ratios to look for in those standardized accounts. Moreover, such standards, after discussion with the provincial AGs, might evolve into national standards for use at all levels. This would make it possible to produce a complete set of "public accounts" that would take stock of all levels of governments in one single document.

OAG as agent of consolidation

The role of the OAG as agent of consolidation of the financial accounts of the nation has received extremely strong and wide-ranging support. Colloquium participants felt that one of the major weaknesses of the present reporting system is that it provides incomplete information in a checkerboard fashion and that neither Parliament nor the public have an accurate portrait of the overall financial picture of the country.

Some groups have pieced together such portraits, but none has the credibility to make them stand out as a true picture of reality. One of the central roles of the OAG might be to coordinate the production of these accounts. It might draw on other agencies (e.g. CICA), but it should be in a position to either put its stamp of approval on those consolidated accounts or at least refer to them in its Annual Report to provide the public and Parliament with the global financial picture.

OAG as storyteller and educator

The OAG has become famous for its horror stories and exposés of administrative pathology. It has served Parliament and the citizenry well in so far as it has reduced such aberrations. However, the emphasis on horror stories may have run into diminishing returns. Beyond its role as *ex post* censor, the OAG has a positive role as *ex ante* educator.

OAG as program evaluator

The OAG's mandate has been to gauge whether things have been done right. Its guideposts have been efficiency, economy and effectiveness, i.e., reporting on the government's ability to assess its own program performance. Some workshop participants suggested that the time has come to go one step further in auditing and have the Auditor General participate directly in measuring program effectiveness.

OAG as watchdog and whistle blower for Parliament

There was a very heated debate on the obligation of the OAG to blow the whistle when the economy reaches the danger point. This was seen as the moment of truth for the OAG if, as a result of his interpretation of his responsibilities to Parliament, he would feel compelled to do this. Some felt that this Cassandra role might hurt permanently the credibility of the OAG. Whistle blowing is a form of forecasting that disaster is imminent.

There was no clear consensus on this issue. Some participants felt it was a duty of a modern auditor to sound the alarm; others felt that it was sufficient for the OAG to hammer away at the deficits/debt issue through the publication of extensive information on the problem; others were suggesting that the OAG engage in "negotiated threat" with government agencies: the threat to expose the matter in its Annual Report unless action is initiated (very much as the threat by the auditor to add a note to the financial statements may prove a persuasive argument with management).

OAG as force for change in parliamentary fiscal control

There was extensive discussion of the futility of only providing information to Parliament as long as the process of parliamentary fiscal management is flawed. What is the point of providing extraordinarily rich information to Parliament when estimates are routinely okayed by parliamentary committees because they are aware that the government can ignore all their recommendations.

Unless the machinery of government is streamlined so that responsible fiscal control can return to Parliament, the efforts of the OAG are bound to be fruitless. Consequently, it was argued that the OAG must press for a change in the process of examination and approval of public expenditure plans, a change that would really re-empower Parliament in the realm of fiscal control. Otherwise, even if the OAG were to improve the quality of its inputs, fiscal control would remain flawed, and the deficits/debt problem insoluble.

What should the OAG do?

How far the OAG should go on the deficits/debt issue was the central question posed to the participants of the colloquium.

The following positions represent the views heard at the colloquium, covering the full continuum from the least interventionist to the most interventionist notion of the role of the OAG.

Some participants would be satisfied to see the OAG stay with a prudent, non-adventurous role; others wish to see the OAG grind out numbers and standards, and be the agent of consolidation of financial accounts; yet others wish the OAG could go beyond its role as agent of Parliament into a public education role addressed to the broader citizenry; a more adventurous group would like the OAG to enter squarely into program evaluation and to act not only as a watchdog for

Parliament but as whistle blower when the Canadian socio-economy or polity enters the danger zone; finally, the most ardent supporters of a very active role for the OAG suggest that it should lead a charge for the reform of fiscal management by Parliament.

At a time when fiscal constraints dictate cuts and downsizing, and when the information and advice of an honest broker armed with incontrovertible and certified data would be most valuable, this most proactive role found a number of ardent supporters.

It would be unfair to identify a centre of gravity on this continuum. The colloquium might best be characterized as bi-modal. Most certainly, however, the vast majority of participants expressed the wish that the OAG move to the left of its present position on the continuum to take on a more proactive role.

Conclusion

It is not in the nature of a colloquium, which brings together a wide assortment of academics and practitioners, to elicit a simple consensus. In one area, there was a plea for the Auditor General to promote the production of a small battery of indicators that are consistent, regularly reported over time, and national in character. No such common ground emerged on whether this was something the Auditor General should do directly or encourage others to do.

Overall, our general synthesis of viewpoints reflects a cautious plea for activism by the whole group, with a vehement plea for much greater activism by a few participants and an equally vehement plea for extreme caution by a small minority of participants.

The diverse points of view were also evident when the participants were asked where we would be in 10 years. Some said that the debt would still be a problem, while others stated that Canadians would have recognized the urgency of the debt problem, would have established solutions and would be in the throes of carrying them out.

We are not surmising what the OAG will extract from this colloquium. However, we will state that participants expressed an implicit but strong support for an active role by the OAG in the whole process of fiscal control.

Post-scriptum in the summer of 2017

On many of these fronts, the views have evolved since 1993. The consultation process, through this colloquium initiated by Denis Desautels, the Auditor General in 1993, proved to be a wise way to play its role as educator. It had an immense impact on the government policies in the following years. Later, the OAG adopted even more of an activist role. This generated some serious criticism at the time, before it moved back, more recently, to a more explicitly *ex post* stance in its focus. For a bit of an update, see "The penumbra of super-bureaucracies in Canada: a governance analysis," written by Ruth Hubbard and Gilles Paquet *(www.optimumonline.ca,* September 2017).

CHAPTER 19

The Task of Stewardship: Real Cultural Change in the Public Service

The critical challenge facing the public service is changing its culture. This is a direct consequence of the complexities and intricacies of the new kind of work required by the 'new governance' in the 21st century. At stake is not simply a change in attitude, but a new awareness that change is not, and will not, be a one-time thing. The inter-relationships among all levels of government, departments, stakeholders and citizens, as well as among jobs and functions within the public service, are bound to be more complex, unspecified, and ever-changing in the digital era.

These days, there is a great deal of loose talk about "stewardship" in the public service as if it were some sort of passive activity designed to ensure that things don't fall apart. It should be a lot more than that. It should be about breathing new life into structures. *The task of stewardship is to ensure that the new governance system works well.* But it is crucial to recognize that it is fruitless to be an executive in an organization that is poorly designed: stewardship entails, therefore, some concern for design and continuous interaction with the construction of the governance system.

Even though I like to refer mostly to persons in positions of authority, it should also be clear that stewardship is not the sole preserve of executives, senior managers and supervisors.

Stewardship is a process (neither a task nor a position) in which persons at all levels of the organization must partake. By focusing on those who are expected to effect change, I want to emphasize two main points: (1) that those in authority may, because of their authority, make or break the new governance; and (2) that those who wish to institute change cannot do it at arms' length and be themselves untouched by the change. It's about "do as I do", not "do as I say."

The context has changed

The new governance requires making sense of people's experience by putting it into a larger context. For the public service, first, this means providing a sense of purpose, a sensitivity to why people do what they do, and a way to shape the organization by building a shared understanding with the many stakeholders. Meaning-making is about reflecting meanings that existed in the partners, and connecting them to one another in new ways appropriate to the demands of the new situation.

Second, community-building is about establishing, developing, maintaining, sustaining and nourishing relationships within and between organizations. It is all about skillfully working interfaces where dilemmas, inconsistencies, contradictions and paradoxes are omnipresent. This requires the mastery of dialogue, the capacity to suspend judgment, and the ability to question one's assumptions.

Thirdly, stewardship cannot emerge unless the public service can improve its ability to adapt rather than simply rely on its traditional authority. This means an ability to 'nudge', to help the community address its particular challenges. As many observers of government have noted over the past quarter century, this means more contact between the public service and the people it serves.

The heart of the matter is not goal-seeking and control, but intelligence and innovation: the definition of standards and norms, and the negotiation of a moral, intellectual and emotional norm-holding pact, built on a multi-level dialogue. The whole institutional process becomes itself the learning process and the source of the redefinition of norms and standards as a result of experience.

Modest proposals

I'm not denying that there has been some progress on this front, particularly at the local levels of government. But the provincial and federal levels are lagging badly. For the new governance system to take hold, it requires a thorough renewal of our way of selecting, evaluating and coaching executives.

The first proposal has to do with the selection, promotion and deployment of executives. While this requires no change in legislation or policy, it would call for a significant modification in practice. The definition of the executive position and the choice of the incumbent would be made in effect not only by the supervisor and the Public Service Commission, but also by representatives of the different stakeholders (employees, peers, major client groups, etc.) under the guidance of the PSC to ensure due process and impartiality.

The inclusion of the stakeholders would force dialogue among them, which can only help anchor the process of organizational learning. Critics will argue that this would require time and dilute management's authority to deploy personnel as it seems fit. That is precisely the point. Meaning-making, shared understanding, community building, and organizational learning cannot occur without dialogue.

Dialogue takes time and is costly (and I am aware that recruitment in the federal service is already absurdly long). But poor selection, based on a very partial identification of needs and leading to demotivated employees, can only translate into organizational sclerosis or in-fighting, reduced productivity, low creativity and innovation, and dissatisfied clients. This is much more costly.

Our second proposal deals with how, once appointed, managers are supported, coached, mentored and developed. At the risk of generalizing, the current model is one of "sink or swim." Executives are expected to be quick studies, and to possess almost instantly all the knowledge and skills of their new positions. Some managers at all levels are known to boast not only that they expect instant high performance, but expect such performance instantly under the most extreme and demanding conditions.

This sort of situation has led to organizational disaster, and would, if anything, be exacerbated by a shift to the market employment (or contract-employment) model. This proposal calls for personal development to be regarded as a planned process of learning, through feedback, coaching and mentoring, as well as other self-directed activities.

The third proposal calls for a new process of evaluation for executives, and a rethinking of the whole incentive-reward system for this category of personnel. Just as the stakeholders must be involved in selecting executives, so they must also be involved in evaluating them. The 360 degree appraisal must become the norm and, as a result of it, a process of dialogue and values clarification must be instituted. Deputies and central agencies will be expected to reward both formally and informally those persons who meet all aspects of the successful profile and to avoid celebrating those who excel in certain areas only to the detriment of others.

This proposal is the kingpin of the transformation process. No cultural change will occur if employees continue to perceive that rewards go mostly to those whose policy skills and political savvy are geared entirely to serving mindlessly the whims of their superiors, irrespective of their capability for meaning-making, their capacity for community-building and their ability to inspire trust and confidence, and to deal with people at all levels.

What is at stake is nothing short of a new covenant for the public service. The traditional employment framework cannot simply be replaced by a nexus of market employment contracts. We have to provide some basis for the development of the new moral framework that will be required as an essential complement to the market contracts. This process depends first on the recognition that market employment contracts will not suffice.

The moral framework has to provide two things:. first, a way of dealing with multiple loyalties by public servants in the modern age and, second, ways of affecting the moral contracts for the new moral framework to coalesce.

To forge the new moral framework, a *six-step process* can be anticipated. Each of these steps will be very difficult because each calls for a genuine revolution in the mind, a new *manière de voir*.

On the governance front, wide-ranging consultations can lead:

1) to a reconfiguration of the new federal public service (a sort of Program Review, Phase II);

2) to the replacement of the Westminster model by a more modern version, taking fully into account the multiple loyalties of public servants;

3) a major redirection in the guiding principles of public administration toward a social learning process is absolutely necessary.

On the stewardship front, the general features of the new stewardship in a new non-centralized, distributed governance system would require dramatic modifications in the machineries that govern:

4) the entry and promotion of executives in the federal public service;

5) the nature of the support and training they get in the process; and

6) the process of evaluation and the whole incentive-reward system for executives.

These changes point the way to a new moral framework that would appear to fall half-way between the old model and the idea that public servants only be hired on contract that is often presented as the only workable alternative.

This may provide for the federal public service what has been provided by successful private sector enterprises for their employees: not a naked market-based employment contract, but a two-tier contract, with a tacit unwritten but centrally important component to ensure a reasonable degree of risk-sharing between employer and employee. The full burden of risk will not be shouldered entirely by the employer, as in the old moral contract, nor by the employee, as in the market-type employment contract, but will be shared after extensive negotiations involving not only those two parties, but by many of the stakeholders who have such an interest in these negotiations that they will no longer permit that negotiations be carried on without them.

CHAPTER 20

Stationary Population as *Fata Morgana*

"être dans le vent … une ambition de feuille morte"

– Gustave Thibon

Introduction

The notion of *fata morgana* has generally quite a negative connotation – it refers to a mirage, an optical illusion, and artificial, unreliable, and misleading knowledge. According to this point of view, mirages induce self-deception and should be dispensed with as quickly as possible.

There is, however, a much more positive connotation attached to an interpretation developed by Albert Hirschman. For him, human beings, especially in a world marred by deep complexity and uncertainty, have a tendency to underestimate their creativity and inner strengths in the face of those difficult circumstances. In such predicaments, simplistic utopian visions and mirages (hiding or minimizing the costs and difficulties ahead, and/ or exaggerating the potential ease of overcoming them) may helpfully compensate for these infirmities of man's imagination – in much the same way that the beautiful imaginary oasis, seen by members of a caravan deep in the desert, increases their efforts to the point that, in spite of their sufferings, they reach the next real oasis (Hirschman 1967: 32ff).

Those of the Hirschman persuasion (like me) do not malign these sorts of *êtres de raison* or simplified chromos that often play a crucial role in keeping the attention on certain key issues, and imbue the exploratory drive with new energy. That is why one must be grateful to senior scholars, who, no longer feeling the need to be *dans le vent*, dare to work on exploratory essays built on controversial reference points, to help reframe the debates in times when most participants and observers would appear to be at a loss as to the most effective way to proceed.

This sort of bold exploratory work shakes off excessive prudence in order to allow the mind not to be unduly restrained by the barnacles of traditional scholarly rules. The objective is not to build a full-fledged theory or model, but only to provide a *conceptual framework* – a set of relationships that may not be specific enough to lead to testable propositions about the world of events, but that provides the mold out of which specific theories are constructed by adventurous critical thinking (Leibenstein 1976: 17-18).

Anatole Romaniuk has provided us with one such valuable exploratory essay.

In such a work, it is difficult to be at the same time general, simple, and precise. Romaniuk's "advocacy paper" (his words) has chosen to be general and simple. It aims at nothing less than suggesting a demographic rule – stationary population – as likely to generate optimality in all perspectives – ecological, economic, social cohesion and national identity. Special attention is paid to Canada in this paper, but the rule is meant to be of universal application in the West. And while the author inserts, in passing, a cautious remark about this rule not being a panacea or a sufficient condition – for there may be other supplementary conditions needed to reach these optima – it is not unfair to say that this rule is meant to do much of the heavy lifting (Romaniuk 2017).

This is quite a daunting endeavour, especially in a relatively short paper. So, even the favourably disposed reader would reasonably expect that Romaniuk's *tour de force* might not be without some lacunae – if only as a result of the author's not having been provided with sufficient space to develop his argument as fully as he might have wished.

In gauging the contribution of the Romaniuk paper, a fair but critical reader should be expected to deal with it fully recognizing the particularities of the genre, and not only draw attention to the most enlightening and useful components of the paper, but also taking notice of these lacunae – separating those strictly due to the condensed and necessarily incomplete nature of any such short paper, on the one hand, from those ascribable to the author's decision to under-emphasise other fundamentally determining factors, on the other.

The lay of the land in three movements

Fortissimo

In the front end of the paper, Romaniuk presents a clinical synthetic sketch of a broad canvas of forces that needs to be taken into account in any reasonable attempt to assess the recent turn toward mass indiscriminate immigration, over the last 25 years – in Canada particularly – but also in other countries of the Western world.

Romaniuk draws from recent studies (including his own) a clear picture of the process unfolding in Canada:
- declining fertility;
- net immigration making up some 60 percent of population growth between 1996 and 2011 in Canada;
- a deliberate mass immigration policy, falsely purported by government officials to generate economic progress, and to compensate for the ageing of the population, but failing at both tasks;
- a displacement of the old Canadian stock by newcomers that is in the process of dramatically changing the cultural make-up of the country;
- the ideology of diversity elevated by federal public officials and a significant segment of the intelligentsia and the media to the status of an absolute unifying virtue, and used by the Canadian government to underpin the propaganda of the multiculturalism ideology, claiming that it would organically generate the miracle of unity from diversity.

Many of these points are well established in the literature, but assembling them in one place gives the whole a greater *force de frappe.* Many stakeholders are in denial about the whole dynamic that these factors create. Romaniuk`s counter-attack is therefore value-adding in exposing some of the flawed assumptions of those proposing what he calls a *populationist agenda.*

Glissando

The next section in Romaniuk's paper is a quick windshield survey of "a number of things that are in need of reconsideration in order to find a response to the population conundrum."

These "things" are underlined as part of a soft *remise en question* of the *populationist agenda* by setting its discussion within a loose conceptual framework that brings into focus important forces at work in the context.

These observations (for lack of a better word) are a mix of bare facts, hunches developed from experience or conventional wisdom, some inferences from the general discussion at the front end of the paper, and some normative suggestions. They are brought to the attention of the reader in a Van Goghian manner to flesh out a more comprehensive appreciation of the socio-demographic context:

- immigration is not a solution to all our socio-economic problems, but it can be a part of it;
- more attention needs to be paid to matters of quality of life (harmony, cohesion, security);
- immigration may not be as important to economic growth as presumed;
- more equal distribution of wealth would reduce migration;
- we should be mindful of the ecological health of the planet (limits to population growth);
- motherhood should be regarded as a public good, and more appropriately rewarded;
- family law needs a recast;
- given the fact that a number of women choose not to have children, three babies each for the rest of the country's women would be optimal to ensure a stationary population.

All these points are relevant to the central theme of the debate – which is the impact of mass indiscriminate immigration – and they constitute avenues both for enriching the perspectives on the debate, and for a potential rethinking of the public sector interventions that might be called for. Romaniuk does not present these various elements as part of a precise program, nor is he always declarative about the exact type of interventions he would favour. The impression left with the reader is that modifying a multiplicity of arrangements would be called for, and that these many re-arrangements would need to be intelligently coordinated and integrated into a 'visionary population policy'. In fact, the need for a *vision* is squarely put forward as mandatory, but details of such a vision are not spelled out. As a result, at the end of this section on the broadening of perspectives, the reader is left somewhat unequipped to develop his own brand of vision, and to respond to the question – what should we do next? Indeed, he is more likely to be overwhelmed by the immensity of the ill-defined task with which he is confronted.

Moderato

The last portion of the paper brings it to a conclusion in a telescopic way by stating:

> *Given this paper's conclusion that stationary population policies are **optimal** (GP's emphasis) for maintaining national identity, social cohesion and material well-being, the question remains whether the robust pro-family policies to achieve childbearing at the generational replacement level are doable.*

This is at the same time an *overstatement* – for the foundations presented for Romaniuk's optimality theorem are quite elliptic – and *somewhat short on the implementation front* – for it provides little practical guidance as to what might make this operationalization phase doable.

In closing the paper, Romaniuk vibrantly expresses his optimism about the possibility of his fundamental and revolutionary proposal materializing. Yet after a last excursus in the worlds of Kondratieff and Oswald Spengler, this vibrant optimism appears to have faltered *un tant soi peu*, for he concludes:

> *Let us hope though that against all the odds the implementation of stationary population policies offers a prospect of stabilizing and, perhaps, reversing it.*

Hope is still there, but it appears somewhat thin. Indeed, by the end of the penultimate paragraph of the paper, Anatole

Romaniuk seems ready to settle for a rather important but very modest small step:

Western governments at the very least should moderate the impulses for ever greater immigration and take a more critical view of diversity as a social construct in nationhood building.

Lacunae

As mentioned earlier, this sort of short exploratory paper, as a genre, is bound to be at times more suggestive than comprehensive, and it allows the author more licence than usual for ignoring or underplaying some aspects of the problem that other observers might regard as essential pieces of the puzzle. This section suggests some flats and sharps that might provoke Romaniuk (in a possible sequel to the present paper) into reconsidering some avenues that he is quite familiar with, but to which he has chosen to give less attention here.

Some flats

- It must be said that so little of substance is adduced about social cohesion and national identity – matters of great importance, indeed – that it must be underlined as a lacuna that considerably weakens the thrust of the paper, and that, by itself, would appear to call for a sequel to this paper.
- Even when the impact of the mass immigration policy on the cultural make-up of the country is referred to – for example, on the occasion of writing about the Dion *et al.* 1995 paper – the author fails to present anything like an explicitation of the consequences that may be derived from the results. This would appear to follow from the limited attention given to social cohesion and national identity.
- It is difficult to understand why the author has paid so little attention to the whole richly-federal-government-financed, brain-washing exercise by the diversity/ multiculturalism clan, and, in particular, to its erasure of English Canadian culture by the likes of Charles Taylor (Duchesne 2016). This erasure is probably the main source of the *lack of effective resistance* to these toxic new

policies. Significant segments of the politicos, the federal bureaucracy, academia and the media have swallowed this imposture and played a toxic role in *disinforming* the citizens and in preventing a critical debate about the policies in good currency (Paquet 2012, 2017).

- Romaniuk has also chosen not to probe further the *electoral gauntlet* in which the Canadian federal government has entrapped itself: it has allowed the proportion of the Canadian population born outside the country to grow unduly rapidly to become one out of five – and much higher in large cities like Toronto and Vancouver – thereby taxing the absorptive capacity of the country. This situation has left Canadian federal governments of all stripes at risk of paying a high price at the polls if they were to give any hint of a tightening of the immigration policy. This, in turn, has paralyzed government action in the face of the current predicament, and put Canada in a position where it is drifting toward an irreversible vortex, since an ill-informed citizenry is unlikely to force the Canadian government to take any corrective action soon (Paquet 2008).

Some sharps

- Some attention should perhaps have been focused on the *absorptive capacity philosophy* that was in good currency in Canada until the last few decades. This might take some of the lustre off the stationary population solution by relaxing it, but it would appear to be *incontournable* in such a paper, since this softer and more flexible approach might appear immensely easier to sell and implement than the more radical solution.
- More also might have been usefully said about *integration*, since more effective integration would make a great difference in gauging the impact of mass indiscriminate immigration. If many more newcomers could be expected to integrate (not to assimilate) with the Canadian old stock – i.e., if they could be expected not to play such havoc with the Canadian cultural make-up – this might modify the notion of what is a workable absorptive capacity.

- Romaniuk should not have avoided the question of screening of newcomers. Canada already does it, but the whole question of the *conditions of admission* of newcomers is shunned for fear of falling into the trap of a Charter of Values *à la* Quebec's PQ (Paquet 2012: chapter 4). This caution has made the whole question a taboo topic, when it is clearly in the back of the minds of all Canadians, old and new.

- Even though Romaniuk makes a case for soft demography, and is intellectually committed to it, there is still a *demometric twist* in the discipline of demography that parallels quantophrenia in the social sciences in general (Paquet 2014: chapter 3). These modes have generated an immense caution when it comes to probing the most qualitative and complex dimensions of culture. As a result, the paper avoids tackling head-on the bizarre proposition propounded by Charles Taylor *et al.* – and senselessly repeated by the likes of Justin Trudeau – that Canada has no culture of its own (Duchesne 2016; Paquet 2017). According to this insanity, Quebeckers have a culture, Aboriginals have a culture, and immigrants have a culture – and therefore cultural rights – while Canadians (at least those in the rest of Canada) do not. This bizarre proposition underpins the very notion that mass indiscriminate immigration *cannot,* by definition, erode social cohesion and Canadian culture, because such a thing as Canadian culture does not exist. A culturally sensitive and refined scholar like Romaniuk cannot be expected to ignore this ignoble elephant in the room.

Conclusion

Romaniuk has succeeded in bringing forth in a high-quality scholarly journal an intelligent discussion of what has been almost a taboo topic in Canada. This is quite an accomplishment. However, as my flats and sharps underlined, the occlusion of certain crucial forces at work, and the proclivity to overprotect the stationary population approach as *primus inter pares* in the list of important solutions, may have weakened the *force de frappe* of the paper.

Four points may be useful in closing.

First, the idea of hoping to resolve such a complex problem as the immigration policy by a simple radical rule like a stationary population policy may be a good way to start a most necessary conversation about Canada's immigration policy, but it is unlikely that the final answer that will eventually emerge from intelligent conversations will be that simple. As Romaniuk himself mentions, many additional re-arrangements will be necessary, and it is most likely that they will not materialize by direct state action but through oblique interventions and nudging (Kay 2011; Thaler and Sunstein 2008).

Second, this sort of bias for simplicity – however minor and however unwittingly it may emerge – is not a danger for Romaniuk, who is intent on launching a serious conversation leading to much social learning. He knows from experience that genuine conversations and fruitful exchanges triggered by pioneers like himself often lead to an outcome that almost completely leaves out the proposal that has served as the point of origin of the discussion: what survives is the sum of the criticisms that it has elicited – what Gaston Bachelard calls le *surobjet* (Bachelard 1949: 138ff). This is not a failure of the originator, but a sign of the heuristic fruifulness of the conversation he has initiated. Therefore, it would be a pity to fetishize the original proposal and thereby block social learning.

Thirdly, the tendency to unduly de-emphasize the most sensitive psycho-social-cultural issues in the way that exploratory papers, like the one by Romaniuk, tend to do, may prove extraordinarily costly. Most often, meaningful issues are contentious, paradoxical, difficult to disentangle, and a privileged terrain for ideological frictions. But they are also the loci where the resolution of the problems must and should be debated. Intellectual gumption should prevail.

Finally, such exploratory, open-ended inquiries into wicked policy problems (Paquet 2013) should be conducted neither in accordance with the diktats of hyper-politeness nor with the blinders of hyper-positivism.

First, because, as Adam Kahane suggests: "Politeness is a way of not talking. When we are being polite, we say what we think we should say ... Politeness maintains *status quo*" (Kahane 2007:

56). This is not the sort of conversation that Anatole Romaniuk wants to initiate.

Second, as the conversation unfolds, one should be particularly diligent in not blocking out a whole range of usable information emerging from intuition, sensitivity, imagination or even unreliable folk knowledge. All these sources of imperfect knowledge and intuition pumps cannot be ignored (Dennett 2013). Fritz Schumacher conveys this point most effectively in his story about the two types of cartographers: the Type I cartographer who would not agree to record a piece of information on the map unless it has been trebly cross-checked, and the Type II cartographer who, in case of doubt in the face of unverified information, would be led to record the information on the map prominently (Schumacher 1978). In our world of continuous surprises, scholars proposing to conduct an inquiry that goes well beyond the short run need to adopt a Type II cartographer frame of mind. Anything might serve along the way. Explorers, as they board their canoes to discover what there is down the river (or as they join a conversation of discovery), might find it useful that their documents factor in the hearsay of the natives about the existence of a 200-meter water fall maybe way down there (or its conversational equivalent in terms of pitfalls). I hope that an adventurous scholar like Anatole Romaniuk would concur.

References

Bachelard, Gaston. 1949. *La philosophie du non*. Paris, FR: Presses Universitaires de France.

Dennett, Daniel C. 2013. *Intuition Pumps and Other Tools for Thinking*. New York, NY: Norton.

Dion, P., E. Caron-Malenfant, C. Grondin and D. Grenier. 2015. "Long-term Contribution of Immigration to Population Renewal in Canada: A Simulation," *Population and Development Review*, 41(1): 109-126.

Duchesne, Ricardo. 2016. "Charles Taylor's Philosophy of Minority Ethnic Identity and the Suppression of Eurocanadian Identity," *The Occidental Quarterly*, 16(2): 3-19.

Hirschman, Albert O. 1967. "The Principle of the Hiding Hand" in A.O. Hirschman. *Development Projects Observed*. Washington, D.C.: The Brookings Institution, p. 9-34.

Kahane, Adam. 2007. *Solving Tough Problems – An open way of talking, listening, and creating new realities*. San Francisco, CA: Berrett-Koehler.

Kay, John. 2011. *Obliquity – Why goals are best achieved indirectly*. New York, NY: The Penguin Press.

Leibenstein, Harvey. 1976. *Beyond Economic Man*. Cambridge, MA: Harvard University Press.

Paquet, Gilles. 2008. *Deep Cultural Diversity – A Governance Challenge*. Ottawa, ON: The University of Ottawa Press.

Paquet, Gilles. 2012. "Toward Principled Governance of the Immigration Regime" in G. Paquet. *Moderato Cantabile – Toward Principled Governance for Canada's Immigration Policy*. Ottawa, ON: Invenire, p. 79-108.

Paquet, Gilles. 2013. *Tackling Wicked Policy Problems – Equality, Diversity, and Sustainability*. Ottawa, ON: Invenire.

Paquet, Gilles. 2014. "On Quantophrenia" in G. Paquet. *Unusual Suspects – Essays on Social Learning Disabilities*. Ottawa, ON: Invenire, p. 69-89.

Paquet, Gilles. 2017. "The obscenity of hyper-toleration," *www.optimumonline.ca*, 47(2): 13-32.

Romaniuk, Anatole. 2017. "Stationary Population, Immigration, Social Cohesion, and National Identity: What are the links and the policy implications? With special attention to Canada. – A demographer's point of view," *Canadian Studies in Population*, 44(3-4).

Schumacher, E.F. 1978. *A Guide for the Perplexed*. New York, NY: Harper.

Thaler, Richard H. and Cass R. Sunstein. 2008. *Nudge*. New Haven, CN: Yale University Press.

Toward a New Cosmology

There is a rearguard action in many schools of public administration and clutches of political scientists that is systematically blocking the development of critical governance studies. These clubs have been fighting for so long to establish their difference with business schools that they have felt aggressed by a governance problematique that is, to a very great extent, challenging this very specificity. As a result, many schools of public administration have allowed themselves to become nothing more than propagandists for a brand of *political science of state-centric regimes*. As a matter of consequence, in those circles, governance has become either a taboo topic, or a target for intellectual condescension, or, at its most intellectually dishonest, an emasculated *fourre-tout*, a weaselword deprived of any analytical content, a symbolic Alice-in-Wonderland label used only to bestow a certain *grandeur* and honourability on any do-gooding initiative that can be remotely associated with routine administration or management.

This reaction is mostly ideological, and the echo effect of the Jacobine cosmology in good currency in such units. This canonical cosmology is based on the assumption that the State (always spelled with a capital S) is a hierarchical, accountable, transparent and oversight-heavy apparatus, in which elected officials and technocrats are in charge. These entities are supposedly imbued with special qualities that enable them to play a transcendent role in defining the public interest on the basis of shared values, and are presumed to impeccably perform their functions top-down, and through the 'magic' of institutionalized compassion.

Any observer who has been paying even minimal attention to the real-world experience of the last few decades has long recognized that the characterization in the last paragraph is a grotesque misrepresentation of what happens in public administration, and that the discombobulation of the notion of governance in the first paragraph constitutes an intellectual imposture. The presumptions on which these elucubrations are built are generally ill-founded, and the explanatory power of the caricatures of the public administration built on these assumptions is bogus.

In our complex and pluralist world, nobody has all the information, all the resources, or all the power – and therefore nobody is in charge. Collaborative governance, defined as effective coordination when power, resources, and information are widely distributed, is therefore the new imperative, and it entails the need for less state-centric, more decentralized and more participative arrangements.

In a book published a few years ago in collaboration with Ruth Hubbard, we tackled this Jacobine cosmology head-on, and showed that the presumptions on which much of the current public administration gospel is built (someone in charge, shared values, state-centricity, presumed perfect alignment between politicians and bureaucrats, superiority of the performance of the state sector, etc.) are mostly unfounded (Hubbard and Paquet 2010).

The black hole of public administration

In the Hubbard-Paquet book, the challenge we have mounted to expose the state of public administration as a black hole has mostly used Canada as a laboratory, but most of the discussion is of general applicability, and the pathologies exposed are quite common. This section summarizes our caustic diagnosis (*Ibid.*).

First, we exposed the general transformation of the public administration enterprise over the last while:

- the drift from Big G government to small g governance;
- the concurrent transformation of the government apparatus *stricto sensu* from G_1 processes emphasizing reliability, to G_2 processes emphasizing innovation;

- the ways in which the realities of public administration have slowly been perverted by a process of fictionalization of real politico-administrative processes (often by academics or uninformed, perhaps incompetent, adjudicators);
- the way those fictions were imposed on the real world has driven public administrators to engage a large portion of their energies in responding to the demands of senior public sector potentates, intent on implementing, in a Quixotic way, the diktats of this self-centred fictional administrative apparatus on the real world, rather than focusing on meeting real societal demands and needs; and
- the slow process of substitution of agile, decentralized and self-governed organizations to replace the centralized and oversight-heavy organizations in good currency in state-centric and therapeutic states – a slow process emerging in the first decade of the century, but a process that has been accelerating in the second one (Laloux 2014).

All those trends (Big G to small g, G_1 to G_2, the dialectics between reality and fiction, the evolution of the relationships between politicians and bureaucrats, decentralization, movement toward open-source governance, etc.) have been bucked by a formidable, dynamic conservatism on the part of both public administration academics and practitioners. They have not stalled these processes completely, but have slowed them down significantly.

Second, we reviewed a variety of pathologies that have ensued. Some of those illustrations were obtained from direct conversations with senior executives; others were revealed by the study of certain policy files. This ethnographic work revealed an array of bad habits (quantophrenia, disloyalty, neurotic state, etc.) that have come to be in good currency. Those bad habits have translated into pathologies of governance.

The examination of recent policy files provided not only damaging evidence about the current state of affairs, but has also suggested potential repairs (private-public partnerships, better organizational design, ombudsmanship, etc.). So the black hole exists, but all is not doomed.

Mental prisons blocking possible change

Public administration is broken, but there is still a general denial about it, especially in Canada. This is because the administrative machine still performs routine functions as a kind of *organic automatic pilot*. Conservatorship *à la* Terry stands on guard for us. What is failing is action that would appear to require agency, as when the automatic pilot must be shut down, and human piloting is required anew to change direction. These more active functions depend a good deal on effective political-bureaucratic collaboration, and would require a refurbished organizational design for the public household. At this level, system failures are obvious, and the negative echo effect on regulation and service delivery is already beginning to be visible.

Two most important mental prisons are blocking the possibility for change:

- the refusal to question the assumption of the *public service as a sort of new clergy*, and
- the presumption that *misalignment* between the priorities of the legitimately elected officials and the interests (personal or tribal) of the public servants is *a quasi-logical impossibility*.

In fact, bureaucratic disloyalty, while being sanctimoniously denied, has developed to the point where it is, at times, self-righteously celebrated in the open by individuals in the managerial class (and by their academic and media acolytes) as a welcome corrective to the wishes of elected officials who have come to be regarded in certain quarters as unreliable (and even illegitimate) definers of the public interest.

In the last 25 years, any form of criticism of the state (however mild and constructive) has come too often to be considered a form of treason by the federal public service in Canada. As a result, a majority of executives have chosen to shun critical thinking completely, and have withdrawn into the "technical" aspects of their work – to *hibernate,* as some have called it – seeing no merit in engaging in discussions that would lead nowhere, and could only be career-arresting.

In the 2010 book, we injected at times a whiff of humour and irony in our indictment of what a majority of scholars and practitioners, with missionary zeal, continue to regard as a superior model of public administration – all the while working busily at denying stridently any sign of its deliquescence, and actively working at suppressing any evidence that it might not be working that well.

Even though our clinical 2010 exposé was fairly hard-hitting, it was broadly ineffective.

We may have been unduly paralyzed by our *bonnes manières* in attacking the well-oiled propaganda machine in place that presents Canadian public administration as a model of efficiency, effectiveness and economy. But it may also be that we have been unwilling to recognize the full extent to which the Canadian federal public administration apparatus had succeeded by 2010 in immunizing itself from external criticisms: by keeping a low profile and standing ready to take the citizenry as hostage as soon as the government of Canada might show signs of would be tempted to abandon its main objective since 1967 – being a 'model employer' – to focus on what should be its only legitimate objective – running an effective and efficient governing apparatus.

Even our caustically publicizing the results of official reports showing that the Canadian federal government pay system costs 15 times more per employee to operate than the industry standard failed to shake off the torpor of the Canadian citizenry and the media!

Aristophanes failed, more of Diogenes may be needed

In the years between 2010 and 2017, I have done much additional critical work – work on which I have amply reported in *Pasquinades in E*. The attentive reader will have noted that the tone of voice has changed. From the dry humor or slight deprecation, in the manner of Aristophanes, that transpired throughout *The Black Hole*, the recent papers have taken a more caustic and acerbic tone – not quite as sharp and brutal as Diogenes – another Athenian of the same period, but one immensely more irreverent and hard-hitting than Aristophanes.

The degree of harshness of the message had to increase because it had become obvious that the Canadian citizenry appears unwilling to see and hear our messages about the grotesque in the traditional public administration ways when they were couched in more guarded terms. As I mentioned a few times earlier in this book as an echo of a Somali proverb: it is very difficult to wake up someone who is only pretending to sleep.

Even though collaborative governance raises questions about the phony mystique of personal leadership, and calls for a form of collective stewardship – a new systemic relational stewardship, capable of feeding a meaningful organic, ongoing, direction-finding process – any attempt to denounce the imposture of the mystical notion of leadership, and to replace it by a more practical notion of stewardship, has proven very difficult. This mental blockage has much to do with the cultural and psychological barriers on the road to collaborative governance.

Some 50 years of the therapeutic state have led citizens to a learned dependency on the state. Over time, citizens have lost the confidence that they are able to handle their problems themselves (collectively and/or individually), leading them to expect that any problems they face can be unloaded onto the state apparatus.

This has by now contaminated the psyche of the Canadian citizenry. Intellectually, citizens recognize that they are producers of governance in a democracy, and that collaborative governance is the superior approach, but they seem to share the sad fate of citizens diagnosed more than 150 years ago by Proudhon (1850) as congenitally suffering from *"la paresse des masses"* and *"le préjugé gouvernemental"* – the unwillingness of the citizenry to get involved as producers of governance because it requires too much effort, and the consequent propensity to lean automatically in the direction of government to demand that it take care of the problems. Fifty years of therapeutic state and the gospel of progressivism have further catatonized the citizenry: citizenship has now morphed strictly into a source of entitlements.

Breaking these cultural and psychological barriers – and the sense of learned helplessness that has emerged from them and is generating so much harm – is a daunting task. Much in the Hubbard-Paquet 2010 book was dedicated to analytically persuading the reader that collaborative governance is not unworkable.

This being established, *Pasquinades in E* has spoken louder and more sharply in its attack on those cultural, psychological, and ideological blinders at the source of key blockages on the road to collaborative governance – while the organizational apparatus likely to produce collaborative governance is being painfully constructed. The hope has been that a part-Aristophanes part-Diogenes discourse can be a catalyst in this process of change.

If it does not work, Diogenes may have to be fully unleashed.

References

Hubbard, Ruth and Gilles Paquet. 2010. *The Black Hole of Public Administration*. Ottawa, ON: The University of Ottawa Press.

Laloux, Frédéric. 2014. *Reinventing Organizations*. Brussels, BE: Nelson Parker.

Acknowledgements

Earlier versions of the different chapters have appeared elsewhere, as shown in the list below.

Gilles Paquet. 2007. "The Charter as governance story" *Canadian Diversity*, fall, p. 80-83.

Gilles Paquet. 2010. "Bouchard-Taylor as hyper-tolerance," website of *Metropolis May*.

Gilles Paquet. 2008. "The betrayal of super-bureaucrats," *Canadian Government Executive,* June.

Robin Higham and Gilles Paquet. 2014. "Unmasking legal corruption and legal extortion," *www.optimumonline.ca*, 44(2): 1-3.

Gilles Paquet. 2015. "The Don Quixote syndrome," *www. optimumonline.ca*, 45(2): 25-29.

Gilles Paquet. 2013. "Columnists vs Academics: a value-adding flip?" *www.optimumonline.ca*, 43(3): 38-41.

Gilles Paquet. 2015. "Laments of two fundamentalists," *www. optimumonline.ca*, 45(4): 52-60.

Gilles Paquet. 2015. "The demonization of Stephen Harper," *www.optimumonline.ca*, 45(1): 16-25.

Gilles Paquet. 2010. "The long form census psychosis as revelateur of governance failure," *www.optimumonline.ca*, 40(3): 1-7.

Gilles Paquet. 2016. "About the new rhetoric of promiscuity," *www.optimumonline.ca*, 46(4): 6-20.

Gary Caldwell and Gilles Paquet. 2016. "Disinformative, ideological and oikophobic: about a piece of storytelling by Quixotic John Ibbitson," *www.optimumonline.ca*, 46(3): 57-66.

Gilles Paquet. 2017. "The obscenity of hyper-toleration," *www. optimumonline.ca*, 47(2): 13-32.

Gilles Paquet. 2017 "The perils of the politics of guilt," *www. optimumonline.ca,* 47(3): 62-74.

Gilles Paquet. 2011. "Getting the Governance of Canada's Federal Capital Right," *INROADS,* vol. 30, p. 70-77.

Gilles Paquet. 2010. "Ontario Higher Education as Governance Failure," *www.optimumonline.ca,* 40(1): 60-67.

Robin Higham and Gilles Paquet. 2000. "The challenge of 2020 for the Canadian Armed Forces –A citizen's perspective," 8p.

Gilles Paquet. 2007. Background paper prepared for the Task Force on Governance and Cultural Change in the RCMP, 22p.

Lorna Marsden and Gilles Paquet. 1993. "Two workshops, one set of concerns" in *Deficits and Debts.* Ottawa, ON: Office of the Auditor General of Canada, p. 19-25.

Gilles Paquet. 2017. "Real culture change in the public service," *Canadian Government Executive,* January.

Gilles Paquet. 2010. "Toward a new cosmology," *PUBLIC* (ESADE's Institute of Public Governance and Management e-bulletin), Ramon Lull University (Barcelona), No. 23, May, 3p.

Gilles Paquet. 2017. "Stationary Population as *Fata Morgana,*" *Canadian Studies in Population,* 44(3-4), in press.

About La Maison
Gouvernance

L A MAISON GOUVERNANCE is the name of the new collective which has taken over the responsibility for *Optimum, The Journal of Critical Governance Studies*, and for the publishing house, Invenire, as of July 2017.

As is well-known to readers of the *Journal* and to those familiar with the books published by Invenire, governance is a *manière de voir*, an analytical framework, a clinically useful apparatus, and a new mental toolbox. But, fundamentally, it is a subversive approach: it aims at permanently and critically analyzing all governance arrangements in place – in particular, the hierarchical and coercive ones like the state.

This interest in *critical governance studies* emerged in the National Capital Region in the 1980s. In the colloquial exchanges of the colleagues who partook in these palavers about governance since then, La Maison Gouvernance has been the informal moniker used to refer to the virtual and shifting rally points around which most of the activities crystallized. This label has also served to identify the disparate group of hundreds of academics, technocrats, professionals and practitioners who met semi-regularly to debate problems of pathologies of governance. Colleagues from other parts of the country joined in on occasions of diverse forums organized in Ottawa.

None of these aficionados ever felt the need to formalize or patent the moniker, nor the collegium for which it stood. They felt comfortable with the openness and the continually renewed composition of the group, its evolving interests, and the organization of meetings only when it was felt useful. Its informality fit the *humeur vagabonde* of the group well, and the various projects that brought them together more or less regularly.

Some will remember the activities organized by the Canadian Higher Education Research Network, the meetings of the Lunar Society, the projects carried out under the aegis of PRIME (Program of Research in International Management and Economy), and the multiplicity of events – some relatively private, others mobilizing significant audiences – in association with the Institute for Research on Public Policy (then located in Ottawa) or the Canadian Centre for Management Development, etc. – all mobilizing moments built on impermanent arrangements to discuss issues pertaining to the governance of private, public, social or civic organizations that generated consequential results.

In the 1990s, there was a general changing of the guard on the Ottawa scene: the Economic Council of Canada and the Science Council of Canada – two poles of critical discussion at the centre of heated debates – disappeared, but other loci like the Canadian Centre for Management Development stepped in. La Maison Gouvernance both expanded and spread out, with the result that its activities also branched out in a number of directions.

At that time, a particularly active research group in critical governance studies came together at the University of Ottawa's Faculty of Administration (now the Telfer School of Management). It was the time when *Optimum* became a flagship publication of the Faculty, when a good number of colleagues in management and elsewhere at the University began to bring in graduate students interested in governance studies, and when the University of Ottawa, at the request of Gilles Paquet and colleagues, agreed to create the Centre on Governance (COG) in 1997.

LA MAISON GOUVERNANCE then, more or less, faded away in the shadow of the Centre on Governance.

The worksite created by Gilles Paquet and his colleagues in 1997 has generated important research products, but it has also, over the years, triggered resistance in a university framework where the progressive ideology and political correctness were becoming ever more present. The COG was and remained a privileged locus of critical thinking – as much of the excesses of the fetishism of the market, of the state, as of blind compassion. It became, over time, the target of persiflage, and less than well-tolerated in quarters where market, state or compassion are revered.

After some 20 years of enlightening but critical books and papers, some academic units – imperceptibly in certain cases, savagely in others – have been led to abandon support for these heretical activities. When the COG abruptly terminated its support for our activities, this signalled an opportune moment to resuscitate LA MAISON GOUVERNANCE, to get it to rise like the mythical Phoenix from its nominal ashes. And since we are in 2017, a website is obviously in order. It is up and running at www.lamaisongouvernance.org. In addition, interested parties can keep informed of the circumstances of this renaissance by consulting www.gouvernance.ca or www.invenire.ca.

For it must be said, loudly and clearly, that critical studies in governance will go on. Gilles Paquet, the *animateur* of LA MAISON GOUVERNANCE remains associated with the Telfer School of Management and with the Graduate School of Public and International Affairs at the University of Ottawa, and a new team associated with other institutions from the National Capital Region have formally joined him in carrying forward activities on the critical governance studies front.

It would be tragic, however, if because of an unfortunate administrative hiatus, the body of work accomplished over the last 30 years were to disappear from sight. The spirit of LA MAISON GOUVERNANCE, invested in the ventures pursued between 1988 and 1997, and temporarily attached between 1999 and 2017 to the Centre on Governance, has left an indelible impact on the governance scene. The group of colleagues that has been the soul of the Centre since its inception has been responsible for a refereed quarterly journal on governance and public management which has profoundly permeated the public debate about governance in Canada and abroad, producing hundreds of papers and reports over the last 25 years, and publishing some 70 books, authored by colleagues from Canada and elsewhere, under different banners.

As *ground zero* of the new incarnation of LA MAISON GOUVERNANCE, it may be useful to remind the members of the *Optimum* community and those who have followed the publications of Invenire of some of the works produced in the period of incubation of governance studies of LA MAISON GOUVERNANCE from the mid-1980s to 1997. These works, listed below, may be said to be the foundation on which the Centre on Governance was built. The period from 1999 to 2017 saw critical governance studies prosper. We provide also below a list of the main books and reports that this group and their associates across Canada and elsewhere have produced since 1997, in collaboration with a number of publishing houses. Most of these books are available through www.amazon.ca.

Under diverse banners during the incubation period before 1998

B. Bazoge & G. Paquet (sld). 1986. *Administration : unité et diversité.* Ottawa, ON: University of Ottawa Press, 350 p.

G. Paquet & M. von Zur Muehlen (eds.). 1987. *Education Canada? Higher Education on the Brink.* Ottawa, ON: Canadian Higher Education Research Network, 300 p.

G. Paquet (sld). 1989. *La pensée économique au Québec français : témoignages et perspectives.* Montreal, QC: Association canadienne-française pour l'avancement des sciences, 364 p.

G. Paquet & M. von Zur Muehlen (eds.). 1989. *Edging Towards the Year 2000: Management Research and Education in Canada.* Ottawa, ON: Canadian Federation of Deans of Management and Administrative Studies, 130 p.

G. Paquet *et al.* (sld). 1990. *Éducation et formation à l'heure de la compétitivité internationale.* Montreal, QC: QC Association des économistes québécois, 217 p.

G. Paquet & O. Gélinier (sld). 1991. *Management en crise : pour une formation proche de l'action.* Paris, FR: Economica, 162 p.

C. Andrew, L. Cardinal, F. Houle & G. Paquet (sld). 1992. *L'ethnicité à l'heure de la mondialisation.* Ottawa, ON: Association canadienne-française pour l'avancement des sciences, 114 p.

J.A. Boulet, C.E. Forget, J.P. Langlois & G. Paquet (sld). 1992. *Les grands défis économiques de la fin du siècle.* Montreal, QC : Association des économistes québécois, 340 p.

G. Paquet & J.-P. Voyer (sld). 1993. *La crise des finances publiques et le désengagement de l'État.* Montreal, QC : Association des économistes québécois, 380 p.

D. Côté, G. Paquet & J.-P. Souque (sld). 1993. *Décrochage scolaire, décrochage technique : la prospérité en péril.* Ottawa, ON: ACFAS-Outaouais, 135 p.

J. de la Mothe & G. Paquet (eds.). 1995. *Technology, Trade and the New Economy.* Ottawa, ON: PRIME, 125 p.

S. Coulombe & G. Paquet (sld). 1996. *La ré-invention des institutions et le rôle de l'État.* Montreal, QC : Association des économistes québécois, 480 p.

J. de la Mothe & G. Paquet (eds.). 1996. *Evolutionary Economics and the New International Political Economy.* London, UK: Pinter, 319 p.

J. de la Mothe & G. Paquet (eds.). 1996. *Corporate Governance and the New Competition.* Ottawa, ON: PRIME, 117 p.

J. de la Mothe & G. Paquet (eds.). 1997. *Challenges Unmet in the New Production of Knowledge.* Ottawa, ON: PRIME, 112 p.

J. de la Mothe & G. Paquet (eds.). 1998. *Local and Regional Systems of Innovation.* Boston, MA: Kluwer Academic Publishers, 341 p.

J. de la Mothe & G. Paquet (eds.). 1999. *Information, Innovation and Impacts.* Boston, MA: Kluwer Academic Publishers, 339 p.

Under the banner of the University of Ottawa Press (1999-2010)

D. McInnes. 1999. *Taking it to the Hill – The Complete Guide to Appearing before Parliamentary Committees*

G. Paquet. 1999. *Governance through Social Learning*

L. Cardinal & C. Andrew (sld). 2001. *La démocratie à l'épreuve de la gouvernance*

L. Cardinal & D. Headon (eds.). 2002. *Shaping Nations – Constitutionalism and Society in Australia and Canada*

P. Boyer *et al.* (eds.). 2004. *From Subjects to Citizens – A hundred years of citizenship in Australia and Canada*

C. Andrew *et al.* (eds.). 2005. *Accounting for Culture – Thinking though Cultural Citizenship*

G. Paquet. 2005. *The New Geo-Governance: A Baroque Approach*

J. Roy. 2005. *E-government in Canada*

C. Rouillard *et al.* 2006. *Re-engineering the State – Toward an Impoverishment of Quebec Governance*

E. Brunet-Jailly (ed.). 2007. *Borderlands – Comparing Border Security in North America and Europe*

R. Hubbard & G. Paquet. 2007. *Gomery's Blinders and Canadian Federalism*

N. Brown & L. Cardinal (eds.). 2007. *Managing Diversity – Practices of Citizenship*

J. Roy. 2007. *Business and Government in Canada*

T. Brzustowski. 2008. *The Way Ahead – Meeting Canada's Productivity Challenge*

G. Paquet. 2008. *Tableau d'avancement – Petite ethnographie interprétative d'un certain Canada français*

P. Schafer. 2008. *Revolution or Renaissance – Making the transition from an economic age to a cultural age*

G. Paquet. 2008. *Deep Cultural Diversity – A Governance Challenge*

L. Juillet & K. Rasmussen. 2008. *A la défense d'un idéal contesté – le principe de mérite et la CFP 1908-2008*

L. Juillet & K. Rasmussen. 2008. *Defending a Contested Ideal – Merit and the Public Service Commission 1908-2008*

C. Andrew *et al.* (eds.). *Gilles Paquet – Homo Hereticus*

O.P. Dvivedi *et al.* (eds.). 2009. *The Evolving Physiology of Government – Canadian Public Administration in Transition*

G. Paquet. 2009. *Crippling Epistemologies and Governance Failures – A Plea for Experimentalism*

M. Small. 2009. *The Forgotten Peace – Mediation at Niagara Falls 1914*

R. Hubbard & G. Paquet. 2010. *The Black Hole of Public Administration*

P. Dutil *et al.* 2010. *The Service State: Rhetoric, Reality, and Promises*

G. DiGiacomo & M. Flumian (eds.). 2010. *The Case for Centralized Federalism*

R. Hubbard & G. Paquet (eds.). 2010. *The Case for Decentralized Federalism*

Under the banner of Invenire (2009-)

R. Higham. 2009. *Who do we think we are: Canada's reasonable (and less reasonable) accommodation debates*

R. Hubbard. 2009. *Profession: Public Servant*

G. Paquet. 2009. *Scheming Virtuously: The Road to Collaborative Governance*

J. Bowen (ed.). 2009. *The Entrepreneurial Effect: Ottawa*

F. Lapointe. 2011. *Cities as Crucibles: Reflections on Canada's Urban Future*

J. Bowen. 2011. *The Entrepreneurial Effect: Waterloo*

G. Paquet. 2011. *Tableau d'avancement II – Essais exploratoires sur la gouvernance d'un certain Canada français*

R. Chattopadhyay & G. Paquet (eds.). 2011. *The Unimagined Canadian Capital – Challenges for the Federal Capital Region*

P. Camu. 2011. *La Flotte Blanche – Histoire de la Compagnie de la navigation du Richelieu et d'Ontario 1845-1913*

M. Behiels & F. Rocher (eds.). 2011. *The State in Transition – Challenges for Canadian Federalism*

R. Clément & C. Andrew (eds.). 2012. *Cities and Languages: Governance and Policy – International Symposium*

R. Clément & C. Andrew (sld). 2012. *Villes et langues : gouvernance et politiques – Symposium international*

C.M. Rocan. 2012. *Challenges in Public Health Governance: The Canadian Experience*

T. Brzustowski. 2012. *Why we need more innovation in Canada and what we must do to get it*

C. Andrew *et al.* 2012. *Gouvernance comunautaire : innovations dans le Canada français hors Québec*

M. Gervais. 2012. *Challenges of Minority Governments in Canada*

R. Hubbard *et al.* (eds.). 2012. *Stewardship: Collaborative decentred metagovernance and inquiring systems*

G. Paquet. 2012. *Moderato cantabile: Toward principled governance for Canada's immigration policy*

G. Paquet & T. Ragan. 2012. *Through the Detox Prism: Exploring organizational failures and design responses*

G. Paquet. 2013. *Tackling Wicked Policy Problems: Equality, Diversity and Sustainability*

G. Paquet. 2013. *Gouvernance corporative : une entrée en matières*

G. Paquet. 2014. *Tableau d'avancement III – Pour une diaspora canadienne-française antifragile*

R. Clément & P. Foucher. 2014. *50 years of official bilingualism: challenges, analyses and testimonies*

R. Clément & P. Foucher. 2014. *50 ans de bilinguisme official : défis,analyses et témoignages*

R. Hubbard & G. Paquet. 2014. *Probing the Bureaucratic Mind: About Canadian Federal Executives*

G. Paquet. 2014. *Unusual Suspects: Essays on Social Learning Disabilities*

R. Hubbard & G. Paquet. 2015. *Irregular Governance: A Plea for Bold Organizational Experimentation*

L. Cardinal & P. Devette (sld). 2015. *Autour de Chantal Mouffe – Le politique en conflit*

R. Higham. 2015. *What would you say? ... as guest speaker at the next Canadian citizenship ceremony*

D. Gordon. 2015. *Town and Crown – An Illustrated History of Canada's Capital*

G. Paquet & R.A. Perrault. 2016. *The Tainted-Blood Tragedy in Canada: A Cascade of Governance Failures*

G. Paquet & C. Wilson. 2016. *Intelligent Governance: A Prototype for Social Coordination*

R. Hubbard & G. Paquet. 2016. *Driving the Fake Out of Public Administration: Detoxing HR in the Canadian Federal Public Sector*

C. Maule (ed.). 2017. *A Future for Economics – more encompassing, more institutional, more practical.*

G. Paquet. 2017. *Tableau d'avancement IV : un Canada français à ré-inventer.*

G. Paquet. 2017. *Pasquinades in E – Slaughtering Some Sacred Cows*

With other publishing houses

Éditions Liber

G. Paquet. 1999. *Oublier la Révolution tranquille – Pour une nouvelle socialité*

G. Paquet. 2004. *Pathologies de gouvernance – Essais de technologie sociale*

G. Paquet. 2005. *Gouvernance : une invitation à la subversion*

G. Paquet. 2008. *Gouvernance : mode d'emploi*

G. Paquet. 2011. *Gouvernance collaborative : un anti-manuel*

Éditions Vrin

P. Laurent & G. Paquet. 1998. *Épistémologie et économie de la relation – coordination et gouvernance distribuée*

Éditions H.M.H.

G. Paquet & J.P. Wallot. 2007. *Un Québec moderne 1760-1840 : Essai d'histoire économique et sociale*

Government of Canada

G. Paquet. 2006 (en collaboration). *The National Capital Commission: Charting a New Course*

Report of the NCC Mandate Review Panel

A selection of the main research reports

J. Roy & C. Wilson. 1998. *Strategic Localism and Competitive Advantage*

COG. 1999. *Corporate Governance & Spin-in Ventures*

COG. 1999. *The Borough Model: Municipal Restructuring for Ottawa*

COG. 2000. *Governance in the 21st Century* (The Royal Society of Canada)

COG. 2000. *The Governance of the Ethical Process for Research – A study for the Tri-council*

G. Paquet. 2001. *Si Montfort m'était conté ... Essais de pathologie administrative et de rétroprospective*

Talentworks Project (under the supervision of Christopher Wilson)

COG. 2001. *Evaluating TalentWorks: Creating a Foundation for Successful Collaboration*

COG. 2002. *Ottawa's Workforce Environment, Report I of Ottawa Works: A Mosaic of Ottawa's Economic and Workforce Landscape*

COG. 2002. *Profiling Ottawa's Workforce, Report II of Ottawa Works: A Mosaic of Ottawa's Economic and Workforce Landscape*

COG. 2002. *Ottawa's Workforce Development Strategy, Report III of Ottawa Works: A Mosaic of Ottawa's Economic and Workforce Landscape*

A. Chaiton & G. Paquet (eds.). 2002. *Ottawa 2020 – A synthesis of the Smart Growth Summit*

G. Paquet & Kevin Wilkins. 2002. *Ocean governance ... An inquiry into stakeholding*

B. Collins *et al.* 2003. *Assessment of Public Internet Access in Ottawa: Report of Key Findings*

COG. 2003. *SmartCapital Evaluation Guidelines Report*

COG. 2003. *SmartCapital Baseline Assessment*

R. Hubbard, G. Paquet & C. Wilson. 2004. *CIPO: Reaching the World of SMEs*

COG. 2004. *SmartCapital: A Smart Community Assessment*

G. Paquet & J. Roy. 2005. *CIPO as an Innovation Catalyst*